The Women of Homer

By

Walter Copland Perry
Author of
"Greek and Roman Sculpture"

With Illustrations

New York
Dodd, Mead & Company
1898

Copyright, 1898
BY DODD, MEAD AND COMPANY

University Press
JOHN WILSON AND SON, CAMBRIDGE, U.S.A.

HOMER.

To

Her Most Gracious Majesty

𝔙𝔦𝔠𝔱𝔬𝔯𝔦𝔞

δίη γυναικῶν

*Queen of Great Britain and Ireland
Empress of India, etc.*

This little work is dedicated, by her kind permission, in grateful remembrance of sixty years passed under her most glorious and beneficent reign, by her humble, loyal, and devoted servant

THE AUTHOR

PREFACE

THE following pages are intended principally for English readers, and all that appeals exclusively to Greek scholars is relegated to the Appendices.

How lively and thorough may be the sense and understanding of classical antiquity in those who have little or no knowledge of the Greek language, is exemplified in very numerous instances. Who has portrayed Greek and Roman heroes so faithfully as Shakespeare, with his "small Latin and less Greek"? Whose heart has been thrilled with greater rapture by the divine songs of Homer than those of Goethe and Schiller? Who has ever shown a more subtle instinct for Greek art and Greek poetry than Keats, in his "Ode to a Grecian Urn," his "Psyche" and "Endymion"? Yet none of these were classical scholars; they derived their knowledge of Greek literature chiefly from translations. The same may be predicated of many of our most popular modern artists, who delight to take their subjects from the two grand Epics of Homer.

The portraits of Greek goddesses and women in this work may be considered inconsistent with what I have said about the essential difference between the dress of Homeric ladies — Andromache, Helen, &c. — and that of Greek women of the so-called classical period. But

Preface

pictorial and plastic remains of the Heroic age do not furnish sufficient examples of Homeric dress from which to derive satisfactory illustrations. We have been obliged, therefore, to forego archæological correctness, and to look to suitability and beauty alone.

We have used throughout, with some variations, the admirable translation of the Odyssey by Messrs. Butcher and Lang, and that of the Iliad by Messrs. Lang, Leaf, and Myers, the quaint phraseology of which is well suited to give the reader an idea of Homer's simple Biblical style.

We have generally, not always, given the Greek names of the personages of the two Epics, but we subjoin their more familiar Latin epuivalents.

Zeus	= Jupiter.		Dionysos	= Bacchus.
Hera	= Juno.		Demeter	= Ceres.
Athene	= Minerva.		Persephone	= Proserpine.
Aphrodite	= Venus.		Hekabe	= Hecuba.
Poseidon	= Neptune.		Odysseus	= Ulysses.
Hephaistos	= Vulcan.		Kirke	= Circe.
Hermes	= Mercury.			

ATHENÆUM CLUB, 1897.

TABLE OF CONTENTS

CHAPTER I

HOMER

PAGE

Introduction—Homeric questions—Opinions of the ancients regarding Homer's birthplace, and the authorship of the Iliad and Odyssey—Views of Bentley—Great importance of Wolf's *Prolegomena*—Dorian migration—Ionian migration to Asia Minor—Kernel of the Iliad and Odyssey—Primary Iliad—Views of Hermann—Greek literature begins with masterpieces—Earlier poets—Cyclic poets—Style of Homer—Dialect and rhythm of Iliad and Odyssey—Homer as historian and geographer—Homer mainly a poet—Views of Ampère, Leake, Dodwell, Choiseul-Gouffier, Winckelmann—Limited knowledge of Homer concerning Greece itself—Ancient myths in Homer 1–17

CHAPTER II

THE WONDERLAND OF HOMER

The wonderland of Homer—Honorific epithets universally applied to good and bad—Homer as theologian, moralist, orator, physician, &c.—Reputation of Homer in ancient world—Opinions of the philosophers, tragedians, poets—Homer thought to possess a divine soul—Pindar, Milton—Influence of Homer on Roman literature—Lucretius, Virgil, Horace, Propertius, Quintilian, &c.—Revilers of Homer—Zoilus—Modern French Zoilists—Scaliger—Italian detractors: Cesarotti, Beni, &c.—Boileau's caustic epigram on French Zoilists—Charge of grossness against Homer—Compared with Shakespeare—Remains of barbarism in the Epics—Hera, Hekabe, Achilles, Priam, Telemachos, Penelope—Enduring fame of Homer—Still, after three thousand years, the chief delight of young and old in every civilised nation—Milton, Herder, Lessing, Goethe   18–32

Table of Contents

CHAPTER III

THE MAGIC OF HOMER

PAGE

Sources of Homer's magic influence—His gods still our gods—Schiller, in *Picolomini*, on the gods of Greece—Advantages enjoyed by Homer—No predecessors and no rivals—Perfect language, dialect, and metre—Homer's broad and deep humanity—*Naïveté* of his characters—Weeping heroes—Frank egotism and boastfulness—Love of eating and drinking—Love of gifts—Achilles—Odysseus—The latter especially remarkable for his desire of acquisition—Even Penelope shows traces of this passion, and Telemachos—Homer's wonderful power of personification and creation of types—He prepares the way for the painter and sculptor—Pheidias and Homer—Absence of all reference to himself in Homer's Iliad and Odyssey—Shakespeare—Modern authors appear too much in their works—They are too subjective—The skill with which Homer makes us accept the most impossible tales—Pindar—Homer draws no very hard and fast line between gods and men, or between men and the lower animals—The loves of gods and women, of heroes and goddesses—Gods frequently assume the form not only of men, but also of beasts and birds—Heroes compared to beasts—Horses especially valued—No cavalry in the Epics, and rare mention of riding—Divine horses and cattle—The varied interest of Homer's tales—The music of his verse—Contrast between the free and joyous Ionian Greek and the Oriental of the same period . . . 33-49

CHAPTER IV

POSITION OF WOMEN IN THE ILIAD AND ODYSSEY

Position of women in the Iliad and Odyssey—Progress of civilisation mainly dependent on women—The women of Homer superior to the women of the classical period of Greece—Eternal types of the women of all ages of the world—Patriarchal simplicity of life in Homer—Rare mention of children in the Epics—Children regarded as blessings, and signs of the favour of the gods—Niobe and Leto—References to children—Achilles, Menelaos, Andromache, and Astyanax—Birth of a child—The Εἰλείθυιαι μογοστόκοι—Nurses—Simple education of girls—Their early years full of joy—Dancing,

Table of Contents

PAGE

music, and song—Comprehensive meaning of the term μουσική—Value set on music—Strong family affection—Achilles and Priam—The mother of Odysseus—Nausicaa as the representative of the Greek maiden—Dancing portrayed by Hephaistos on the shield of Achilles—Frequent mention of the dancing of youths and maidens—Monument at Troy to the dancer Myrine—Women of Homer careful of the *convenances*—Great ladies always attended by handmaidens—Love of beauty characteristic of Greek race—Epithets of beautiful women—Magical effect of Helen's beauty—Kleitos—Endymion and Selene—Chryseis and Agamemnon—Value set on skill in needlework, embroidery, &c.—Athene, Helen, Penelope, Calypso, Circe 50-61

CHAPTER V

MARRIAGE

Position of women in the Epics—Their entire dependence on the men—Their influence only personal—Arētē, wife of King Alcinoos—Marriage a matter of arrangement and barter—The marriageable girls generally given to the highest bidders—The ἕδνα ("gifts of wooing")—Gifts of the suitors to Penelope—Women offered as prizes to victors in athletic contests—Women always under the tutelage of some man—Telemachos has full power to bestow his mother Penelope's hand in marriage—Woman captured in war, however high her rank, becomes the slave of her captor—She has no "rights" whatever—Patience of women under absolute subjection to their lords—Briseis and Achilles—High position attained by some slaves—Eurycleia, the trusted friend and *confidante* of Penelope, Odysseus, and Telemachos—Different occupations of slaves in a household—Though a matter of purchase, marriage regarded as a desirable and honourable estate—No polygamy, except in the case of Priam, king of Troy—Yet concubinage not dishonourable—Women generally faithful wives—Greater latitude allowed to men—Happy relation between Hector and Andromache—Joyous celebration of marriage—A bride the precious "gift of the gods"—Marriage of Peleus and Thetis—Marriage of Menelaos' sons and daughters—Duties of married women—Absence of sentimentalism in Homeric maiden—Case of Briseis and Calypso—The attitude of the latter compared with that of Dido, after her desertion by Æneas—The case of Nausicaa 62-75

Table of Contents

CHAPTER VI

DRESS OF WOMEN IN HOMER

PAGE

Love of beauty leads to love of dress—Epithets applied to noble women's attire—Dress of Homeric women was that of the Æolico-Ionians down to eighth or ninth century B.C.—Mistake to look on Homer's women as dressed like the figures in the Parthenon sculptures—The one garment of women in the Iliad and Odyssey was the *peplos* or *heanos*—Dress of Athene—The φᾶρος—Dress of Circe and Athene—The *chiton*—The train of Eastern origin—The ζώνη (girdle)—The hundred tassels of Hera's girdle—Aphrodite's magic girdle, the κεστός—The κόλπος (bosom)—The κρήδεμνον (veil)—Penelope and the suitors—The κρήδεμνον laid aside in action or vehement emotion—The στεφάνη (coronal) and ἄμπυξ (snood)—The κεκρύφαλον and πλεκτὴ ἀναδέσμη—The ἴσθμιον and ὅρμος (necklaces)—The τρίγληνα (earrings)—The κάλυκες worn by Hera—The ἕλικες (spiral ornaments of some kind)—The πόρπαι (brooches or buckles)—The περόναι and ἐνεταί (safety pins)—The πέδιλα (sandals)—Did the Homeric Achaians wear gloves?—Hair worn long—Golden hair of divine and noble personages—Cosmetics—Hera's toilet—Did the Achaian women use rouge?—Dress of Helen on the walls of Troy; and of Andromache—Whence did the Achaians derive their works of art?—Opinions of Helbig and Pottier—Mention of Phœnician (Sidonian) art in Holy Scriptures—The work of Carians and Mæonians mentioned in the Epics—Colours of dress—Views of Professor Helbig on works of art found at Mykenai   76-92

CHAPTER VII

SOME HOMERIC WOMEN

We include the goddesses—Hera, Athene, Artemis, Aphrodite, Calypso, Circe, Thetis, Andromache, Hekabe, Helen, Penelope, Nausicaa .   93
HERA—Cause of her hatred to Troy—Her grand position and great power—Her opposition to her consort Zeus, who favours the Trojans—Perpetual quarrels between the august pair—Her treatment of the minor deities, Artemis and Aphrodite, &c.—She deludes Zeus by the aid of Aphrodite and Hypnos (Sleep), that she may give victory to the Greeks—Her toilet—Borrows Aphrodite's *cestus*, and bribes Hypnos—Zeus' fury on awakening   94-103

Table of Contents

CHAPTER VIII

ATHENE

PAGE

Her birth—Her mighty power and high position—Her epithets—Goddess of war—Superior to Ares—Her warlike dress—Goddess of reflection and prudence—Patroness of science, literature, art, and of all mechanical work, and female handiwork—She defeats and prostrates Ares—She attacks and beats Aphrodite—She loves the strong and brave: Diomed, Achilles, &c.—But still more she loves the prudent and cunning, especially Odysseus, the man "of many wiles"—She procures for him the favour of Nausicaa and the Phæacian king and queen, Alcinoos and Arētē—She aids him in his struggle with the suitors 104-113

CHAPTER IX

APHRODITE

First worshipped at Ascalon: also at Paphos, Amathus, and Idalion, in Cyprus—Temples in Egypt, Chaldæa, and Phœnicia—No temples found in Mykenai, Tiryns, and Hissarlik—Her rising from the sea—In Homer she is daughter of Zeus and Dione—Her epithets and character—Her entrancing beauty and charm—Not a favourite of Homer, who presents her in a less favourable light than later writers—Good-natured, but could be harsh when opposed, as by Helen—She is wounded by Diomed, when she saves her son Aineias—Appeals to her mother Dione, who tells her gods often maltreated by mortals—Her intrigue with Ares—In Pindar called wife of Ares, and her statue placed in same temple as that of Ares at Argos and Athens 114-122

ARTEMIS (DIANA)—The daughter of Zeus and Leto—Her ephithets—Her appearance and character—Favours the Trojans, but plays subordinate part—Beaten by Hera—Appeals to Zeus—All painless deaths attributed to her "gentle shafts"—Could send pestilence, and also heal—Though huntress, was regarded as protectress of young animals—Worship of her as moon universal—Homer knows nothing of the love of Selene for the "ever-sleeping Endymion" 122-126

Table of Contents

CHAPTER X

THE DEMI-GODDESSES OR NYMPHS — CALYPSO, KIRKE (CIRCE), THETIS

PAGE

The Nymphs play a great, and generally beneficent, part in the life of Odysseus and of Achilles 127

CALYPSO—Her epithets—Reception of Odysseus, whom she keeps with her for seven years—Her cave and garden—Zeus sends Hermes to order her to let Odysseus return home—Her generosity to him, and his suspicious caution—Compares herself with Penelope—Helps him to build his raft 127-132

KIRKE (CIRCE) of Aia, or Æaea, an enchantress, daughter of Helios and Perse—Her epithets—Odysseus escapes to her island of Æaea—Circe transforms his men into beasts—Odysseus saved by magic herb given him by Hermes—She restores his companions to their human shape, and they all remain with her a year—Odysseus' descent to Hades—His conference with Teiresias, who tells him what to do to regain his home 132-141

THETIS, daughter of Nereus—Her epithets—Forced by gods to marry the mortal Peleus—Her son Achilles destined to be short-lived—She begs Zeus, whom she had saved from the other gods, to avenge her son on Agamemnon—Prophetic power of marine deities—When Hector kills Patroklos, and carries off the divine armour which Achilles had lent him, Thetis goes to Hephaistos, and procures for him a new and better suit—She leads the lament for Patroklos—Her reception by Hephaistos—The splendid decoration of the new shield—Zeus sends her to her son Achilles to persuade him to receive a ransom from Priam for Hector's body—Her grief at the prospect of her son's untimely death 141-152

CHAPTER XI

ANDROMACHE

Pattern of devoted wife and mother—Daughter of Eëtion, king of Kilikia—Her sad meeting with Hector on the wall—Her son Astyanax—Her piteous plaint at the prospect of being left a widow with her orphaned boy—Hector's touching prayer for his son—Her frantic grief on hearing of Hector's death—She leads the lamentation at Hector's funeral 153-160

Table of Contents

PAGE

HELEN, daughter of Zeus and Leda; sister of Polydeukes (Pollux) and Castor—Her epithets—Her entrancing beauty—Its effect on Priam and the Trojan sages on the tower of Troy—Homer's skill in exciting the imagination—Her humble and penitent address to Priam, and his gentleness to her—Her admiration for Hector, and contempt for her lover Paris—She is the third to lead the lament at Hector's obsequies—Her gratitude for his kindness—Helen in the Odyssey restored to her husband Menelaos and her old home in Sparta—Character of Menelaos—Declines to fight with Hector—Like Priam and Hector, he regards Helen as the helpless victim of Aphrodite and the Fates—Visit of Telemachos to Sparta—Kindly received by Helen—Splendour of Menelaos' palace—She sees the likeness of Telemachos to his father Odysseus—Helen's soothing draught $νηπενθής$—She loads Telemachos with gifts—Her skill in augury—The portent of the eagle and the goose—Enduring fame of Helen—Her character—Denunciation of her by Euripides, the Cyclic poets, and Virgil—Mr. Gladstone's estimate of her compared with that of Colonel Mure 160–172

CHAPTER XII

HELEN—*continued*

Debate on the age of Helen in Troy and Sparta—Lucian and Bayle make her as old as Hekabe—Sara in the Old Testament—Futility of the discussion—Helen's embroidered representation of Trojan war—Supposed to be followed by Homer in the Iliad—Stesichorus, the Spartans, and Dion Chrysostom maintained the chastity of Helen, and held that she was not carried off to Troy, but only a counterfeit image of her 173–176

PENELOPE—The faithful, long-suffering wife of Odysseus—Daughter of Icarios and Periboea—Her epithets—Her difficult position, all men urging her to marry one of the numerous suitors—She is subject to her son, who only does not exercise his legal right of giving her in marriage from filial affection—Her artifice with the web to put off the day of re-marriage—Her beauty, and its effect on suitors—Her courage in upbraiding Antinoos—She gives way at last, and promises to marry the man who could string and use Odysseus' bow—Odysseus' delay in revealing himself to his wife—Her doubts of his identity overcome at last by his description of the bed which he himself had made—Their joyful reunion—Warm eulogy of the

Table of Contents

shade of Agamemnon in Hades on the virtues of Penelope—Was Odysseus worthy of such a wife?—The high estimate of him by Menelaos—He was a favourite of goddesses and women . . 176-190

CHAPTER XIII

HEKABE

Daughter of Dymas, king of Phrygia, and wife of Priam—All *mother!* —More solicitous about the life than the honour of husband and son—She supplicates Athene in vain—When Hector is slain she no longer wishes to live—She dissuades Priam from going to Achilles to ransom Hector's body—Hekabe in later literature—Euripides, Virgil, Ovid 191-194

NAUSICAA, daughter of Alcinoos, king of Scheria, and Queen Arētē —Description of the land and people of Phæacia—The palace and gardens of Alcinoos—The frieze of κύανος (blue enamel)—The gold and silver hounds—The ever-bearing fruit-trees and vineyards—No indication of sculpture proper in the palace—Nausicaa plays an important part in the adventures of Odysseus—Odysseus is cast alone and naked on the shore of Scheria, near a stream—Athene counsels Nausicaa to go to the same spot to wash her clothes—Odysseus is awakened by the cry of Nausicaa and her maidens when they lose their ball—First meeting of Nausicaa and Odysseus—Odysseus' prayer to Nausicaa for help—She gives him raiment and food—Is favourably impressed by the stranger, and tells her maidens she wished that such a man might one day be her husband—They all return to the town—Nausicaa instructs Odysseus how to gain the favour of her parents—Her fear of being the talk of the town— Odysseus reaches the palace, and is well received by Alcinoos and Arētē, who take him for a god—The king wishes that Odysseus would abide in Phæacia and marry Nausicaa—Odysseus contends with the young Phæacian nobles in athletic feats—Hedonist nature of the Phæacians—The song of the minstrel Demodocos—Ares and Aphrodite—The admiration of Alcinoos and Arētē for Odysseus— They send him home in one of the wise barques of the Phæacian mariners—Effect of Odysseus' high qualities on the hitherto untouched heart of Nausicaa—Her indifference to the suit of her countrymen—Her quiet resignation on Odysseus' departure—The Greek αἰδώς—Her pathetic farewell—Nausicaa as asteroid . 194-212

THE "NAUSICAA" OF SOPHOCLES—Only fragments extant—Supposed plot and action—Goethe also tried to write a play of which Nausicaa

Table of Contents

PAGE

was the central figure—Much struck by the glorious vegetation of Sicily and the famous gardens of Palermo, which reminded him of those of Alcinoos—He sketched his drama, but never completed it—This he afterwards regretted—Different treatment of the subject from Homer's—His plot in six acts—The charm of Nausicaa   212–219

EXCURSUS

Singular deterioration in the character and position of women as portrayed by post-Homeric writers, and especially by the Attic dramatists of the classical period—Dignified *status* of women in the Homeric Epics—Andromache, Hekabe, Helen, Penelope, Arētē, Nausicaa—In the highest period of Attic culture the great mass of women have become mere ignorant household drudges—The passion of love plays a very subordinate part even in Æschylus and Sophocles—Love regarded as a violent pernicious disease (νόσος)—Case of Sophocles' "Antigone"—Her strange reasons for preferring a brother to a husband or child—The similar case of Intaphernes' wife in Herodotus—Controversy on the genuineness of the passage in the "Antigone"—Similar strange reasoning in Æschylus' "Eumenides"—If passage is genuine, it is partly owing to the low estimate of love and marriage—Strange bearing of the lover Hæmon—Case of Medea in Euripides—His views of the proper position of women—Absolute subjection—Case of Alcestis and Admetus—Women appear in a still worse light in Attic comedy—Early comedy chiefly political—Women almost ignored, and when brought on stage make a most unfavourable impression—The *hetairai*—Cratinus opponent of Pericles—Crates and the *hetairai*—Aristophanes brings women on the stage incontinent and drunken—Women reach the lowest degradation in Middle Comedy—Marriage despised and ridiculed—*Hetaira* preferred to wife—Marriage "worse than disfranchisement"—Reaction in favour of pure love and honourable marriage in New Comedy—Antimachus of Colophon supposed to have been the originator of the new and better style of comedy—His "Thebais" and "Lyde" Menander and Philemon—Among the chief followers of Antimachus are mentioned Philetas and Callimachus—The "Stichus" of Menander . . . 220–232

APPENDICES 233–242

LIST OF ILLUSTRATIONS

HOMER	*Frontispiece*
APHRODITE	*on p.* 15
NIOBE AND HER YOUNGEST DAUGHTER	*to face p.* 52
A DANCE	*on p.* 57
From the new relief in the Phigaleian Room, British Museum	
BRISEIS AND AGAMEMNON	„ 67
MINERVA MEDICI	*to face p.* 93
ATHENE IN CAPITOLINE MUSEUM	„ 104
ODYSSEUS AND THE SIRENS	*on p.* 112
Reproduced, by permission of the Publishers, from "The Journal of Hellenic Studies," vol. xiii.	
HEAD OF VENUS	„ 115
VENUS	„ 117
ATHENE, HERA, AND APHRODITE	„ 120
DIANE À LA BICHE	*to face p.* 122
CIRCE	*on p.* 133
Reproduced, by permission of the Publishers, from "The Journal of Hellenic Studies," vol. xiii.	
NEREID ON THE SEA-BULL	*to face p.* 141
ANDROMACHE	*on p.* 154
Reproduced, by permission of the Publishers, from "The Journal of Hellenic Studies," vol. ix.	

List of Illustrations

Harpy Tomb in the British Museum	. . .	*on p.* 163
Helen Pursued by Menelaos	. . . . .	,, 170
Paris leading Helen Away	. . . . .	,, 173
Penelope	. . . .	,, 180
Athene Farnesi	. . . . . .	*to face p.* 187
Key to Noble Maidens	. . . . .	*on p.* 194
Train of Noble Maidens	. . . . .	*to face p.* 194

    From the Parthenon Frieze.

THE WOMEN OF HOMER

CHAPTER I

HOMER

ONE of the strongest inherent tendencies in the human mind is that which impels us to search for the origin of all the more striking phenomena of external nature, and all the more brilliant developments of the human intellect.

We are not content with seeing the Nile in its full strength and glory, as the source of life and joy to countless generations of a wise and mighty people; to see on its banks the temples of primæval gods, the palaces and sepulchres of wide-ruling monarchs, and the gigantic colossi in their awful silence and mystery, and their eternal duration. This does not satisfy us; men have been ready in all ages to risk life and fortune in the effort to reach its source, to see it in its weak infancy in the mountain fastnesses.

And so it is with Homer: we know him as the origin of Greek (*i.e.* of European) literature, as the perennial spring of lofty thoughts and beautiful images, from which the greatest poets — Pindar, Æschylus, Sophocles, Euripides, — the greatest philosophers — Plato and Aristotle — drew their inspiring draughts. We know him as

The Women of Homer

the creator of the gods of the most gifted of human races, as the mighty genius who gave them personal and moral character, and brought them within the reach of human comprehension and the artist's chisel; and we know that his works were the delight and solace of mighty conquerors — of Alexander the Great, of Hannibal and Napoleon — in the intervals of their warlike labours.

But this is not enough. Whole libraries have been written in the past, and will be written in the future, on what are called "the Homeric questions;" — where was Homer born? to what country and race did he belong? where and how and with whom did he live? did he only sing, or also write his lays? were the Iliad and the Odyssey the work of the same man? and did he write the whole or only part of each?

And although the subject of the present work, "The Position and Character of the Women of Homer," renders any minute inquiry into these vexed questions unnecessary, we cannot altogether ignore them. We shall content ourselves, however, with briefly proposing such answers to them as seem to us to be warranted by the most trustworthy evidence, external and internal.

These questions will seem futile to many minds, and not least so to some who derive the keenest enjoyment from the works themselves. "What does it matter?" they say; "we have our Homer — one of the most precious gifts which God has vouchsafed to man. Why seek to drag him forth from behind the veil which he has purposely drawn? — for he never speaks of himself — his clear sweet voice rings in our ears from the unfathomable depths of the ages, and, like the voice of Nature herself, thrills our hearts with ineffable delight."[1] We know that seven cities of Asia disputed for the glory of being his birthplace, yet the ancients were in as much doubt as we are about the place of his birth: "For Homer was not a product of the earth, but the muses sent him to us creatures of a day as a much-desired gift."[2]

The best answer perhaps to the question, Where was Homer born? is given in this well-known epigram: "To what country shall we ascribe Homer, towards whom all cities stretch out their hands? This we know not, for the great godlike hero has left his birth and his country to the muses."[3]

Yet, as I have said, these questions have occupied the thoughts of countless generations of learned men. Even in this materialistic and prosaic age, there are scholars in England, and far more in Germany, who, under the name of Homerologists, spend their lives in striving to find a satisfactory answer to them.

The ancient world in general accepted the Iliad and the Odyssey as the work of the same man; and this view has been taken by many scholars of our own times. Even Bentley, the most illustrious of European scholars, the greatest master of analytical criticism, held that Homer lived about the year 1050 B.C., and composed both the Iliad and Odyssey in writing.

We cannot but think that had he lived to read the

---

[1] We should observe here that the "lives of Homer" by Plutarch, Porphyrius, Proclus Diadochus, Suidas, and three anonymous, are all fictitious. The Christian fathers mention Homer.

[2] See Appendix I.; *Anthol. Pal.* ii. 715.

[3] See Appendix II.; *Anthol. Pal.* ii. 715.

The Women of Homer

famous *Prolegomena* of F. A. Wolf, published in 1795 A.D., he would have modified his opinions.

Wolf endeavours to show that the two great Epics were handed down by oral recitation to the year 550 B.C., during which period they naturally underwent many alterations. In that year, he thought, they were committed to writing, and received further additions and alterations. He proves, as we think, that the Iliad and Odyssey were not by the same author. He does not, indeed, deny the existence of an inspired poet called Homer, who wrote most of the lays, which, he thought, were afterwards collected, and, with more or less skill and success, moulded into a harmonious whole.

The main propositions of Wolf's great work have been accepted by most of the later commentators, and form the basis of modern criticism. Yet the old faith in the Homeric unity still lingers amongst us, and especially in the minds of poets; for the ground on which it rests is mainly sentimental and æsthetic. Mr. Matthew Arnold, for instance, who naturally takes the subjective view, declares that "the insurmountable obstacle to believing that the Iliad is a consolidated work of several poets is this: 'that the work of great masters is unique; and the Iliad has a great master's genuine stamp, and that stamp is the grand style.'"

How powerfully this sentiment acts on the minds of the lovers of Homer, how reluctant we all feel to seem to detract from the sole unapproachable majesty of the great god of poetry, is strikingly manifested in the case of Wolf himself. In a magnificent passage, in his pre-

Wolf's Prolegomena

face to the Iliad,[1] quoted by Professor Jebb,[2] Wolf shows how truly he sympathised with the indignation aroused by his anatomical dissection of the sacred body of Homer. "As often," he says, "as I immerse myself in that stream of action and narration which flows with even course down its prone and liquid bed; whenever I reflect how uniform is the colour which permeates these lines, no one could be much more angry with me than I am with myself."[3]

It is said of Villoison — whose publication of the Venetian Scholia furnished Wolf with the chief arguments for his theory — that he could not contain his indignation against the audacious assailant of his idol, nor the regret he felt at having unwittingly furnished him with his keenest weapons.

We are warranted in supposing that the events related in the Iliad and Odyssey — in so far as they are historical — took place before the Dorian migration of 1100 B.C., and therefore at a time when the Peloponnesus was ruled by Achaian kings. The migration of the Dorians, who are only once mentioned in the Epics,[4] drove the Ionians, who inhabited the north and east coasts of the Peloponnesus, Megaris, Attica, and Eubœa from their old homes in Greece to Asia Minor, where their minds and manners were greatly modified and softened by Oriental influences. The Ionians before their expulsion were probably the old pre-Hellenic, or

---

[1] Page xxii.
[2] In his admirable "Introduction to the Iliad," so succinct, and yet so exhaustive.
[3] See Appendix II. [4] Od. xix. 177.

The Women of Homer

Pelasgian population, Hellenised by the Achaian conquerors.

The kernel of the Iliad, or "The Primary Iliad," was probably written by a poet called Homer, residing, as some think, in Thessaly, before the emigration of the Ionians to Asia Minor, to which no allusion is made in the Epics.

It is true, indeed, that Homer was regarded as a poet of Asiatic Ionia, and, as we have said above, many cities in that country contended for the honour of being his birthplace.[1] But Professor Jebb has shown that the European origin of his poems may be reconciled with the Asiatic.

The Thessalian poet having composed the Primary Iliad in Greece, took it with him to Ionia, where it received large additions, and underwent such important changes in dialect and style as to account for its being regarded as a product of Ionia.[2]

This kernel of the Iliad consisted of Books I., XI., XVI.–XXII. Books II.–VII. were probably the earliest additions, not including "The Catalogue of the Ships," which is evidently of a much later date. Some of these interpolations — and notably Books IX. and XXIV. — are so grand in style, and so eminently fitted for the place they occupy, that some writers, in spite of some important differences, ascribe them to the original European Homer, writing in his later years in Ionia.

---

[1] Thucydides, iii. 104. quotes Hymn to Apollo, and thinks that Homer was the blind man "who dwelt in rocky Chios" —

τυφλὸς ἀνὴρ οἰκεῖ δὲ Χίῳ ἔνι παιπαλοέσσῃ.

[2] See Professor Jebb's "Introduction."

The Primary Iliad

The Odyssey, too, was probably written before the Dorian migration, and taken, like the Iliad, to Asia Minor, where it was greatly modified. It was not by the author of the Primary Iliad, from which it differs considerably in language, in general tone, and in the pictures it presents of divine and human life. It is, in short, far more Ionian and far more modern than the Iliad, and far better adapted to Ionian tastes — to their love of maritime adventure, and their keener sympathy with the wily and resourceful character of Odysseus. Yet the poet who enlarged the Odyssey may have written some of the interpolations in the Iliad; there is a great similarity between "The Return of Odysseus" and Books IX. and XXIV. of the Iliad.

The fact of the different authorship of the two grand Epics was recognised at a very early period by Xenon and Hellanicus; and in modern times it has been very emphatically affirmed by the illustrious German scholar and critic, Gottfried Hermann. "That the whole Iliad and Odyssey," he says, "were not written by the same poet appears to me so beyond all doubt, that I should think that the man who disputed it had not carefully read the verses." The Odyssey, however, is far more of one piece than the Iliad, and was evidently put together by one man. The main additions are the so-called "Telemachy" in Books I.–IV., the latter part of Book XXIII., and the whole of Book XXIV.

One of the many marvels of Homer's Epics is that with them Greek literature, as far as it has come down to us, begins with these works of unrivalled grandeur and beauty. The splendid constellation rises suddenly

The Women of Homer

on the horizon, apparently without forerunners, without any warning portents visible to our eyes. We know nothing of the stages by which epic poetry reached the height of perfection in which we find it in Homer. We know, in fact, nothing of it but what we learn from Homer himself. We hear, indeed, of what some regard as earlier poets, under the names of Orpheus, Musæus, and Linos,[1] but these names are entirely mythical, and the poems ascribed to them in antiquity, and of which some fragments remain, are apocryphal and forged. Homer himself speaks of the κλέα ἀνδρῶν[2] ("the glories of heroes"), lays in celebration of the many brave men who lived *ante Agamemnona;* and we must believe that there existed in pre-Homeric times a number of mystic poets who sang in the service of religion and in praise of the deeds of mighty warriors.

The Cyclic poets — so called because they related in chronological order the origin and history of gods and men — are of a later date than Homer. A writer of the middle of the second century B.C. wrote an analysis of these poems, fragments of which are extant.[3] He included the Iliad and the Odyssey in the number of the Cyclic poems; yet we know that it was in comparison with them that the latter were exposed to ridicule and contempt.[4]

The very style of the great Epics surely indicates a long succession of bards who were bound by tradition and custom to certain schematic formulæ. Homer,

---

[1] Il. xviii. 570.   [2] Il. ix. 189.
[3] See Mr. Munro, "Journal of Hellenic Studies," iv. 305 and v. 1.
[4] Horace, *Ars Poet.* 136; see Appendix III.

Dialect and Metre of Homer

therefore, rose, as has been well said, "in a firmament already lustrous," but all other luminaries paled their ineffectual fires before the great sun of poesy, and are lost in the dark night of oblivion.

The dialect in which the Primary Iliad was written was no doubt Achaian, whatever that may mean; whether the earliest Ionian, or the Pelasgic. This ancient dialect underwent great changes in the direction of Asiatic Ionian and Æolian, of which latter the Iliad and Odyssey show many unmistakable traces.[1]

The strongest proof, perhaps, of the existence of still earlier epic bards is the exquisite perfection of the metre and rhythm of the Iliad and Odyssey. Metre — the general laws of rhythm — must have been cultivated for many ages, and by no inconsiderable poets, before it could acquire the ineffable beauty and grace of Homer's versification.

Another Homeric question of great interest and no little difficulty is concerning the value of Homer as an historian. We have seen reason to believe that the most important parts of both Iliad and Odyssey were written before the Dorian conquest. The old Achaian civilisation was destroyed by that event, to which there is no allusion in either of the Epics. The polity and the social life which Homer describes is essentially pre-Dorian. He is the faithful echo of traditions older than himself, and he is evidently describing a state of transition in which Oriental luxury and rude and squalid barbarism existed side by side. He gives us the history of his Present and the hoary remains of a still older Past.

[1] Mr. Munro, "Journal of Philology," ix. 252.

The Women of Homer

We are naturally inclined to attribute to the great minds which have achieved distinction in any one sphere an almost universal knowledge. It is not surprising, therefore, that Homer, who is above all things a poet, should have been hailed by his worshippers as historian, geographer, theologian, moralist, orator, and physician. The ancient Greeks rightly regarded him as their first historian, but they took an exaggerated and utterly untenable view of the historic accuracy of his writings. Solon appealed to his authority to settle a dispute with the Megarians. Herodotus and Thucydides regarded his persons as real, and hardly questioned the accuracy of his facts. Yet Thucydides[1] exercised criticism. He was well aware that the poets who sang the great deeds of forefathers were not to be implicitly trusted. Pindar, too, though he thinks the songs of Homer immortal, allows that they contain exaggerations. "I think," he says, "that more is said about Odysseus than he really suffered, in the sweet tale of Homer. For his lies, by their winged art, have a certain dignity and wisdom which alluringly cheat us by fiction."[2] Even in our own day there are scholars who incline to believe in the historical accuracy of Homer. Happily for us, Dr. Schliemann — who, though not a scholar in the usual sense, has greatly aided historical research — regarded the great Epics as trustworthy annals of real events. He believed in their plenary inspiration, and it was this unreasoning, childlike faith which awakened his unerring, truffle-dog-

---

[1] i. 21; i. 9, 10.
[2] ἐγὼ δὲ πλέον ἔλπομαι
Λόγου Ὀδυσσέος ἢ πάθεν διὰ τὸν ἁδυεπῆ γενέσθαι Ὅμηρον.

Homer as Historian

like instinct and supported him under his arduous and exhausting labours.

In one very important sense, Homer is one of the greatest, as he was the first, of Greek historians; for without him we should know nothing of the heroic period of Greek history. He opens for us a vista through the dark clouds of the past — a vista of ineffable charm and beauty. In page after page we see the blessed gods,[1] seated on their thrones on the bright summit of Olympus, quaffing their nectar, listening to Apollo's lyre and the choir of the muses, or indulging in inextinguishable laughter at the clumsy Hephaistos ladling out the nectar, and bustling with halting steps through the radiant palace of his father Zeus. He brings before us in bright array wise counsellors "like Zeus in wisdom," majestic heroes "equal to Ares" in strength and prowess, and lovely women like the slim and graceful Artemis and "golden" Aphrodite. In the Iliad we witness the death-struggle of brave warriors, we hear the rattle of clashing armour, the triumphant shouts of victors, and the despairing cry of the vanquished and the dying. In the Odyssey we watch the passage of the much-enduring, patient Odysseus through perilous adventures by sea and land, and his hairbreadth escapes from angry gods and enchanted monsters — the Cyclopes, Scylla, and Charybdis — and from the gentler but no less dangerous enchantments of Circe and Calypso, until we see him safely landed in Phæacia, and received with generous hospitality by Alcinoos and his wise and beautiful consort Arētē, and by the lovely Nausicaa, the pearl and flower of maidenhood.

[1] Od. vi. 42; Lucretius, iii. 18; Appendix IV.

The Women of Homer

All this is history, and very important history — a history of opinions, life, and manners; but it is not history in the same sense as the writings of Herodotus aud Thucydides.

What, then, in Homer, are we to take as history, and what as fiction? We are told with the same certainty that the Greeks spent ten years in the siege of Troy, that Achilles slew Hector by the aid of Athene, and that Diomed overthrew Ares in battle and wounded Aphrodite. Are all these statements true, or none of them? Pascal said: "Homer wrote a romance; for nobody can believe that Troy and Agamemnon had any more existence than the golden apples of the Hesperides. He had no intention to write a history, but only to amuse us."

This is the very extreme of scepticism. Yet Homer was above all things a poet, whose imagination was fired by what he saw at the courts of Achaian kings, by what he learned from tradition and the earlier poets of the great deeds and romantic adventures of Achaian heroes. His charming visions are like the dream which follows the waking contemplation of actual scenes. It is on his true picture of a vanishing phase of an early civilisation that the discoveries of Schliemann throw such a welcome and precious light. It has been well said that he "rediscovered" the age of Agamemnon, Achilles, and Odysseus. The stupendous walls of Mykenæ and Tiryns, which the ancients thought that only Cyclopean giants could have reared — which bid fair to endure as long as the globe itself on which they lie so heavily — attest the power and wealth of the pre-

Schliemann's Discoveries

Dorian monarchs; while the tender beauty of the golden flower on a silver stalk, picked up near a grave at Mykenæ, bears witness to their taste and skill in decorative art, and to the beauty and splendour of their regal mansions.

The Homeric poems are woven out of three main threads — real events as groundwork, skilful arrangement, and pure fiction. Epic poetry must always rest on a basis of great events; but the Greek ῥαψῳδοί, like the Troubadours and the Minnesänger of the Middle Ages, dressed up real events, and gave them the form and colour best calculated to strike the fancy and to please the ear of a courtly audience. The lively Ionian was peculiarly fitted by his restless, roving imagination, and his national loquacity, to invent such tales, and to gather them from the "yarns" of Phœnician sailors, adventurous travellers and merchants.

The limits we have set to this introduction to our proper subject forbids us to discuss at any length the interesting question of the place of Homer as a historian. We must, however, also speak of him, very briefly, as a geographer, for his title to that character has been very warmly upheld, not only in ancient but in very recent times.

That very popular, but hardly very trustworthy, writer, Ampère, tells us that Homer, Æschylus, and Pindar " *s'assujettissaient à faire de la nature un portrait ressemblant; les poètes de la décadence semblent trouver au-dessous d'eux cet esclavage du vrai; dans leur liberté stérile, ils ne tracent que des descriptions vagues.*" He also speaks of Homer's geographical " *fidelité dont le voyageur est frappé aujourd'hui.*"

The Women of Homer

Mr. Leake, the highly distinguished traveller and archæologist, thought that the Ithaca of to-day corresponds to that of the Odyssey, except that it is not now covered with forests. He was much struck by the epithet πολυτρήρωνα (abounding in doves) applied to Thisbe, and he brought away two pigeons from Kakolia, which he took to be the ancient Thisbe, as ocular proofs of Homer's extraordinary accuracy.[1] Mr. Dodwell, in his "Classical and Topographical Tour through Greece," writes in the same strain. Choiseul-Gouffier, the great French diplomatist, who combated the views of Wolf, used the Homeric Epics as guide-books, and discovered the nook in Mount Ida where Paris reviewed the three goddesses and gave judgment in favour of Aphrodite; and also the spot where Zeus was deluded by the wiles of Hera and Hypnos.

It is very remarkable how slight are the foundations on which the fame of Homer as a geographer rests. The strongest argument perhaps is derived from his calling Tiryns τειχιόεσσαν (strong-walled) which he also applies to Gortyna.[2] But is it necessary that Homer should have *seen* Tiryns before he could use the word; or should have known more about it than he could learn from travellers? Do we not glibly talk of the sandy Libyan desert and the muddy Nile, though we may never have been in Africa? In fact, we find no geographical description, either in the Iliad or the Odyssey, sufficient to prove that Homer was an extensive traveller or a close observer. His descriptions of different parts of Greece are essen-

---

[1] See Professor Jebb, "Introduction to the Study of Homer," p. 44.
[2] Il. ii. 646.

tially meagre and vague, and for the most part fashioned after a preconceived idea, a fixed and arbitrary canon. We may fairly say of Homer what Winckelmann says of the Archaic artists: "*Donnant sans ménagement dans l'idéal, ils travaillèrent d'après un système généralement adopté, que d'après la nature; ils s'étaient fait une nature particulière.*" Homer had in his mind the type of an island, a mountain, a river, after which all these objects, when he mentions them, must be moulded. Almost every mountain is σκιόεν or αἰπύ; the islands of Calypso, Circe, and Phæacia are all woody; all ships are swift and well-found; all rivers are broad and clear. We can understand that the Nile[1]

STATUETTE OF APHRODITE.

[1] Od. IV. 477.

should be descended from Jove; but the Xanthos, the Spercheios,[1] and the stream in which the lovely Nausicaa washed her clothes, are all likewise διιπετής. A great many rivers — the Axios, the Enipeus, and others — are the most beautiful on earth.[2] To Homer, as to children and most poets, the last seen person or natural object is the grandest or most beautiful.

Homer's ideas of distance would be very strange in a great traveller, or even in one who had heard much of foreign countries from others. Thus he tells us that Menelaos, on his return from Troy to Sparta, came from so great a distance that "even a bird would spend a year on the way." He calls the distance from Lesbos to Pylos, and even to Argos, long,[3] and speaks of the voyage of Telemachos as bold and perilous.[4] Penelope, too, is astonished that her sister, married in Thessaly, should undertake the long journey to Ithaca to see her.[5]

Homer, then, is not a historian in the common sense of the word. Where can we draw the line between the palpably fictitious and marvellous and the faithful record of real events?

Still less is he a geographer. If we omit the Catalogue of the Ships and the Allies of Troy, which all admit to be of a much later date, there is surprisingly little geography in the Iliad, though somewhat more in the Odyssey. Homer tells us very little of the countries which his heroes traverse — Laconia, Messene, Argos — but very much of regions and peoples, manifestly fabulous — the Læstrygones, the Lotus-eaters, the Cyclopes,

[1] Il. xvi. 174; Od. vii. 284.   [2] Od. xi. 238.
[3] Od. iii. 169.   [4] Od. iv. 483.   [5] Od. iv. 410.

Homer, above all things, a Poet

the island of Calypso, the floating island of Æolus, and the gardens of Phæacia. In speaking of Ithaca his statements are vague and contradictory. He tells us very truly that it is a rugged country, unfit for horses, but good for goats. But in other passages he speaks of it as a "rich land,"[1] bearing corn and wine in abundance, and covered with flocks. We learn, too, that it is capable of supporting eighteen mighty lords, with property enough to aspire to the hand of Penelope.

The mistake he makes in representing Poseidon as viewing the plains of Troy from the heights of Samothrace, in spite of the intervening island of Imbros, is surprising; but perhaps we ought to remember that a god might see an object at any distance and through any obstacle!

Homer is a poet; and though a great historic event has been rescued for us by him from the dark waves of oblivion, though some of the actors on his stage may have really existed, their characters and their actions are drawn from the inexhaustible resources of his fruitful genius.

[1] Od. xix. 399.

CHAPTER II

THE WONDERLAND OF HOMER

THE moment we enter the wonderland of Homer we tread enchanted ground, we mingle with a godlike company. His imagination teems with the popular fables of a preceding age. We see the giant of fable in the Cyclopes and Briareus; the witch with her magic salve in Circe. We see the magic wand of Athene, the magic girdle of Aphrodite, the wonder-working herb of Hermes, the shoes of Hermes, the sword of Poseidon, the song of the Seirens, the thinking-ships of Phæacia, and the golden dogs and youths of the palace of Alcinous. We see Hermes leading his ghosts to Hades, Æolus and his bag of winds, the εἴδωλα of the shades below, the tokens by eagles, and the "second sight." We see the vampire superstition in the blood-drinking of the disembodied shades below, and the blood-sucking harpies. And even where not supernatural, all is glorious and beautiful. All his heroes are of the grandest stature, noble in bearing, magnanimous in spirit, and "equal to the gods." All strangers and guests have the mien of " sons of the gods," and the beholder is constantly in doubt whether they are human or divine. All the women, young and old, are of noble lineage, stately and graceful, beautiful in form, "like chaste Artemis or golden

His application of Epithets

Aphrodite." They have flowing hair or braided locks, white arms, lovely cheeks, and beautiful ankles. They are all sweet and amiable, loving and tender, and they move across the resplendent stage, the everlasting types of all that is most enchanting in the women of all succeeding ages.

Nor is it only kings and heroes and princely dames who are adorned with honorific epithets. Odysseus's faithful swineherd, Eumæos, is called ἀρίγνωτε[1] (far-famed) and δῖον[2] (divine). Even the hated murderer, Ægisthus, is called ἀμύμων (blameless), and Menelaos speaks of Deiphobos, one of the lovers of his wife Helen, as θεοείκελος (godlike).

This ennobling and purifying process is extended to what we call the lower animals, and even to inanimate objects. All the horses have beautiful manes and outstrip the winds. Some of them are descended from the gods and are immortal; they talk and weep and even prophesy.[3]

In external nature all is serene and beautiful. All the dawns are rose-coloured, all the sunsets pure and glorious. The banquets are all rich and joyous, the wine is old and honey-sweet,[4] and "fit for the table of the gods." And as the joyous revellers satisfy their hunger with delicious food and quaff the "flashing" wine—"the marrow of men"—from golden cups, they listen with delight to the inspired, melodious song of the sacred minstrel.

Into Homer's claims to be also theologian, moralist,

---

[1] Od. xvii. 80.
[2] Od. xxi. 8.
[3] Il. xix. 405.
[4] Μελιηδὴς ἡδίποτος.

The Women of Homer

orator, physician, and surgeon, our limits will not allow us to inquire. Theologian he was in a very practical and emphatic sense, since he created the Olympian gods, and influenced the faith of the most gifted of mankind for centuries. Some writers see a close affinity between the Epics and the Hebrew Scriptures, and this view is advocated by Mr. Gladstone and many learned German Homerologists. The Christian fathers, as we know, accused him of framing fables from the works of Moses.[1] Plato, followed by Plutarch, pretends that Homer possessed all the knowledge of more civilised ages; and the old Stoic, Crates, made him author of treatises on astronomy, medicine, and geography. Plato found allegorical meanings in Homer's writings, and the neo-platonists of the third century A.D. discovered in them their own strange, mystic doctrines. The Stoics claimed him as one who valued virtue alone and scorned all pleasures. Epicurus praised him as one passing his life in a quiet state, amidst feasts and songs; and the Academy as one who regarded all things as uncertain.[2] Ephorus distrusted all statements made before the Dorian migration; but Polybius, Strabo, and Diodorus saw a kernel of truth in all the current myths.

We have still to speak of the vast and enduring influence, and the widely extended reputation, of the greatest of ancient poets. With the exception of Shakespeare perhaps, he is the only bard who has been appreciated to the full, and whose fame is almost as great as his merit. He is *laudatus a laudatis*. His

---

[1] See Bogan, Ὅμηρος ἑβραΐζων Οξ, 1658.
[2] Seneca, *Ep.* 88; Dio. Chrysost. *Orat.* 53.

Fame of Homer in Antiquity

readers in all ages and nations have been the noblest of mankind. Plato thought so highly of the Epics that he burnt his own verses, in despair of rivalling the glorious hexameters in which Homer describes the contest between the river Scamander and Achilles.[1]

His own countrymen acknowledged him as the founder of Greek civilisation; as the great spiritual father of the illustrious poets, philosophers, historians, and orators who succeeded him. He was revered and imitated by Pindar, Æschylus, Sophocles, Euripides, Socrates,[2] Plato, Aristotle, Zeno, Chrysippus, Democritus, and Anaxagoras, by Hesiod, Herodotus, and Thucydides, Xenophon[3] and Demosthenes,[4] and Æschines, Moschus, Theocritus, Antipater Sidonius. The last of these calls him: "Herald of the valour of heroes and the fame of blessed prophets, second sun to the life of Greeks, immortal splendour of the muses."[5] Dio. Chrysostom.[6] says: "Homer, the first and middle and last for every child and man and greybeard."

According to Athenæus,[7] Æschylus used to say that his own tragedies were "the best slices from the rich banquet which Homer had served up." He drew from his great master not only the kernel of the heroic myths,

[1] Il. xxi. 234.
[2] Socrates said, "I admire Homer most of the epic poets."—Xenophon, *Mem.* i. 43.
[3] Xenophon mentions Homer several times in his *Memorabilia* and *Symposium*.
[4] Plato was called the Homer of philosophy. Dionysius Halicarnassus says that Demosthenes imitated Homer. *Cf.* Verb. 24, *Ars Rhetor.* 10, 19; Longinus, *Subl.* cap. 13, 14, 36.
[5] Appendix V. [6] *Orat.* 18.
[7] 8, 39. For the dependence of tragedy on Homer, *cf.* Welcker, *De Epico Cyclo*, and Nitzsch, *Die Sagenpoesie der Griechen*.

The Women of Homer

but also the ideal picture of the heroic age. The same may be said of Sophocles, who has been called "Poeta Ὁμηρικώτατος." To some writers "Sophocles alone seemed a real disciple of Homer; he alone sipped the splendour of his verse, whence he was called Μέλιττα (the bee)."[1] Nor was it only by his immediate countrymen that the influence of Homer was felt. It was owing to the fame of his works that the Greek language and literature, and with them Greek arts and modes of thought and life, were so widely spread in Italy, in Asia, especially India, and in Carthage, where Hannibal wrote his commentaries in Greek.

Dio. Chrysostom. tells us that when Philip of Macedon asked his son Alexander why he read Homer so constantly, he replied: "Not every poem suits a king, any more than every dress. Other poems may give good counsel to private persons, but to us they are of little use. Homer's poetry alone do I find truly noble, grand, and royal. Whoever, therefore, aspires to rule others must betake himself to Homer." In Xenophon's *Symposium* one of the company says: "My father, wishing me to be a good man, made me learn all the poems of Homer, and I can say the Iliad and Odyssey by heart."[2] Athenæus,[3] quoting from Carystius the historian, says that Cassander was so great a lover of Homer (φιλόμηρος) as to know by heart much of the Iliad and Odyssey. In the same chapter he quotes Jason, who wrote that in the sacred rites offered to the god Alexander in the great theatre at Alexandria, Hegesias the player acted

---

[1] See Appendix VI.   [2] 3, 5.
[3] xiv. 620 and xiv. 638.

Homer's 'divine soul'

"scenes from Herodotus," and Hermophantus scenes from Homer. Timomachus relates that Stesander was the first to sing the lays of Homer at Delphi, beginning with the Odyssey.

The ancients thought that noble works could only be achieved under the influence of higher beings. Democritus taught that Homer had received a divine nature; that divine things could only come from a divine soul. Plato[1] declares that ἀμουσία (Muselessness) differs little from godlessness, and describes the ἄμουσον and μισολόγον as akin to the lawless, godless Cyclopes and Centaurs. Pindar,[2] too, says: "He whom Zeus does not love shrinks back from the song of the Muses." Milton, we know, had a somewhat similar conviction: "No one should presume to sing of heroes and famous cities unless he has in himself the experience and the practice of all that is praiseworthy."

We need hardly point out the mighty influence of Homer on the greatest minds of Rome. Without the Iliad we should not have had the Æneid of Virgil, nor indeed any other of his works. Horace holds him up as the great pattern for all poets.[3] Lucretius speaks "semper florentis Homeri" as "sceptra potitus."[4] Propertius says: "Nescio quid majus nascitur quam Iliade" (I know nothing greater than the Iliad), and Cicero[5] agrees with him.

Quintilian found the elements of all the arts in the works of Homer; and at a later period, in the

---

[1] *De Rep.* iii. 313. [2] *Pyth.* i. 25; *Isthm.* iv. 37. [3] *Ars Poet.* 148.
[4] iii. 1050. [5] See Appendices VII. and VIII.

The Women of Homer

Pandects of Justinian, where we should least expect to find poetic enthusiasm, Homer is called "Pater omnis virtutis."

It is indeed difficult to contemplate the image of Homer without a feeling akin to adoration, when we consider the unspeakable blessings, the glorious privileges, he has conferred upon us. He first expressed and widely diffused that spirit of freedom and self-respect which distinguishes the West from the East. To him we owe the Greek tragedians, and in fact all that is best in Attic literature. He created the gods who formed the models for the inimitable works of Grecian sculpture. He inspired the noblest of the Roman poets. To him we owe the mediæval Renaissance, the French classical tragedies of Corneille and Racine, and very much that is best in Dante and Tasso, in Shakespeare and Milton, in Lessing, Goethe, Schiller, Herder, and a host of minor poets of every civilised nation. How poor the world would be without him!

It is not wonderful that such great and widespread fame should excite the envy of detractors. The most notorious of these was Zoilus, who visited Alexandria in 278 B.C., and wrote a work in nine books called ψόγος (Censure), against Homer, and was therefore called Ὁμηρομάστιξ (Scourge of Homer). He tried, it is said, to obtain a hearing at Olympia before assembled Greece, but failed, and, according to an unsupported tradition, was thrown from the Scyronian rocks and then burned, with a copy of his work.[1]

The greatest of modern Zoilists was the illustrious

---

[1] The critics of the present day get off more easily.

Zoilus and French Zoilists

scholar and critic, Julius Cæsar Scaliger (born on Lake Garda in 1484 A.D.), who preferred Virgil to Homer (the moon to the sun), and Seneca to Euripides. Although the greatest of Latinists, he was not so great a Grecian, and was essentially French in his literary perceptions and tastes. "Homer," he says, "is a country wench, Virgil a noble matron; the one is lead, the other gold; the first a mere ballad-singer, the second a true and sublime poet: Homer a shapeless chaos, Virgil the divinity which informed it with life and beauty."

The works of Homer naturally attracted the chief attention of the leaders of the Renaissance, and the admiration they caused did the most to encourage the enthusiastic study of Greek literature.

Dante places Homer in limbo, but speaks of him as "Poeta sovrano"—

"Che sovra gli altri com' aquila vola."

Tasso said that no poet "came nearer to eternity" than Homer, who is more secure from opposition and malevolence than the summit of Olympus from the winds and storms.

At the end of the seventeenth century A.D. there existed a whole school of French Zoilists, and among them many able and popular writers—La Mothe, St. Evremond, Fontenelle, St. Hyacinthe, Terrasson, and Cesarotti. On the other side, as defenders of Homer, we find Boileau, Gacon, Madame Dacier, and others. Boileau's caustic epigram is well known:—

"Clio vint l'autre jour se plaindre au Dieu des vers,
Qu'en certain lieu de l'Univers,

The Women of Homer

On traitait d'auteurs froids, de poètes stériles
    Les Homères et les Virgiles.
' Cela ne saurait être, on s'est moqué de vous,'
    Reprit Apollo en courroux
Ou peut on avoir dit une telle infamie?
' Est-ce chez les Hurons, chez les Topinambours?'
' C'est à Paris.' ' C'est donc dans l'Hôpital des Fous?'
' Non; c'est au Louvre en pleine Académie.'"

Cesarotti, who translated Homer, is quite amusing in his self-conceit: "La traduzione poetica diede al sentimento un torno piu conveniente."

Paolo Beni of Padua greatly preferred Torquato Tasso to Virgil, and Ariosto to Homer: "Ma perche abastanza per aventura, si e mostrato che il nostro Torquato nell' idea del perfetto Capitano et Eroe, meriti ampia lode con restar di non poco superiore a Virgilio, e di gran lungo parimenti ad Homero."

One of the strangest and least justified charges brought against Homer by the Zoilists, ancient and modern, is that of grossness of conception and expression. This is a singular fault to be found by the countrymen of Rabelais and Zola, and by the English, the worshippers of Shakespeare! In support of this charge, reference is made to the speech of Nausicaa to her maidens after her first meeting with Odysseus by the river-side: "Listen, my white-armed maidens, and I will say somewhat. . . . Would that *such a one* might be called my husband, abiding here."[1] She does not even say, "Would that this man were my husband," but only "such a one." What more natural than that

---

[1] Od. vi. 244.

Was Homer coarse?

she should utter such a wish to her familiar comrades, and to them alone? It is well, perhaps, that we do not hear the confidential whispers of even the most modest of maidens to their friends and their maids. If this speech is unmaidenly, what shall we say of Rosalind, that exquisite creation of Shakespeare, who, after seeing Orlando for a few minutes, when he threw the great wrestler Charles, calls him to her, gives him a chain, and says, "Sir, you have wrestled well, and thrown more than your adversaries;" or what shall we think of her still bolder utterances in the 4th Act, Scene 1, of "As You Like It"?

The great scholar Heyne is more just:[1] "Miror verecundiam Homericarum versuum, qui pro illa ætate castissimi sunt" (I wonder at the modesty of the Homeric verses, which, for that age, are most pure).

The wonder is that there should be so little in Homer's lines to shock our moral sense. They are purity itself compared with the filthy stuff which passes current for literature in the plays and novels of the present day in France, and alas! in England too. People who read Zola and the Diabolist poets of France will find little—too little, they will think—to shock them in Homer. With the exception of the Episode in the Eighth Book of the Odyssey, of which the grossest part (ver. 333-343) is rejected by many commentators, there are but few passages in Homer which can wound the most delicate sensibility. There is no trace in Homer of the loathsome vices which polluted the Greeks of the classical period, no lubricous fauns or satyrs. There is

[1] *Ad Homerum*, viii. 405.

The Women of Homer

no attempt on the part of the poet to inflame the imagination or to corrupt the heart; nothing that lowers our respect for the man, and we may safely say that no one was ever the worse for reading his works.

But while we may easily exonerate Homer from the imputation of grossness and sensuality, we must admit that there are traces in his lays of the rudeness, and occasionally of the brutality, of an age anterior to his own.

The reverend spouse of Priam, Hekabe, speaking of Achilles, says: "One whose inmost vitals I were fain to fasten and feed upon."[1]

So Achilles, in answer to Hector's piteous prayer for honourable burial: "Entreat me not, dog, by knees or parents! Would that my heart's desire could so bid me myself to carve and eat raw thy flesh, for the evil thou hast done me."[2]

Even the "wise and prudent" Penelope comes down from her upper chamber, with her maidens, saying: "Come let us go to my child (Telemachus), that I may see the suitors dead, and him that slew them."[3]

Poor Priam, too, in his desperate anxiety for his son Hector, who is about to meet Achilles before the walls, exclaims with bitter irony: "Would that the gods loved him (Achilles) as I do; then would dogs and vultures quickly devour him on the field."[4]

We must acknowledge, in mitigation of the enormity of these atrocious sayings, that they were wrung from

---

[1] Il. xxiv. 212. [2] Il. xxii. 345.
[3] Od. xxiii. 84. [4] Il. xxii. 42.

Remnants of Barbarism in the Epics

the hearts of the utterers by the direst agony, and the sense of intolerable wrong. We may forgive a father and a mother for being driven to madness by the slaughter of a son, and that son a Hector!

There are, indeed, other signs of a barbarism which contrasts strangely with the general civility of manners and courtly grace.

Athene, under the assumed form of Mentes, tells Telemachos that the "goodly" Odysseus goes to Ephyra to ask Ilos, son of Mermeros, for a deadly drug with which to smear his bronze-shod arrows," and adds: "But Ilos would in nowise give it him, for he had in awe the everlasting gods; but my father, Anchialos, gave it him, for he bare him wondrous love."[1]

Telemachos, generally considerate and affectionate to his mother, is on some occasions harsh and rude.

In reply to Athene, as Mentes, who asks him whether he is the son of Odysseus, he answers: "My mother, indeed, saith that I am his; for myself I know not; for never man yet knew, of himself, his own descent."[2]

The admiration accorded to Homer's Epics in the past has been fully maintained in modern times. They have stood the test of the most searching criticism of the most enlightened nations. They remain, after 3000 years, the study of our youth, the delight and solace of our age. As the boys of the grand period of Greek history were trained by Homer, so now his works form a chief study of the children of the ruling classes in England, and still more so in Germany.

Our Milton speaks of him in the same strain as the

[1] Od. i. 260.   [2] Od. i. 215.

The Women of Homer

noblest of the ancients, as the father of all kinds of poetry —tragedy, comedy, ode, and epitaph :—

> "And varied measured verse,
> Æolian charms and Dorian lyric odes;
> And his who gave them breath, but higher sung,
> Blind Melesigenes, thence Homer called,
> Whose poem Phœbus challenged for his own."

Schol. Alcibiad. (I. cap. 1, ed. Tur. p. 916, B. 33) says: "Homer, to whom Apollo himself lent his bow."[1]

Herder and Lessing were zealous Homerologists, and it was from them that Goethe derived his knowledge of the great poet, and his enthusiastic admiration and love of his works. Herder says that Homer was for a long period "the source of all divine and human wisdom, the great centre of Greek and Roman literature."

Goethe, in his beautiful domestic epic, "Hermann and Dorothea," in which he has caught so much of the spirit and colour of the Odyssey, and imitated the metre and rhythm of the Epics as successfully as may be done in a modern language, modestly says: "Doch Homeride zu sein, auch nur als der letzte, ist schön." And again: "Ein Vers Homer's, selbst der unbedeutendste, ist ein Ton aus einem Lande, das wir als ein Besseres, und doch uns nicht fernes, anerkennen."

Goethe tried to write an Achilleis, but failed. Only one song from it is extant, which he sent to Schiller. Bötticher damned it utterly: "Seine Achilleis," he says, "fliesst im Ganzen weder tief noch anmuthig; sie ist *effœta senectutis debilitas.*"

---

[1] *Vide* Appendix IX.

The Opinions of Goethe and Schiller

Although Goethe was no great Greek scholar, he was so imbued with the spirit of Homer that all his utterances about the great poet are of the highest interest. This is warmly acknowledged by the illustrious philologian Hermann, who calls him " Spiritus Graiæ tenuis Camenæ Germanis monstrator."

"While reading Homer," says Goethe, "I feel as if I were in a balloon, raised far above all earthly things, poised in the intermediate space, between heaven and earth, where gods flit to and fro." And again : "The gods of Homer do not wander from star to star, but from mountain to mountain."

According to Lavater, it was Goethe who uttered the well-known fine and pregnant words, when looking at the bust of Homer in the Vatican : "Dieser ist der Schädel, worin die ungeheuren Götter und Heroen eben so viel Raum finden, als im weiten Himmel" (This is the skull in which the mighty gods and heroes found as much room as in the wide heavens).

Goethe sought refreshment and repose in the calm bright world of Homer : "What mean all this pain, this pleasure ? Let us take refuge in the world of Homer's poetry. The spirit must have some relief under the weight of this ruffled, crinkle-crankle life" (krausverworrenen Lebens). "Even to this very day the songs of Homer have the power, at least for a few moments, to free us from the fearful burden of the knowledge, experience, and speculation, which thousands of years have laid on our weary shoulders . . . and to let us sip the dew of the early morn of creation."[1]

[1] *Ethisches*, Abth. 5.

The Women of Homer

Goethe strove to give additional zest even to his favourite pastime, skating, by connecting it with Homer's verses. He recited a curiously applicable passage in the Odyssey describing Hermes, the swift messenger of the gods, putting on his sandals[1]: "Straightway he bound beneath his feet his lovely golden sandals that wax not old, that bare him alike over the wet sea and the limitless land swift as the breath of the wind."[2]

[1] Appendix X. [2] Od. v. 44.

CHAPTER III

THE MAGIC OF HOMER

WHENCE then this magic influence of Homer's lays over all the noblest and highest spirits of every age and clime? How is it that, after two thousand years of Christianity, his gods are still, to a certain extent, *our* gods, the gods of our poetic fancy?

Schiller, in his *Picolomini*, makes Max and Thekla express this truth in beautiful language: " Deeper significance," says Max, "lies in the fables of my childhood's years than in the truths which life teaches us" (Tiefere Bedeutung liegt in den Mährchen meiner Kinderjahre, als in der Wahrheit die das Leben lehrt). And again—

"Fable is the home of Love."

"Die Fabel ist der Liebe Heimatwelt."

"Jove still brings all that is great,
And Venus all that is fair."

"Und jedes Grosse bringt uns Jupiter
Noch diesen Tag, und Venus jedes Schöne."

It is in age, when we begin to look back with regretful longing to our lost childhood, that we feel all the charm of this purest representation of the infancy of the human race. Whence then, I repeat, this irresistible fascination, by which child and sage—the earliest and the latest ages

The Women of Homer

of the world—are equally enthralled? The answer is a long one, for the sources of the charm are numerous and manifold.

In the first place, Homer has no forerunner known to us; he is absolutely original; our attention is not distracted and confused by a multitude of competitors. In the next place, he wielded, with full mastery, the most perfect and beautiful language which the mind of man has ever conceived, which only the ancient Greeks could invent or use—a language of infinite strength, flexibility, and grace; and of that language, a dialect—the Ionico-Æolic—peculiarly suited by its union of softness and strength for the epic verse of Homer, majestic, harmonious, and picturesque.[1]

Again, he found ready to his hand a perfect metre and rhythm, formed by the experience and practice of many generations—a metre which in his hands acquired new beauty, variety, and polish. All that was wanting was a divine genius which could wield all these powerful instruments, and fashion with them an eternal monument of surpassing grandeur and beauty.

Perhaps what gives Homer his greatest power over his hearers is his intense and broad humanity. What chord in the human heart does not vibrate beneath his touch? His songs stir the soul of every human creature, not as Greek or barbarian Jew or Gentile, ancient or modern, but as *man*. He brings us down to the bedrock of human nature, with its strength and its weakness, its joys and its sorrows, its virtues and its vices. We

[1] The epigram says: "Orpheus gained the greatest glory by his lyre, Nestor by his wisdom, but the divine Homer by his mastery in the structure of words" (τεκτοσύνῃ δ'ἐπέων πόλυιστωρ θεῖος Ὅμηρος).

Sources of Homer's Charm

understand and sympathise with the characters he draws so clearly, because they are so like ourselves; not the dressed-up counterfeits we present to the world, but what we know ourselves to be. We delight in his picture of the simple patriarchal life, with its entire freedom from all affectation and hypocrisy, all attempt to simulate or dissimulate emotion.

When Odysseus goes down to Hades and converses with the shades of the glorious dead, Achilles eagerly asks for news of his son Neoptolemus. Odysseus answers: "When the best and bravest of the Argives were about to enter the belly of the Wooden Horse, 'which Epeios constructed for the ruin of Troy,' then did the other princes and counsellors of the Danaans wipe away their tears, and the limbs of each one tremble beneath him; but never once did I see thy son's fair face wax pale, nor did he wipe the tears from *his* cheeks."[1]

Achilles, that mighty man of valour, weeps in his tent for the loss of Briseis, his slave; and in his mourning for his friend Patroklos, he pours black ashes on his head and grovels in the dust, "tearing his hair with both his hands."[2]

Patroklos weeps over the havoc which Hector is making in the Achaian ranks, and Achilles compares him to "a fond little maid who runs crying by the side of its mother, begging to be taken up."[3]

The royal Priam sat in the midst of his sons and daughters, wrapped in his cloak, "and on his head and neck was much mire, which he had gathered in his hands as he grovelled on the ground."

[1] Od. xi. 526.   [2] Il. xviii. 22.   [3] Il. xvi. 7.

The Women of Homer

Priam and Achilles weep copiously together in the tent of the latter,[1] the one for the loss of his son, the incomparable Hector, the other at the mention of his aged father Peleus, whom he was never to see again.

It would never occur to Priam to play the Stoic, and to say with Anaxagoras, "I knew that my son was born a mortal."

In the Odyssey, Odysseus and his hardy crew are perpetually weeping over their manifold misfortunes by land and sea.

Another phase of the frankness with which they give vent to their feelings is their unconcealed egoism, which, although we control it by higher motives, is natural to all men.

Agamemnon[2] says to Teukros, "I will give you a prize, first after myself." So Odysseus, having shot many goats, distributes nine to each ship, and keeps ten for himself alone.[3]

The Homeric heroes openly boast, and praise themselves: "I am Odysseus, son of Laertes, who am in men's minds for all manner of wiles, and my fame reaches unto heaven."[4]

Again, when speaking in disguise to his wife, he says: "Many a woman weeps who has lost her husband ... albeit a far other man than Odysseus, who, they say, is like the gods."[5] So when he spoke in high terms of praise of Neoptolemus to his father's ghost, he says: "He was ever first to speak, and no word missed the mark; the godlike Nestor and I alone surpassed him."[6]

[1] Il. xxiv. 507.   [2] Il. viii. 289.   [3] Od. ix. 160.
[4] Od. ix. 19.   [5] Od. xix. 267. [6] Od. xi. 512.

Frank Boasting of Homer's Heroes

And, again, to the Phæacians he says: "I avow myself far the most excellent of all the mortals that are now upon the earth."[1]

Hector speaks of himself as φαίδιμος (glorious) Hector.

The almost childlike simplicity (naïveté) of Homer's characters is further shown in what we should consider an entire want of reticence and discretion. The Phæacian king Alcinous, on his first meeting with Odysseus, before he knew who he was or whence he came, breaks out with the extraordinary wish, "Would to Father Zeus, and Athene, and Apollo! would that so goodly a man as thou art, and like-minded with me, thou wouldst wed my daughter, and be called my son, here abiding."[2]

Another prominent trait of Homer's character — a trait common to all primitive people — is the immense value set on food and drink.

We read that Menelaos stirs the hearts of his hearers by reminiscences of the lost Odysseus: "Argive Helen wept, and Telemachos wept, and Menelaos, the son of Atreus; nor did the son of Nestor keep tearless."[3] But soon the son of Nestor rouses them: "And now," he said, "be persuaded by me, who for one has no pleasure in weeping *at supper time.*"

So during the terrible interview between the aged Priam and Achilles, when the former ventures into the Achaian camp to beg for the body of his glorious son. After copious weeping, Achilles says: "But now let us think of our meal; for even Niobe thought of eating when she had wept herself tired over her twelve children."[4]

---

[1] Od. viii. 221.
[2] Od. vii. 311.
[3] Od. iv. 183.
[4] Il. xxiv. 601.

The Women of Homer

Odysseus in his dire anxiety—just rescued from a terrible death by the nymph Ino Leucothea and the maiden Nausicaa—even on his first arrival at the palace of Alcinous, is entirely dominated by the desire of food. "There is nothing," he cries, "more shameless than a ravening stomach, which biddeth a man perforce be mindful of it, though one be worn and sorrowful of spirit; yet evermore it biddeth me eat and drink, and maketh me utterly forget all my sufferings, and commandeth me to take my fill."[1] In another place the same Hero says: "Nay, as for me, I say there is no more gracious and perfect delight than when a whole people makes merry, and the men sit orderly at a feast in the halls and listen to a singer; and the tables by them are laden with bread and flesh, and a wine-bearer, drawing the wine, serves it round, and pours it into the cups. *This fashion seems to me the fairest thing in the World.*"[2]

The winecup, too, was held in the highest estimation. Æolus, god of the winds, sits enthroned on his floating island, with his six sons and his six daughters, "feasting evermore by their dear father and their kind mother, and dainties innumerable lie ready at their hands. And the house is full of the savour of feasting, and the noise thereof rings around."[3]

Nausicaa, when describing her father's palace to Odysseus, says: "And there is my father's throne, where he sits and drinks his wine with pleasure, like an immortal god."[4] Agamemnon reminds Idomeneus of the

[1] Od. vii. 216. [2] Od. ix. 4.
[3] Od. x. 5. [4] Od. vi. 308.

Love of Property

honour he had shown him at the banquets of the chiefs: "I honour thee, whether in war . . . or at the feast, when the chieftains of the Argives mingle in the bowl the gleaming wine of the counsellors.[1] For even though all the other long-haired Achaians drink only one allotted portion, thy cup standeth ever full, even as mine, to drink as oft as thy soul biddeth thee."

Another very marked trait in Homeric society is the ardent love of property, the eagerness to acquire. When Athene checks Achilles, who, in his blind fury at the loss of Briseis, is drawing his sword to slay Agamemnon, she tells him that he shall one day receive splendid gifts, three times the value of his captive maiden.[2] And when he reluctantly consents to restore the body of Hector to his suppliant father, he is evidently influenced by the splendid ransom which Priam brings.[3] He thinks it necessary to apologise to the shade of Patroklos, and entreats him not to be angry, "*because he had received no mean ransom.*"[4]

Yet Achilles was not always to be softened by rich gifts. When Agamemnon strives to appease his wrath by noble offers of treasure, he tells the envoys: "Not even if he gave me ten times, nay twenty times, all that now is his, and all that may come to him otherwhence, even all the revenue of Orchomenos, or Egyptian Thebes . . . nay nor gifts in number as the sand or dust . . . neither all the treasure that the stone threshold of the archer Phœbus Apollo encompasseth in rocky Pytho; not even so shall Agamemnon persuade

---

[1] Il. iv. 259 (γερούσιον οἶνον).   [2] Il. i. 213.
[3] Il. xxiv. 138.   [4] Il. xxiv. 592.

The Women of Homer

my soul, till he have paid me back all the bitter despite."[1]

Odysseus is especially remarkable for his love of gifts. When he is landed asleep in Ithaca, his first thought is to hide the rich treasure he had brought with him from Phæacia. "Whither," he wails, "shall I bear all this wealth? ... I know not where to bestow my treasure; yet I will not leave it here behind me, lest haply other men make spoil of it.... But come, I will reckon up these goods and look to them, lest the men be gone and have taken back some of their gifts to the hollow ships."[2] And when Athene appears to him in the guise of a young herdsman, his first prayer is: "Save this my substance"! When he goes, in the guise of a beggar, to his own palace, and sees Penelope conversing with the suitors, he rejoices "that she beguiles their souls and draws rich gifts from them."[3]

It would seem, indeed, that the desire of acquisition was sometimes stronger in him than the love of home and wife. When still unrecognised by her, he recounts his adventures to Penelope. He tells her that her husband is nigh at hand, "and is bringing with him many choice treasures which he begs for through the land." And he adds that "Odysseus would have been with her long since, but that he thought it more profitable to gather wealth as he journeyed over distant lands."[4] He proudly boasts that he was "skilled in gainful arts above all men upon earth."

Even Penelope occasionally shows traces of this

[1] Il. ix. 379.
[2] Od. xiii. 203.
[3] Od. xviii. 281.
[4] Od. xix. 282.

Homer's power of creating Types

passion. When she thinks that she must at last yield to the importunity of the suitors, her chief regret is at leaving the house of Odysseus—"this honourable house, so very fair, and filled with all livelihood, which methinks I shall remember aye, even in my dreams."[1]

Telemachos, in the midst of his anxiety about his father's fate, thinks most of the waste which the wooers of his mother are making of his property. In the Assembly of the Ithacans, when he addresses the lord Ægyptus, and bemoans his own sad fate, he says: "First I have lost my noble father . . . and now there is an evil *greater far*, which surely shall soon make grievous havoc of my whole house, and ruin all my livelihood."[2] One of his chief objections to the remarriage of his mother is, that he would have to return the marriage gift to her father, Icarius.[3]

On another occasion he wishes that he had been "the son of some blessed (wealthy) man whom old age overtook among his own possessions; but now I am the son of him that is the most hapless of men."[4]

What strikes us with the greatest admiration in the works of Homer is his unrivalled power of personification. He fills the heavens with gods, and the earth with demi-gods and heroes, so clearly cut, so distinctly characterised, that we hardly regard them as figments of the fancy. He does not merely describe, he paints and chisels them; the work of the sculptor and the painter is half done for them by the poet. Zeus and Hera, Ares, Poseidon, Hephaistos and Apollo, Athene, Aphrodite and

---

[1] Od. xix. 579. [2] Od. ii. 46.
[3] Od. ii. 132. [4] Od. i. 218.

The Women of Homer

Artemis, Agamemnon, Menelaos, Achilles, Odysseus, Priam, Hector and Paris, Andromache, Penelope, Helen and Nausicaa, are more real and better known to us than nine-tenths of the people with whom we live, of whom we see so much and know so little.

It is true that ages passed away in slow preparation before the sculptor's art attained to the perfection which poetry had already reached in Homer—before the Iliad and the Odyssey could be translated into stone. According to the well-known story, Pheidias, the greatest of artists, derived the central idea of his chryselephantine statue of Zeus at Olympia from the greatest of poets. Being asked from what model he had formed his Zeus,[1] he quoted the famous lines of Homer (Il. i. 527):—

> "He said, and nodded with his shadowy brows,
> Waved on the immortal head the ambrosial locks,
> And all Olympos trembled at the nod."

We are sometimes inclined to regret that we learn nothing of the personality of Homer. But does not this absence of all reference to himself add greatly to his power and charm? Lord Tennyson thanked God that we know nothing of Shakespeare but what he himself tells us. Well, may we not, after all, thank God that we learn nothing of Homer even from himself? He is essentially objective; he never appears upon the stage. Like the great Creator of the universe, we see him not; we only see the work of his hands. Homer

[1] Strabo, viii. p. 353; Macrob., *Saturn.* v. 13, p. 23; Valer. Max. iii. 7, ext. 4.

Objectivity of Homer

is hidden from our eyes, but he speaks to us from the inner sanctuary of the gods of nature.[1] In this respect he differs from Shakespeare, of whose inner nature and life, of whose joys and sorrows, of whose love and hatred, of whose high deep thoughts and childlike simplicity, of whose fiery trials and sordid struggles, of whose brilliant hopes and deep despair, we *do* learn much from his Tragedies and Lyrics.

And Homer differs still more widely from most modern poets, who continually obtrude themselves upon the canvas; who, when they scale Parnassus, are thinking of the crowded plain below, and of the reception they will meet with there—of the smiles and the embraces, the feasts and the music, the wine-cups and the garlands which await them.

One of the greatest vices of modern literature is the boastful display of the subjective feelings of the author. It is a positive relief, too, to be freed in Homer from all abstract and metaphysical terms; to listen to him as an old man listens to the simple prattle of a child.

Very remarkable is the beguiling power—noticed by Pindar and Horace—with which he makes us accept, not only without reluctance, but with the greatest delight, the most audacious and impossible tales of gods and giants, sorcerers and witches, miraculous transformations, thinking ships, talking horses, and moving and

---

[1] Among the curious tales about Homer invented by the commentators of a later age is the well-known riddle: " Homer asked some young men whom he saw returning from fishing, how many fishes they had caught. They replied, '$\delta\sigma'$ ἔλομεν λιπόμεσθα $\delta\sigma'$ οὐκ ἔλομεν φερόμεσθά' ('What we caught we left behind. What we did not catch, we have brought away ')."

The Women of Homer

deathless statues of gold. Horace[1] beautifully expresses this fascination—

> "Semper ad eventum festinat et in medias res,
>   Non secus ac notas auditorem rapit . . .
>   Atque ita mentitur, sic veris falsa remiscet
>   Primo ne medium, medio ne discrepat imum."

> "He hurries to the crisis, lets you fall,
>   Where facts crowd thick as if you knew them all.
>
>   . . . . . .
>
>   Truth blent with fiction in one motley scheme,
>   He so contrives, that, when 'tis o'er, you see,
>   Beginning, middle, end alike agree."

The task of thus making us swallow with content and pleasure the most improbable tales is rendered easier to Homer because he draws no hard and fast line between gods and men, nor indeed between men and the lower animals.[2]

Longinus (9, 7) says that Homer made gods of his men, and men of his gods.

Augustine, in his "Confessions," wishes that he had rather made the men divine than the gods human.

Schiller says: "Als die Götter menschlich waren, waren Menschen göttlicher."

Even Zeus has to fight his way to omnipotence, and is the object of conspiracies of the other gods. The gods of Homer eat and drink, sleep and love, quarrel and fight, just like human beings. Cicero[3] remarks that "the Cyclops Polyphemus was no whit wiser than his favourite ram, to whom he talks."[4]

---

[1] *Ars Poet.* 148. [2] Gladstone, "Studies on Homer," ii. 362.
[3] Tusc. v. 39: "Nihilo enim erat ipse Cyclops quam aries ille prudentior."
[4] Od. ix. 447.

Heroes Kindred of the Gods

The heroes are the sons of gods or goddesses, and even when not half divine by descent, they are "like" or "equal to the immortals"—

> "Kinsfolk of gods, not far from Zeus himself,
> Whose is the altar to ancestral Zeus,
> Upon the hill of Ida, in the sky,
> And still within their veins flows blood divine."[1]

When a stranger asks hospitality in the name of Zeus the Protector (ἱκετήσιος), his hosts are often in doubt whether he be man or god. The gods, and even Zeus, are joined in love with mortal heroines,[2] and goddesses mate with human heroes." The "rosy-fingered Dawn"[3] took Orion for her lover; the fair-tressed Demeter, the hero Iasion;[4] Aphrodite, Anchises;[5] Calypso and Circe, the goodly Odysseus. In their encounters with mortals the gods are not always victorious. Poseidon and Apollo built the walls of Troy for Laomedon for a stated wage, which, when the walls were reared, he refused to pay.[6] Diomed wounds Ares and drives him from the field. He also attacks Aphrodite and wounds her in the hand;[7] and when she goes for sympathy and aid to her mother, Dione,[8] the latter reminds her that many of the gods had suffered wrong at the hands of mortals.

The mightiest of the gods assume not only the form of men, but of beasts and birds, and even inanimate objects. Zeus, the great Lord of heaven and earth, in

---

[1] Plato, *Rep.* iii. (Davies and Vaughan's translation), supposed to be from the "Niobe" of Æschylus.   [2] Il. ii. 513.
[3] Od. v. 121.   [4] Od. v. 124.   [5] Il. ii. 820.
[6] Il. xxi. 452.   [7] Il. v. 334.   [8] Il. v. 384.

The Women of Homer

his Don-Juan-like roving becomes a bull, a swan, and even a shower of gold. Athene repeatedly assumes the human form, either to aid and protect, as in the case of Odysseus, or to deceive and destroy, as in the last contest between Hector and Achilles before the walls of Troy.[1] At other times she appears as an eagle,[2] an osprey, and a falcon (ἅρπη[3]). After urging Odysseus to the slaughter of the suitors, she flies up to the rafters of the murky hall, in fashion like a swallow flies, and there sat down.[4] So Thetis sprang down from Olympos like a falcon, bearing new armour for Achilles. Apollo and Poseidon take the shape of the same bird.[5]

In the Iliad and Odyssey man's immeasurable superiority has not yet led him to the reflection by which the gulf between the thinking mind of man and the instinct of the speechless brute is opened and continually deepened. The noblest heroes are compared to beasts: "The son of Peleus rushed upon him like a lion;"[6] Diomed and his companions fall on the Trojans like ravening lions or wild boars;[7] the troops of Aineias follow him like sheep. Hector, Tydeus, and Odysseus are compared to sharp-toothed pursuing hounds.[8]

Agamemnon, after being likened in head and eyes to Zeus, in waist to Ares, and in breast to Poseidon, is compared to a bull standing out foremost amid the herd.[9] Paris is like a stalled horse, full fed at the

---

[1] Il. xxii. 224.   [2] Od. i. 326; iii. 72.
[3] Il. xiii. 350; v. 778: "Hera and Athene went their way with steps like unto turtle-doves." *Cf.* xviii. 616.
[4] Od. xxii. 239.   [5] Il. xv. 237; xiii. 62.
[6] Il. xx. 164.   [7] Il. v. 782.
[8] Il. viii. 338; x. 360.   [9] Il. ii. 480.

Immortal Horses

manger;[1] the Myrmidones swarm like wasps; the Ajantes are like two wine-dark mules struggling at the plough over rough ground.[2] The Trojans flee before Achilles like locusts before fire,[3] and Athene inspires Menelaos with the boldness and fury of a fly.[4] The plague of flies in Arcadia was so great that the people of that country erected special altars to Zeus ἀπύμυιος, the Fly-averter.[5]

Horses were especially loved and cherished. We find no cavalry in the Greek or Trojan army, and no riding on horseback, except where Diomed, after his nocturnal raid into the Trojan camp, sprang upon a horse and "sped to the swift ships of the Achaians."[6] We have indeed mention of what we should call a circus-rider who leaps from horse to horse while they fly along.[7] Riding is more common in the Odyssey.[8] Very remarkable ideas respecting the horse are to be found in the Iliad. The immortal horses of Achilles are hardly to be controlled by a mere mortal hand, but submit to him, "whom an immortal mother bare," and to Patroklos, whom the noble steeds respected and loved as the dearest friend of Achilles. Automedon says to Alkimedon, "What other Achaian had like skill to guide the spirit of immortal steeds save only Patroklos, peer of gods in council, while yet he lived?"[9] These divine horses, Xanthos and Balios, "that fly as swift as the winds; the horses that the harpy Podarge bare to Zephyros, the west wind, as she grazed on the meadow

---

[1] Il. vi. 506.   [2] Il. xiii. 703.   [3] Il. xxii. 12.
[4] Il. xvii. 570.   [5] Pausanias, v. 14, 1.   [6] Il. x. 510.
[7] Il. xv. 684.   [8] Od. v. 371.   [9] Il. xvii. 476.

The Women of Homer

by the stream of Okeanos."[1] So Boreas, the north wind, became the sire of the horses which Aineras inherited from a long line of ancestors: "These, when they bounded over the Earth, the grain-giver, would run upon the topmost ripened ears of corn and break them not," and "they would run upon the crests of the breakers of the hoary brine."[2]

The very cattle are brought into close relationship with deities. The kine and flocks of Helios in the island of Thrinacia "have no part in birth or in corruption, and there are goddesses to shepherd them, nymphs with fair tresses, Phaethusa and Lampetie, whom bright Neæra bare to Helios Hyperion."[3]

The Homeric Greek was surrounded by divinity, and held close communion with his gods—

> "When, whereso'er he moved
> Alone or mated, solitude was not;
> He heard upon the wind the articulate voice of God."

To the interest of the varied matter of the great Epics — the ever-changing kaleidoscope scenes which the poet presents to us—there comes the charm of his sweet style, the music of his incomparable verse, which flows along, now with a smooth and gentle course over shining pebbles and between flowery banks, and now with the rapidity and thunder of a headlong torrent. And everywhere we breathe the free and joyous spirit of the lovely and lively Ionian youth, formed to harmony and beauty by music and gymnastics, by the Muses and the Graces.

[1] Il. xvi. 151.   [2] Il. xx. 226.   [3] Od. xii. 127.

Contrast between Greeks and 'Barbarians'

What a contrast between the Greek of Homer, living in free and happy intercourse not only with his fellow-men but even with his gods,[1] who shared in his feasts and listened to his prayers—and the Egyptian or Assyrian of the same age, struggling in his political and hieratic bonds, the hopeless slave of priests and tyrants.

[1] Φιλοπαίγμονες καὶ οἱ Θεοί.

CHAPTER IV

POSITION OF WOMEN IN THE ILIAD AND ODYSSEY

IN the foregoing pages we have endeavoured to describe the circumstances, the material and moral atmosphere, in which Homer's characters lived and moved, in order to form, as it were, a suitable frame for the lovely female portraits which his vivid imagination and his plastic genius painted, for the wonder and delight of all succeeding ages.

It is hardly necessary to point out that in the primitive as in the modern world, civilisation was in the main fostered and advanced by women. The men were absorbed in war, the chase, and the struggle for existence. On the women devolved the training of the children, the transmission of national customs and traditions from age to age.

The women of Homer show very favourably when compared with the women of Asiatic Ionia, and of Greece in the classic period. Simonides of Amorgos says that "a good woman was an exception." Hipponax covers them with bitter ridicule; and they appear in the worst possible light in the Comedies of Aristophanes.[1]

The female characters of Homer—among whom we

[1] See Excursus.

Patriarchal Simplicity

must include the goddesses—so thoroughly human, so terribly feminine are they—bear witness to his godlike power of creating eternal types. They vary greatly, of course, in form and character, but all are so clearly defined, so harmoniously consistent with themselves in word and action, that they represent not only the beauty, the grace, and the sweetness of the women of all ages, but also their meanness, their folly, their artifice and treachery, their unbridled passions, and even their desperate cruelty and wickedness. In the main, however, the women of Homer, reared in simple patriarchal surroundings, their inclinations controlled by the sanctity of family life, are amiable and well-behaved, eminently moderate, and correct in word and action. The lady of Homer is the true lady of all times and nations.

Indications of the patriarchal simplicity of the Homeric age meet us at every turn. Paris, a wealthy and accomplished Trojan prince, to whom three of the greatest goddesses appeal as a judge of female beauty, was a shepherd. Princesses and even goddesses go out of the city to draw water from the wells.[1] The Princess Nausicaa washes her own clothes in company with her maidens, "treading them down with their lovely feet." Great kings and heroes slay the sheep and oxen with their own hands, and cook their flesh. Even goddesses —Hera and Athene—yoke the horses and prepare their food.

In the two grand Epics—the one devoted to scenes of war, the deeds of mighty heroes and immortal gods; the other to the bold adventures and the terrible suffer-

[1] Od. x. 105.

The Women of Homer

ings of Odysseus, one of the foremost of Achaian chiefs—we cannot expect to find frequent mention of little children.

As in all early uncorrupted ages of the world, children were regarded as blessings sent as a favour by the gods.[1] Dione, the mother of Aphrodite, threatens Tydides with childlessness for daring to fight against the Immortals: "He is not long-lived that fighteth with the Immortals; nor do his children prattle upon his knees at his return from war and the terrible fray."[2] Niobe was elated even to madness by the glory of having given birth to twelve children, and spoke with contempt of Leto, who had only two.

In India childlessness was punished by the loss of eternal happiness, and was regarded as shameful in China. There was a strange superstition in Greece that some children were born in trees, and this is referred to in the Odyssey.[3]

There are, as we have said, very few references to children in Homer; but now and then the blood-red cloud of war is opened for us, and we get a glimpse into the better world of family affection.

Achilles asks Patroklos: "Wherefore weepest thou like a fond little maid that runs by its mother's side, and bids her mother take her up, snatching at her gown and hindering her in her going, and looks tearfully up at her till her mother takes her up? Like her, Patroklos, dost thou let fall soft tears?"[4]

When Athene turns away the arrow of Pandaros

---

[1] *Cf.* Exodus xxiii. 26; Psalm cxxviii. 3.
[2] Il. v. 406.   [3] Od. xix. 163.   [4] Il. xvi. 7.

NIOBE AND HER YOUNGEST DAUGHTER.

Andromache and Astyanax

from Menelaos, she does so "as a mother driveth a fly from her child that lieth in sweet slumber."[1]

Andromache, in her piteous wail over the corpse of her gallant husband, thinks sadly of the future of her little son Astyanax: "The day of orphanage sundereth a child from his fellows, and his head is ever bowed down and his cheeks are wet with tears. In his sore need the child seeketh his dead father's friends, plucking this one by the cloak, and that one by the coat, and one of them that pities him holdeth his cup a little to his mouth and moisteneth his lips, but his palate he moisteneth not. And some child, unorphaned, thrusteth him from the feast with blows and taunting words: 'Out with thee! no father of thine is at our board.' Then weeping to his widowed mother shall he return, even Astyanax, who erst upon his father's knee ate only marrow and fat flesh of sheep, and when sleep fell on him and he ceased from childish play, then in his nurse's arms he would slumber softly nestling, having satisfied his heart with good things."[2]

At the birth of a child the Ἐιλείθυιαι μογοστόκοι (the goddesses of the birth pangs), daughters of Zeus, stood at the mother's side with consolation and help. Children were often nursed by their own mothers, and notably so in the case of Hector and Telemachos.[3] Nurses, however, were in common use. The great goddess Demeter, during her wanderings in search of her daughter Persephone, hired herself to Metaneira to bring up Demophoon.[4]

---

[1] Il. iv. 130. [2] Il. xxii. 490. [3] Il. xxii. 83; Od. xi. 448.
[4] *Hym. Cer.* 101, 218, 236.

The Women of Homer

We may easily imagine what the children of the beautiful Greek race would be when we see into what loveliness they afterwards developed. Their mothers prayed that they might grow up like golden Aphrodite in beauty and charm, and like Athene in wisdom and skill in handiwork.[1] The education of the girls was of the simplest. They grew up in the apartments of the mother, from which all that was foreign was excluded, and learned from her, without any formal intellectual training, all that seemed necessary for their future career —a modest bearing, skill in needlework and in the management of a household, and, above all, in reverence for the gods, and some knowledge of sacrificial usages. Their early years were full of play and mirth. In the description of the shield of Achilles, we read that "the maidens and the striplings, in childish glee, bare the sweet fruit in plaited baskets. And in the midst of them a boy made pleasant music on a clear-toned viol, and sang thereto a sweet Linos-song with delicate voice, while the rest, with feet falling together, kept time with the music and the song."[2]

No doubt music formed an important element in the education of girls as well as boys. Its subduing and entrancing influence is well set forth in the legends of Orpheus, and in the irresistible power attributed to the song of the two Seirens, and in the honour paid to the sacred bards.

The mutual love between parents and children was

---

[1] Il. ix. 389.
[2] Il. xviii. 570. The term μουσική was by no means restricted to *our* music, but included all science and even philosophy. The training in it was not only serious but severe. See Appendix XI.

Parental and Filial Love

strong and enduring. The feeling of the wrecked Odysseus at the sight of land is compared to the joy of children at the recovery of a father "who lies in sickness and strong pains."[1]

When Priam ventures into the Grecian camp and the tent of the terrible Achilles, the slayer of his son, he appeals for mercy in the name of Peleus, the dread hero's father: "'Fear thou the gods, Achilles, and have compassion on me, bethinking thee of thy father.'[2] Thus spake Priam, and stirred within Achilles desire to make lament for his father. . . . And as they bethought them of their dead . . . Achilles wept for his own father . . . and their moan went up through the house."

Odysseus' mother dies of regret for his absence; when he sees her shade in Hades, she says: "It was my sore longing for thee, and for thy counsels, great Odysseus, and for thy loving-kindness, that reft me of sweet life."[3]

In the well-guarded sanctuary of her home the Greek maiden bloomed in the hereditary beauty and stately grace of her richly endowed race.

In his Nausicaa, the daughter of the Phæacian king Alcinous, Homer gives us a perfect picture of the Greek girl in the springtide of her youth and beauty.

Nausicaa was the Greek maiden *in excelsis*, and no English girl, reared by wise and loving parents in a country home, as yet untainted and unsoured by the jealousies, the rivalries, and the heart-aches of a London season, ever stepped from her bower into her garden

---

[1] Od. v. 394.   [2] Il. xxiv. 504; *cf.* xix. 334.   [3] Od. xi. 200.

more lovely, fresh, and joyous than this fair daughter of Alcinous.

But carefully as we see that the Homeric maiden was reared in reverent obedience to her parents, and in piety to the gods, we must not suppose that she was, like the women of the East, immured in walls, or subjected to the rigid surveillance of jealous duennas. She enjoyed far greater freedom in the heroic than in the later classical period, and was in all respects superior to the Attic girl of the fifth and fourth centuries B.C.

Great stress is laid on the joys of dancing, in which the maidens joined with the youths. Thus in the relief on the mighty shield which Hephaistos made for Achilles, we find the representation of a joyous dance: "Also did the glorious lame god devise a dancing place, like to that which, in wide Knossos, Daidalos wrought for Ariadne of the lovely tresses. There were youths dancing, and maidens of costly wooing, their hands upon one another's wrists. Fine linen had the maidens on, and the youths well-woven doublets faintly glistening with oil. Fair wreaths had the maidens, and the youths daggers of gold hanging from silver baldricks." [1]

When the suitors of Odysseus had put from them the desire of meat and drink, they minded them of other things, even of the song and dance, for "these are the crown of the feast." [2] Odysseus, anxious to conceal the slaughter of the suitors from the knowledge of the public, institutes a dance in which youths and maidens join.[3] "'First,' he orders, 'go ye to the bath and array you in your doublets; and bid the maidens in the chambers

---

[1] Il. xviii. 590. [2] Od. i. 152. [3] Od. xxiii. 131.

The Joyous Dance of Youths and Maidens

take to them their garments. Then let the divine minstrel, with his loud lyre in hand, lead off the measure of the joyful dance.' . . . And the divine minstrel took the hollow harp and aroused in them the desire of sweet song and the happy dance. So the great hall rang round them with the sound of the feet of dancing men and fair-girdled women."

Hermes falls in love with the beautiful Polymede,

A DANCE.
From a relief in the Phigaleian Room, British Museum.

"fair in the dance," when he beheld her among the singing maidens in the choir of Artemis.[1] Hector, communing with his own soul whether he should go and conciliate Achilles, decides, "This is no time to dally with him from oak-tree or from rock, as youth and maiden hold dalliance with one another."[2] The skilful dancer

[1] Il. xvi. 180. [2] Il. xxii. 126.

The Women of Homer

was evidently in high repute, and outside the walls of Troy there was a monument to "the bounding Myrine," a famous dancer.[1]

The women of Homer were very careful to observe the *convenances* of their sex and station. They might remain in the room when their husbands received strangers, but they were always accompanied by their attendant maids.

Helen, restored to husband and home in Sparta, "came forth from her fragrant vaulted chamber, like Artemis of the golden arrows; and Adraste set for her the well-wrought chair, and Alcippe bare a rug of soft wool, and Philo a silver basket."[2] So Andromache, even in her dread anxiety about the fate of Hector, does not omit to call on her maidens to follow her to the walls:[3] "Come two of ye this way with me, that I may see what deeds are done."

Penelope, too, is followed by her maidens when she goes to the hall of the men to hear the minstrel Phemios: "And from her upper chamber the wise Penelope caught the glorious strains; and she went down the high stairs, but not alone. 'Bid Autonoe and Hippodameia,' she says, 'come to stand by my side in the halls, for alone I will not go among men, for I am ashamed.'"[4]

The love and worship of physical beauty is one of the most striking characteristics of the Greek race. We see it everywhere throughout their history and literature. A favourite epithet of their country is Ἑλλάδα καλλιγύναικα (Hellas famed for fair women), and we meet with

[1] Il. ii. 814.
[2] Od. iv. 120.
[3] Il. xxii. 450.
[4] Od. xviii. 185.

Greek Love of Beauty

numerous words significant of beauty, as εὔμορφος, εὐειδής (fair in form), καλλιπάρηος (with beautiful cheeks), καλλίστερνος (beautiful breasted), καλλιβλέφαρος (with beautiful eyelids), καλλιπλοκάμος (with beautiful locks), καλλίσφυρος (with beautiful ankles), καλλίπηχυς (with beautiful elbows), &c.

We see this love in the story of Helen, whose entrancing and bewildering beauty electrified the bloodless old Trojan sages, as they sunned themselves on the walls of Troy, "like grasshoppers that sit on a tree and utter their lily-like (delicate) voice."[1] "When they saw Helen coming to the tower they softly spake winged words to one another: 'Small blame is it that Trojans and well-greaved Achaians should, *for such a woman*, long time suffer hardships; marvellously like is she to the immortal gods to look upon."

Nor did they only appreciate the loveliness of *women*. Altars were raised to youths whose beauty seemed to them a godlike thing. The "golden-throned Dawn" snatched away Kleitos "for his very beauty's sake, that he might dwell with the Immortals."[2] The Greeks were astonished at the beauty of Hector's corpse: "And other sons of the Achaians ran up around, who gazed upon the stature and marvellous goodliness of Hector."[3] So, at a later period, the Greeks admired the beauty of the dead Masistos.[4]

The marvellous beauty of Endymion—"the eversleeping"—drew down Selene (the moon) from the skies at night, "that she might kiss him unobserved."

---

[1] Il. iii. 150.
[2] Od. xv. 250.
[3] Il. xxii. 369.
[4] Herod. ix. 25.

The Women of Homer

The exquisite sense of perfection of form revealed to us in the works of Greek sculptors, which we admire even in copies, attest the love of beauty which penetrated the soul of the artists and inspired them with a godlike power. As we should expect in a people only lately emerging from barbarism, the woman was chiefly prized for her personal charms—her beauty of face and form,[1] her fair cheeks and sparkling eyes.

When Agamemnon is called on to resign Chryseis to her father, he expresses his extreme reluctance, saying: " I prefer her to Clytemnestra, my wedded wife, for in nowise is she inferior, neither in favour, nor stature, nor wit, nor skill."[2]

But it was not only for their fair persons that women, and even goddesses, were prized. The great goddess of wisdom, Athene, wove her own garments, and instructed her favourites in the art.[3] All the demi-goddesses, princesses, and heroines are praised for their skill in splendid handiwork.[4] In the haven of Phorkys, in Ithaca, the Naiads "on their great looms of stone weave raiment of purple stain, a marvel to behold."[5]

Achilles, when rejecting the offer of Agamemnon's daughter, declares that he would not wed one of them, "not if she were the rival of golden Aphrodite for fairness, and of the bright-eyed Athene for handiwork."[6]

When Hector goes to rouse Paris to join in the battle, he finds the fair Helen, for whom thousands were risking their lives, sitting with her attendant maidens, all employed in "brave handiwork." She herself was working

---

[1] "δέμας, μέγεθος—μῆκος." [2] Il. i. 113. [3] Il. v. 735.
[4] Il. xiii. 288. [5] Od. xiii. 107. [6] Il. ix. 388.

Skill in Handiwork

at a web, famous through all antiquity, on which the war of the Greeks and Trojans was skilfully depicted. So Penelope, "whom Athene endowed beyond all women with knowledge of handiwork," was busy for years upon the splendid shroud for Laertes with which she deluded the suitors, telling them that she would marry one of them when it was finished.[1]

Eurylochos reports to his chief Odysseus that, on his arrival "at the fair halls of Circe, there was one that fared before a mighty web, singing a sweet song." So Hermes, the messenger of Zeus, when he goes to Calypso's island to set Odysseus free, finds the crafty Nymph within the house "singing with sweet voice, as she fared to and fro before the loom and wove with a shuttle of gold."[2]

[1] Od. ii. 101.   [2] Od. v. 61.

CHAPTER V

MARRIAGE

IT would be a mistake to conclude from the high position held by some of the great ladies we have mentioned—Andromache, Penelope, Helen, and Arētē—that there was anything like equality between the sexes. The women of Homer had really no *rights*, and their position was entirely defined by the will and the requirements of men. The influence of the woman over her husband is entirely personal. Man's will is absolute, but he listens to the wife he loves.

When Arētē, the Phæacian queen, expresses her opinion of Odysseus, Lord Echeneus, the Phæacian elder, defines her exact position, as a beloved and respected wife: "Friends, the speech of our wise queen is not wide of the mark, nor far from our deeming; so hearken thereto. *But on Alcinous here both word and work depend.*"

Marriage was a matter of arrangement and barter between the suitor and his intended father-in-law.[1] The successful wooer was generally the one who offered the most costly marriage gifts (ἔδνα). Much-courted maidens were called παρθένοι ἀλφεσίβοιαι (virgins who brought

[1] How different from our own matrimonial arrangements, in which love and merit alone decide!

Wives purchased from their Father

many oxen to their parents), "maidens of costly wooing."[1]

A common epithet applied to a woman was ὠνητή (purchased), who might be either one bought from her father, or a slave. Raids were continually made to capture women, who were regarded as the most precious booty. The woman thus acquired in war was called δουρικμητή (gained by the spear). Achilles boasts: "Twelve cities of men have I laid waste from shipboard, and from land eleven.... I was wont to watch out many a sleepless night, and pass through many days of battle, warring with folk for their women's sake."

We see that brigandage, the chief objects of which were the women, was highly honourable, and formed the chief occupation of the highest classes. The process was a simple one—the men were put to the sword, the women carried off as booty. "The prize," says Hector, "which Achilles doeth battle for, will be our city and our wives."

The marriageable girl or widow was, in fact, put up to auction. Telemachos says of Penelope: "My mother has divisions of heart, whether to abide here with me, respecting the bed of her lord and the voice of the people, or to go straightway with whomsoever of the Achaians that woo her in the halls, is the best man, and *gives the most bridal gifts.*[2]

---

[1] Very different from the custom of the Romans! Chremes (Terence, *Heauton-Timoroumenos*, act iv. sc. 7) complains that he has to find some one to marry to his daughter, to whom he may give his property:—

> "Quam multa justa injusta fiunt moribus!
> Mihi nunc relictis rebus inveniendus est,
> Aliquis labore inventa mea cui dem bona."

[2] Od. xvi. 77; xx. 335; xxi. 162.

The Women of Homer

Iphidamas, whom Agamemnon slew, gave a hundred kine for his wife, and promised "thereafter to give a thousand goats and sheep together."[1] So Peleus "wedded Chloris, on a time, for her beauty, and brought gifts of wooing past number."[2]

Penelope on one occasion taunts the suitors with their meanness, and tells them that "those who wish for a good lady ought to bring with them oxen of their own and goodly flocks, and a banquet for the friends of the bride, and give splendid gifts."[3] Sometimes, however, as in the days of chivalry, a man might win his bride by *heroic deeds* and *personal merit*.

Othryoneus, who came to defend Troy against the Achaians, sought to gain the hand of Cassandra, "the fairest of Priam's daughters," without gifts of wooing, promising to drive the Achaians out of the land of Troy.[4] Agamemnon, when he offers his daughter to Achilles, not only does not ask for ἕδνα, but promises to give with her a mighty dower "such as no man ever gave," viz. seven well-peopled cities, with flocks and kine innumerable.[5] Alcinous, the Phæacian king, promises to give to the shipwrecked suppliant, Odysseus, his daughter Nausicaa "with house and wealth."[6]

Yet we find no word signifying dowry; for μείλια (soothing things[7]), which Agamemnon offers to Achilles, occurs only once, and cannot be taken to indicate the practice of giving a fortune with the daughter. The women bought from their fathers, or carried off from conquered cities, were at the absolute disposal of their

---

[1] Il. xi. 243.   [2] Od. xi. 282.   [3] Od. xviii. 276.   [4] Il. xiii. 366.
[5] Il. ix. 289.   [6] Od. vii. 314.   [7] Il. ix. 147.

Entire Dependence of Women

husbands or masters. They could be offered as prizes for the victor in athletic games. In those which Achilles celebrated in honour of Patroklos, we read that he brought forth prizes from his ships, "caldrons and tripods, and horses and mules, and strong oxen, and *fair girdled women*, and grey iron."[1] One of the prizes for the charioteers was a woman skilled in handiwork, "a noble prize"[2]; and the consolation prize in the wrestling match was also *a skilled woman, valued at four oxen*.[3]

Dependence on the man was the lot of the woman during her whole life, and there was no escape. From the tutelage of her father she passes into the hands of her husband, who has absolute power over her. The word πόσις meant master as well as husband. When he dies, the grown-up son succeeds to his father's rights. Telemachos, for instance, *could* have given his mother[4] to any one of the suitors, and was well aware of his power; but he was restrained from exercising it, partly by affection and partly by more mercenary motives. To Antinoos, who urges him, he says: "It can in nowise be that I should thrust forth from the house, against her will, the woman that bare me and reared me."[5] And he adds: "Moreover, it is hard for me to make heavy restitution to Icarius" (Penelope's father), "as needs I must if, of my own will, I send my mother away."

If her husband was slain in battle, the widow became the slave of the conqueror, however high her previous

---

[1] Il. xxiii. 260. [2] Il xxiii. 264. [3] Il. xxiii. 705.
[4] Od. ii. 113. [5] Od. ii. 132.

The Women of Homer

rank may have been. Hector paints in the gloomiest colours the condition into which the high-born princess Andromache must fall, when he shall no longer be near to protect her. "Yea, of a surety," he says, "the day shall come for holy Ilios to be laid low. . . . Yet doth the anguish of the Trojans hereafter not so much trouble me, neither Hecabe's own, neither King Priam's, neither my brethren's, the many and brave, . . . as doth *thine* anguish, in the day when some mail-clad Achaian shall lead thee away weeping, and rob thee of the light of freedom. So shalt thou abide in Argos, and ply the loom at another woman's bidding, and bear water from fount Messeis or Hypereia, being grievously tormented."[1]

No doubt the fact that the captive women were often of noble and even royal lineage rendered the relations between them and their masters much more tolerable. These were, of course, as much the slaves of their owners as were the nigger women and quadroons of America. But personally they were on a level with the legitimate wives, and were therefore generally treated with kindness and consideration. We do not read of any instances of brutal violence inflicted on female slaves.

Monstrous as it seems to us that women, both as wives and captives, should be subjected to the caprice of the "predominant partner," it is evident that they looked on their position as quite in the natural order of things, and bore it with wonderful patience and resignation.

Briseis, a maiden of princely descent, and "like to

[1] Il. vi. 451.

Agamemnon, Achilles, and Briseis

golden Aphrodite," is a striking instance of this. Achilles had slain her father and her two brothers, and had taken her from her home by force. Yet she is evidently attached to him; and when the envoys of Agamemnon come to lead her away, their parting is a sad one; she goes with them "all unwilling," and Achilles "wept anon."[1]

When Patroklos is slain, she mourns for him with the most affectionate regret, chiefly because he had promised to make her Achilles' wedded wife and prepare a marriage feast for her among the Myrmidones.[2]

The entire dependence of the woman on her husband, or the master, was never forgotten by either of them. Andromache, the dearly-beloved of Hector, quietly submits to his rebuke, after their last sad meeting on the walls. In piteous terms she entreats him not to meet Achilles before Troy. In reply, he bids her not to meddle with warlike matters: "Go to thy house, and see to thine own tasks—the loom and the distaff—and bid thy handmaids ply their tasks; but for war

BRISEIS AND AGAMEMNON.

[1] Il. i. 346, xix. 132.   [2] Il. xix. 282.

The Women of Homer

shall men provide, and I, the chief of all men who dwell in Ilios."[1]

Among the eminent slaves mentioned in the Epics are Eurymedusa, who reared Nausicaa; Iphis, daughter of Enyeos, king of Scyros, a slave of Patroklos; Alcippe, a handmaid of Helen; Hekamede, daughter of the great-hearted Arsinoos; Autonoe and Hippodameia, slaves of Penelope.[2] Perhaps the most instructive example of the position to which a slave might attain is that of the wise and thoughtful Eurykleia, the nurse of Telemachos, and the trusted friend and confidante of Odysseus and Penelope. She was a woman of noble lineage, daughter of Ops, son of Peisenor,[3] whom Laertes, the father of Odysseus, had bought for twenty oxen while as yet she was in her first youth. Laertes had respected her, although she was his bondwoman, "for he feared the wrath of his lady wife." She became the loving nurse of Telemachos, and the trusted ruler of the house, to whom the other servants looked to assign to them their several tasks. She participated in all the joys and sorrows of the family, and her advice and assistance are of the greatest value to her master and mistress. She calls Penelope "my child," and Penelope calls her "dear little mother."[4] To her alone Telemachos confides the secret of his intended journey in search of his father.[5] It was she who first recognised Odysseus by the scar on his foot, which she was bathing, and, in spite of her excitement, she faithfully kept the secret from Penelope.[6] Yet there is no doubt of her

[1] Il. vi. 490. [2] Od. vii. 8. [3] Od. xx. 149.
[4] Od. xxiii. 5. [5] Od. ii. 349. [6] Od. xix. 380, 390, and 467.

servile condition and absolute dependence. When she comes to the upper chamber of her mistress, "laughing aloud," to tell her that her dear lord was within, "and her knees moved fast for joy, and her feet stumbled one over the other," she finds Penelope asleep. On awaking, Penelope treats her as a mad woman, and harshly chides her: "Get thee down and back to the women's chamber, for if any of the other maids of my house had brought me such tidings, and awakened me from sleep, straightway would I have sent her back right rudely, but old age shall stand thee in good stead."[1]

The case of Eurykleia was, no doubt, an exceptional one, and slavery must have had its hardships and its inevitable demoralising effects. "Thralls," says Eumaios, the goodly swineherd, "are no more inclined to honest service, when their masters have lost their dominions; for Zeus of the far-borne voice takes away the half of a man's virtue, when the day of slavery comes upon him."[2]

The female slaves in a Greek household were divided into several classes, according to their different qualities and abilities. The majority seem to have been employed in handiwork of various kinds. All the garments were made in the house, for the use of the family, or to be laid up in store as presents for guest-friends and strangers. The hardest work performed by women was that of grinding at the mill and drawing water.

---

[1] Od. xxiii. 20.
[2] Od. xvii. 352. *Cf.* Aristoph. *Vesp.* 1337 : Τί δ' ἔστιν ὦ παι; παιδα γὰρ κἂν ᾖ γέρων καλειν δίκαιον ὅστίς αν πληγὰς λάβῃ.

The Women of Homer

Although marriage was, as we have seen, a matter of purchase and barter in the world of Homer, it was evidently considered as an honourable estate, and nowhere do we find more pleasing pictures of conjugal affection and family life. Odysseus says: "He that stayeth away from his wife for a single month in his benched ship, fretteth himself when wintry storms and the furious sea imprison him." The same hero, when supplicating the mercy of Nausicaa, offers up a prayer for her: "May the gods grant thee a husband and a home, and a mind at one with him; for there is nothing nobler than when man and wife are of one heart and mind in a house, a grief to their foes, and to their friends great joy; *but their own hearts know it best.*"[1]

So Achilles, in his bitter lament at the loss of Briseis, asks indignantly: "Do the sons of Atreus alone love their wives? Surely whoever is good and sound of heart loveth his own and cherisheth her, even as I loved mine with all my heart, though but the captive of my spear."[2]

We find hardly any trace of polygamy in Homer, except in the case of King Priam, in whose history there is some oriental colour. Concubinage was more common, and not considered dishonourable. The woman was in general faithful to her husband, and Penelope has been held up to countless generations as the very type and ensample of a loyal wife. So happy had she been in her marriage with Odysseus, that she thought "the gods were jealous that they should abide together and have joy of their youth." Hector, Menelaos, and Odysseus were

[1] Od. vi. 180.   [2] Il. ix. 339.

Licence allowed to the Husband

all regarded as faithful husbands. But observe the difference between what was expected of the woman and the man ; between the sad and sober life of Penelope, who, amidst noble, clamorous, and persistent suitors, never ceased to mourn for her absent lord—and that of Odysseus, consoling himself in the bowers of Calypso and Circe! He yearned, indeed, to see "if it were but the smoke leap upward from his own land," and his face was ever turned towards home, for which he refused the offer of immortality with the charming nymph Calypso.[1] "For myself," he says, "I can see nought beside sweeter than a man's own country . . . though he dwell far off in a rich house in a strange land."[2] But he had no scruple, on his wife's account, in remaining seven years with her and one whole year with Circe. We gather from the narrative that his longing to leave Calypso was quickened by the fact that he was rather tired of her, goddess though she was; "for the nymph *no more* found favour in his sight."[3] But no one, not even Penelope, thought of blaming Odysseus for his infidelities. The same conduct on the part of a wife would have been regarded as altogether shameful, and she or her father would be required to return the ἕδνα to the injured husband.[4] The marriage was celebrated as a joyous event with feasting, dancing, and music ; and sacrifices were offered to the gods, for the bride was their precious gift. Prayers were made to Aphrodite for her assistance, and the wrath of the virgin goddess Athene was deprecated. Athene tells

---

[1] Od. v. 134.
[2] Od. ix. 28, 35.
[3] Od. v. 154.
[4] Od. viii. 349.

The Women of Homer

Telemachos to put all his possessions into the hands of the most trusty of his maids "till the day when the gods shall show thee a glorious bride."[1]

At the wedding of Thetis with Peleus, a mortal husband, all the gods were present, and among them Phœbus Apollo, with his lyre.[2] On the shield of Achilles the divine artist Hephaistos represented such a πομπή at a marriage festival.[3] "Beneath the blaze of torches, they were leading the brides from their chambers through the city, and loud rose the bridal song."[4] The mother of the bride lit the torches, which were borne by servants. Blooming maidens and youths led the procession in a dancing chorus, playing on the lute and singing the Hymenaios; the bride followed, in gold-embroidered garment and shining veil, with a myrtle garland on her head. It was customary for the bride to give garments to those who accompanied her to the bridegroom's house,[5] and for the bidden guests to bring contributions to the marriage feast.

When Telemachos goes to Sparta in search of his father, he finds the king, Menelaos, engaged in the celebration of a double marriage, viz.: of Megapenthes, his son by a slave woman, to the daughter of Alector of Sparta; and of his daughter, whom he was sending away, with chariot and horses, to be the wife of the son of Achilles, in the famous city of the Myrmidones.[6] "They were all feasting through the great vaulted hall, the neighbours and friends of

---

[1] Od. xv. 25. [2] Il. xxiv. 61.
[3] Il. xviii. 492. [4] Il. xviii. 491; see Appendix XII
[5] Od. vi. 30. [6] Od. iv. 3

Joyous and Festive Weddings

renowned Menelaos making merry; and among them a divine minstrel was singing to the lyre, and as he began the song, two tumblers in the company whirled in the midst."

The life of the Greek woman in marriage was simple and patriarchal, and, in the highest class, very much like that of the great ladies in the age of mediæval chivalry. They ruled the house, allotted their tasks to the numerous slaves, reared the children, with the help of nurses both male and female, and spent much of their leisure time at the loom and in the fashioning of garments. Even the rich Helen and Penelope had always the *fuseau* in their hands, and felt that there could be no degradation in work, in which nymphs and goddesses and the great Athene herself were proud to excel.

As a natural result of their peculiar marriage arrangements, and the complete ascendency of man, we mark the entire absence of what we call romance and sentimentalism in the Homeric maiden. She quietly submits to be handed over to the highest bidder, and to be transferred from one master to another, as if she were only conforming to a law of nature. It is only in the married woman, who happened to have a husband she could love, —in an Andromache and a Penelope—that we meet with expressions of strong emotion, and even these are restrained by the Greek αἰδώς.

We have already spoken of Briseis. All that we hear of her feelings when she was torn from the arms of Achilles is that she left him "unwillingly"; there were no shrieks, no hysterics; she was a *woman,*

The Women of Homer

accustomed to see herself disposed of by the arbitrary will and caprice of men. When Hermes comes to the island of Calypso with an order to release Odysseus, "she shudders" at first, and complains that the great gods are hard and jealous, grudging that goddesses should mate openly with mortals. She instances the cases of Orion and the rosy-fingered Dawn, of Iasion and the fair-tressed Demeter.[1] But she very soon recovers her equilibrium, and quietly provides Odysseus with timber and tools to build his raft, and cloth to make the sails, which were to bear him away to her rival Penelope. After bathing him, and clothing him "in fragrant attire," she walks with him to the shore, furnishes the raft with corn and wine and "a great store of dainties," and causes a warm and gentle wind to blow. She does not accuse him of heartlessness; indulges in no recrimination, but wishes him good luck and a safe voyage to his home, and then quietly returns to her cave.[2]

How different is her conduct from that of Queen Dido, under similar circumstances, when Æneas stealthily deserts her!

> "Tum vera infelix fatis exterrita Dido
> Mortem orat; tædet cœli convexa tueri."[3]

> "Dido, oppressed by the fates that await her,
>   wild with affright,
> Prays but to die; she is weary of heaven's blue
>   vault and the light."

---

[1] Od. v. 121. [2] Od. v. 265.
[3] Virg. Æn. iv. 450 and 658.

Calypso and Dido

"Dixit et os impressa
Moriemur inulta, sed moriamur."

"She pressed to the pillow her lips,
And as she pressed them cried: 'Do I die unavenged on the foe?
Yet let me die! Thus, thus, with joy to the shadows I go."[1]

The lovely Nausicaa, though her heart was strangely moved by the noble stranger Odysseus, never loses her self-control. When he departs she calmly bids him farewell: "Nausicaa, dowered with beauty by the gods, stood by the doorpost of the well-builded hall, and marvelled at Odysseus, ... and spake to him winged words: 'Farewell, stranger; see that thou remember me in thine own country on a day, for to me first thou owest the price of life.'"[2] There is no tearing of the hair, no thought of suicide. She is not ready, like many a heroine of modern literature, to risk damnation for a single kiss; nor does Odysseus, though evidently moved by the beauty, grace, and sweetness of this noble girl, desire, like the modern German poet, "to tear a pine-tree from a Northern forest, to dip it in the glow of Etna, and to write in letters of flame across the firmament, '*Agnes, I love thee!*'"

[1] Lord Bowen's Translation.   [2] Od. viii. 461.

CHAPTER VI

DRESS OF WOMEN IN HOMER

THE love of beauty naturally led to the love of dress, by which that beauty is adorned and heightened. Frequent mention is made of δέσματα σιγαλόεντα (shining garments), and the value set on them is shown by numerous epithets, as εὔπεπλος (with beautiful peplos), εὔζωνος (well girdled), καλλίζωνος (with beautiful zone), καλλικρήδεμνος (with beautiful veil), καλλιπέδιλλος (with beautiful sandals). Other terms imply the beauty and the careful dressing of the hair, as εὐπλόκαμος, καλλιπλόκαμος (with goodly locks), λιπαροπλόκαμος (with glossy locks).

The Homeric poems give us the dress of the Æolico-Ionians down to the ninth or eighth century B.C.; nor do we find much change in costume in the hymns attributed to Homer, or in the works of Hesiod.

A great but very common mistake made even by distinguished artists,[1] when carving or painting Homeric heroines, is to transfer to them the ideas they have gained from statues and pictures of the classical period of Greece. The dress of Helen, when she appeared in her radiant beauty before Priam and the Trojan elders, was very different from what we see in the pediments

---

[1] Perhaps for sufficient artistic reasons.

The πέπλος, ἐιανὸς, and φᾶρος

and friezes of the Parthenon, and was much more oriental in its character.[1]

The women of the Iliad and Odyssey wore only one garment, the πέπλος, ἐιανὸς, or ἑανὸς, which continued to be worn by the Dorian women down to a much later period. This dress was, no doubt, brought to Hellas by their noble Aryan forefathers from their homes in Asia.

Euripides[2] speaks of the μονόπεπλος Δῶρις (the simple-robed Dorian woman), and derides the Spartan maiden as unwomanly (μηροῖς καὶ πέπλοις ἀνειμένοις); and Ibycus derisively calls them φαινομηρίδες.

The peplos, or heanos, consisted of an oblong piece of the primitive home-made woollen cloth, unshapen and unsewn, open at the sides, and fastened on the shoulders by fibulæ (περοναι), a kind of safety-pin, and bound by a girdle. The πέπλος evidently left the arms bare, as we gather from the frequent use of the epithet λευκώλενος (white-armed). When Athene prepares for battle, she changes her one garment, the πέπλος, for the chiton or tunic of her father Zeus. "She casts down her many-coloured woven vesture, which she herself had made."[3]

The φᾶρος—probably a *linen* garment of Egyptian origin—sometimes takes the place of the πέπλος. While Odysseus is putting on his chiton, the nymph Calypso "donned a great shining φᾶρος, light of woof and gracious; and about her waist she cast a fair golden girdle, and a veil withal on her head." The same words are used of Circe's dress.[4]

---

[1] See Helbig, Epos, 371. [2] Hekabe, v. 933. [3] Il. v. 732. [4] Od. x. 542.

The Women of Homer

When Hera arrays herself to fascinate her mighty consort Zeus,[1] she girdles her fragrant robe with a zone adorned with a hundred tassels (θύσανοι).

In later times the simple πέπλος gave place to the chiton or tunic, a Semitic garment with a Semitic name. In the Hymn to Apollo we find the expression ἑλκεχίτωνες Ἰάονες [2] (the chiton-trailing Ionian women). This change indicates Oriental influence, which would, of course, be first felt by the more eastern Ionian Greeks.

The noble Greek women also adopted the *train* from the East, as we gather from the term ἑλκεσιπέπλοι (robe-trailing), which Hector applies to the Trojan dames.[3] Those who affected dignity of bearing [4] allowed the train of the πέπλος to drag on the ground behind. The front of the dress remained short enough to allow the feet to appear, as we see from the epithet καλλίσφυρος εὔσφυρος (fair-ankled, applied to Ino Leucothea [5] and Hebe [6] in the Odyssey, and to Demeter in the hymns.[7] Helen herself is called Ἑλένη τανύπεπλος [8] (of the flowing robe).

As we have said above, the πέπλος, being open at the sides and unsewn, required the ζώνη (girdle), which distinguished the women from the men.[9] This was frequently of gold, and richly ornamented with pendent tassels. Mention is made of Calypso's golden girdle, and of the girdle of Hera with its hundred tassels [10]

---

[1] Il. xiv. 181.
[2] v. 147.
[3] Il. vi. 442, and xxii. 105.
[4] τὸ σεμνὸν τῆς περιστολῆς.
[5] Od. v. 333.
[6] Od. xi. 603.
[7] Hym. Cer. 453 (*cf.* Sappho, Fragm. 70 B.).
[8] Od. iv. 305. *Cf.* Il. iii. 228; xviii. 385 (of Thetis).
[9] See Helbig, Epos, 109; and Studniczka, *Beiträge zur Gesch. der altgriech. Tracht.* 122.
[10] Il. ii. 448; xiv. 153.

The Magic Girdle of Aphrodite

"of pure gold, all deftly woven, and each one worth an hundred oxen." But the girdle of girdles was the κεστὸς ἱμὰς (the magic cestus) of golden Aphrodite.[1] The Greeks, with their subtle intelligence, distinguished sharply between beauty and grace or charm. Even Aphrodite had not her full entrancing power without her famous cestus; and with it the stern Hera herself became irresistible—even to her husband.

The tightened girdle naturally made the dress full over the bosom (κόλπος), whence the epithet, so often applied to Homeric dames, of βαθύκολποι (deep-bosomed), or, as some translate it, "with full, swelling bosom."[2] When Aphrodite rescues her beloved son Aineias from Tydides, she covers him with the fold (πτύγμα) of her πέπλος. "About her dear son she wound her white arms, and spread before his face a fold of her radiant garment."[3]

The κόλπος properly denoted the cavity between the two breasts, which, with the top of the πέπλος, formed a receptacle for precious objects, in which Hera hid away the love-inspiring cestus.

Another characteristic article of the dress of Homeric women was the κρήδεμνον,[4] a kind of veil, which, from the epithets applied to it—"glossy" (σιγαλόεις), "glancing" (ἀργής), "shining" (φαεινός)—must have generally been of linen; but may also have been of silk, and very

---

[1] Il. xiv. 215.
[2] Il. xviii. 122, 339; Hym. in Cer. v. 186; Æsch. Sept. con. Thebas, 863 (ἐρατῶν ἐκ βαθυκόλπων, said of Antigone and Ismene); Il. vi. 467. See fig. on Francois Vase, Abth. 25. [3] Il. v. 314.
[4] Od. v. 346, 351, 373, 459. Also called κάλυμμα, καλύπτρη. The word κρήδεμνον was subsequently only used in *cultus* and poetry.

rich. It is sometimes called ὀθόναι. It was, therefore, generally white, but sometimes dark blue.¹ This covering of the head was of Semitic origin, and was used by the Orientals to hide the face. The Ionians, in adopting it as a covering for the head, modified it in accordance with their freer customs. They let it fall some way down the back and the sides of the face, which was left uncovered. This is evident from the frequent use of the word καλλιπάρῃος (fair-cheeked). At a later period, no doubt, the Grecian women did really hide their faces, as we see in Tanagra figures and on some vases.²

Almost the only passage on which those who hold that the κρήδεμνον was a veil, in the Oriental sense, rely, is that in which the poet tells us that when Penelope came down from her upper chamber to the suitors, "she held up her glistening veil (λιπαρὰ κρήδεμνα) before her face."³ But, if really veiled, how could she address the minstrel Phemius, and how could the suitors have been struck dumb by her marvellous beauty?

"Athene gave her gifts immortal, that all the Achaians might marvel at her. . . . Her fair face first she steeped with beauty imperishable, such as that wherewith the crowned Cytherea is anointed when she goes to the lovely dances of the Graces.⁴ . . . But when the fair lady had come to the wooers, she stood by the doorpost of the well-builded room, holding her glistening κρήδεμνον before her face."⁵ "And straightway the knees

---

¹ The noble goddess (Thetis) took to herself a dark-blue (κυάνεον) veil; "no darker garment was there found" (Il. xxiv. 94).
² Studniczka, *Beiträge*, 128.   ³ Od. i. 333; xvi. 14.
⁴ Od. xviii. 190.   ⁵ Od. i. 334; xv. 416; xxi. 265.

The κρήδεμνον or Veil

of the wooers were loosened, and their hearts were enchanted with love, and each one prayed that he might be her husband."[1] This could hardly be said if she were closely veiled.

The nearest approach to the Homeric κρήδεμνον in modern dress is the shawl which the factory-girls of Lancashire wear over their head and down the sides of the face.

The Homeric women had no garment answering to the χλαῖνα, or cloak, which the men wore over the χιτών, or tunic. But as the men, when preparing for action, threw off this upper garment, so the women cast off their mantle-like κρήδεμνον for freer movement, or under the strong excitement of grief. Hekabe, wailing for Hector, "tore her hair and cast far from her her shining veil."[2] When Nausicaa and her maidens, having washed the clothes in the divine stream, are about to dance and sing and play at ball, "they cast off their tyres (κρήδεμνα) and begin the song."[3]

We have more difficulty in forming a clear notion of other ornaments of the head. The Epics make no mention of garlands of fresh flowers. Hesiod, indeed, at a later period, says that the Hours crowned Pandora with flowers.[4] But Homer often speaks of metal ornaments for the head—the στεφάνη (coronal), and the ἄμπυξ (head-band or snood), of which the στεφάνη was the larger and higher. We find the epithets ἐυστέφανος (of the bright coronal) applied to Alcmene,[5] to Aphrodite,

---

[1] Od. xviii. 211.   [2] Il. xxii. 407.
[3] Od. vi. 100.   [4] Ἔργα καὶ Ἡμέραι, 72.
[5] Od. ii. 120.

The Women of Homer

and frequently to Demeter.[1] Χρυσάμπυξ[2] is used in the Iliad only of the golden frontlet of horses; but in the Homeric hymns, and in Hesiod and Pindar, it is an epithet of goddesses. Examples of the στεφάνη and ἄμπυξ have been found by Schliemann and others.[3]

Of much more doubtful interpretation is the κεκρύφαλος. The wretched Andromache, when she first hears of Hector's death, "shook off from her head the bright attire[4] thereof, the frontlet (ἄμπυξ), the net (κεκρύφαλον), and woven band (πλεκτὴν αναδέσμην). According to Professor Helbig,[5] followed by Leaf, Lang and Myers, in their excellent translation of the Iliad, the κεκρύφαλος was a cap-like net, bound by the πλεκτὴ ἀναδέσμη, or woven band.

Among the principal ornaments worn by the high-born Homeric women were the ἴσθμιον and the ὅρμος. The ἴσθμιον[6] was a necklace fitting close to the neck. It is not mentioned in the Iliad, and only once in the Odyssey. The ἴσθμιον[7] is the prototype of the classical necklace.[8] Such necklaces have been found of bronze in the Apennine peninsula and in the Necropolis of Villanova, and are of pre-Hellenic times.[9] The Gallic *torques* belongs to this class.

The Hormos (ὅρμος), also a kind of necklace, was a long chain, sometimes of gold and amber, hanging from

---

[1] Hym. Cer. 224, 236, 307, 384.   *Cf.* Eurip. Hec. 664; Æschyl. Supplices. 431.   [2] Il. v. 358, 363.
[3] Hesiod, Theognis. ix. 16; Pindar, Ol. 719; Pyth. iii. 158; Hym. Ven. 175.
[4] δέσματα σιγαλόεντά (Il. xxii. 468).   [5] Epos, 222, 271; Studniczka, 130.
[6] Od. xviii. 300.   [7] See Appendix XIII.
[8] Schol. in Od. xviii. 300.
[9] Helbig, Epos, 271; Friedereich, *Kleine Kunst*, p. 124, n. 527, 533.

Ornaments worn by Homeric Women

the nape of the neck over the breast.[1] It is found on clay figures of Astarte, the Phœnician Venus, on old Greek and Etruscan figures, on Tanagra figures, and on others from the Necropolis of Kameiros in Sicily.[2]

Earrings were worn by Homeric dames, as we learn from the description of Hera's toilet : " She set earrings in her pierced ears, earrings of three drops (τρίγληνα μορόεντα) and glistening ; therefrom shone grace abundantly."[3] The three drops were probably three balls, like the apple of the eye.[4]

Of the κάλυκες worn by Hera we have no certain information. Some writers suppose that they were earrings in the form of a cup (calix). They are mentioned among the works of art which Hephaistos fashioned during his nine years' sojourn in the depths of ocean, an exile from Olympos.[5]

The Helikes (ἕλικες) are also mentioned only once, in the description of Hera's ornaments. The meaning of the word is much disputed, and cannot be certainly known. As helix (ἕλιξ) means "twisted," "spiral," the Helikes may denote spiral ornaments, such as are found in Greece, Italy, and Central Europe.[6]

These ἕλικες were probably armlets, or they may have been earrings. Hephaistos, the divine artificer, relates to his wife Charis how Thetis had sheltered him from the ill-will of his "shameless mother," Hera, who wished to do away with him because he was lame ; and

---

[1] Il. xviii. 401 ; Hym. Apoll. i. 103. See Appendix XIII.
[2] Helbig, 106.   [3] Il. xiv. 182.
[4] Helbig, Epos, 274.   [5] Il. xviii. 401.
[6] Vide Sacken, " *Grabfeld von Halstatt* ;" Helbig, Epos, 236 ; Studniczka, 14, 266.

how he had lived with her and Eurynome[1] for nine years, during which he had wrought cunning works of bronze—brooches (πόρπας), spiral armbands (γναμπτὰς θἔλικας), cups (κάλυκας), and necklaces (ὅρμους).[2]

Other ornaments mentioned in the Epics are the περόνη and the ἐνετή,[3] which probably answer to our safety-pins. In the nineteenth book of the Odyssey we read that Odysseus fastened his thick purple mantle with a περόνη of gold, with a double covering for the pins, on the face of which was a hound holding a dappled fawn in his fore-paws, and gripping it as it writhed. This was no doubt an exceptionally elaborate work, and more of the nature of a brooch.[4] When Aphrodite was wounded in the hand by Diomed, Hera laughs at her, and supposes that the goddess had torn it on the golden περόνη of some Achaian woman whom she was caressing.[5] It was with their πορπαι that the Trojan women put out the eyes of Polymestor.[6]

When sandals are mentioned it is generally as worn by gods and goddesses. These had golden soles which sped them quickly on their way.[7] Athene, when about to go to Ithaca, bound beneath her feet her lovely golden sandals "that wax not old, and bare her alike over the wet sea and the limitless land, swift as the breath of the wind."[8] But the higher class of Achaians also wore coverings for the feet, which are generally

---

[1] Il. xviii. 398.   [2] Il. xviii. 401.
[3] Il. xiv. 180; Od. xviii. 293.   [4] Od. ix. 225.
[5] Il. v. 425.   [6] Eurip. Hekabe, 1179.
[7] Studniczka, p. 113, Anm. 66; Helbig, Epos, 77.
[8] Od. i. 96; Il. xiv. 186.

Shoes and Gloves?

called πέδιλα, but sometimes ὑποδήματα [1] and εἵματα. The καλὰ πέδιλα of Menelaos [2] are reckoned among his raiment (εἵματα). Even the swineherd Eumaios [3] has "fair sandals"; but his position as a slave was a very exceptional one.

Did the Achaians in the heroic age wear gloves? Of these there are but few indications in the Epos, and the authorities give different answers to the question. Casaubon thought that gloves *were* worn. Winckelmann and others take the opposite view. They are not mentioned in the description of Hera's elaborate toilet, but some figures on urns seem to be holding gloves in their hands. Odysseus on his return to Ithaca finds his aged father, Laertes, in his vineyard, "digging about a plant in a filthy doublet, patched and unseemly . . . with long sleeves or gloves (χειρῖδας)," where the word may mean one or the other.[4] On the whole, we think that there is too little evidence in the Epos to prove the common use of gloves.

In Homer, both gods and mortals, male and female, wore the hair long. When Zeus bows his head in confirmation of his promise to Thetis to honour her son Achilles, "the ambrosial locks waved from the king's immortal head."[5] Hera, when making her well-known toilet, "plaits her shining tresses, fair and ambrosial, flowing from her immortal head."[6] The same is said of Athene, Circe, and Calypso.

[1] Od. xv. 369; xiii. 225; xv. 368; iv. 309; Il. ii. 44.
[2] Od. iv. 309.   [3] Od. xiv. 23; xvi. 154.
[4] Od. xxiv. 230.   [5] Il. i. 529.
[6] Il. xiv. 175. Πλοκάμους here means, not locks of hair, but plaited tresses.

The Women of Homer

The Greek youth wore the hair unshorn up to manhood; and Apollo, the great exemplar of eternal youth, is called "Phoibos of the unshorn hair" ("φοῖβος ἀκερσεκόμης").[1] Achilles, Menelaos, and Odysseus[2] are all called ξανθός. On the Attic stage, "golden hair" marked youths of princely blood. Some of the young warriors adorned their hair. Of Panthoos' son, slain by Menelaos, it is said that his hair was drenched with blood, and his tresses closely knit with bands of silver and gold.[3] When Athene beautifies Odysseus, that he may find favour in the sight of Nausicaa, "she caused deep curling locks to flow from his head, like the hyacinth flower."[4] Yellow or auburn hair seems to have been common. Demeter, Agamede, and others are called ξανθή (golden-haired).[5] The epithet is applied to Ariadne by Hesiod, to Athene and the Graces by Pindar.[6]

There can be little doubt that the women of Homer used artificial means to enhance their beauty. Hera, when making her toilet, anoints herself with olive oil.[7] When Penelope's handmaid exhorts her to dress and anoint herself and go down to her son and the suitors, Penelope replies: "Eurynome, speak not thus comfortably to me, loving as thou art, nor bid me to wash me and be anointed with ointment."[8] Again, when Athene lulls her into a soft slumber, "she made her whiter than newly-sawn ivory."[9] Helbig[10] and other commentators find in these passages a proof that the Homeric ladies used cosmetics, and translate ἀλοιφή by

---

[1] Il. xx. 39.   [2] Il. i. 197; Od. xiii. 399.
[3] Il. xvii. 52.   [4] Od. iv. 230.   [5] Il. v. 500; xi. 740.
[6] Nem. 10, 11.   [7] Il. xiv. 175.   [8] Od. xviii. 179.
[9] Od. xviii. 192.   [10] Epos, 256.

Did Homer's Ladies use Rouge?

rouge. They also attribute the whiteness of her face, "like newly-sawn ivory," to the application of ψιμύθιον (Lat. *cerussa*, white-lead), a word which does not occur in Homer. It is, of course, possible that cosmetics were used by the Homeric ladies, but the passages quoted above are hardly sufficient to prove it. Little spoons have been found in very early Etruscan graves, which probably held rouge, and there are certain indications of its use in the Old Testament.[1]

The Achaians of Homer delighted in strong scents, and the epithet εὐώδης is used of clothes and women's chambers.[2] This taste, too, they derived from their intercourse with the East.

The dress and ornaments of the women of Homer are, as we have seen, very different from those of the classical period of Greek history. We are apt to think of Helen and the Trojan elders on the walls of Troy as clothed very much in the same manner as the old men and the beautiful female forms in the Ionic frieze of the Parthenon. What Homer saw in his age, and what he has depicted in the Epics, was something very different. The elders wore long linen chitons, and over them a richly embroidered mantle, red or purple, contrasting strongly with the white of the lower garment. With regard to Helen's dress, we are justified in supposing that, as a Trojan princess, and wife of Paris, she would wear very much the same attire as Andromache. Andromache, as we have seen, in her despair, on hearing of the death of Hector, tore off the

---

[1] Ezek. xvi. 9; Judith x. 3; Ps. cxxxiii. 2; 2 Sam. xiv. 2; Dan. x. 3.
[2] Il. iii. 382.

The Women of Homer

bright attiring of her head, the frontlet (ἄμπυκα), the cap-like net (κεκρύφαλον) and woven band (πλεκτὴν αναδέσμην), and the veil (κρήδεμνον). We may therefore think of Helen as arrayed in a coloured peplos, richly embroidered and perfumed, the corners of which were drawn tightly over the shoulders, and fastened together by the περόνη or safety-pin. The waist was closely encircled by the zone, which was no doubt of rich material and design. Over her bosom hung the Hormos of dark red amber, set in gold. Her hair hung down in artificial plaits, and on her head was the high stiff κεκρύφιλος, which we have spoken of above, bound in the middle by the πλεκτὴ ἀναδέσμη. Over the forehead was the shining ἄμπυξ, or tiara of gold; and from the top of the head fell the κρήδεμνον, or veil, over the shoulders and back, affording a quiet foil to the glitter of the gold and jewels.[1] It was thus that she appeared on the walls of Troy, dazzling the sight and bewildering the minds of the bloodless sages. The difficulty in this picture of Helen's dress, and, indeed, in that of Andromache, if we are right in our translation of the κεκρύφαλος, is as to the manner in which the κρήδεμνον could be worn without covering the ἄμπυξ or the κεκρύφαλος.

Much controversy has recently arisen respecting the art of the Phœnicians. The last generation of archæologists were inclined to deny them all artistic merit, and to regard them simply as traders who carried works of art from country to country. They held that the Phœnicians had no art of their own, and only exported works of art from the interior of Asia to

[1] Helbig, Epos, 371.

Controversy on Phœnician Art

Greece and other parts of Europe. They thought that the silver vessels of the sixth century B.C. which have been found are Egyptian and Assyrian, and that, for instance, the traders who carried off Ino brought Egyptian and Assyrian wares to Argos. Quite recently, however, the Phœnicians have found favour in the sight of German archæologists, and especially of those very eminent scholars Professor Helbig[1] and M. Pottier.[2] We agree with these writers that the supposed incapacity of the Phœnicians is hardly to be reconciled with statements in ancient literature. Solomon, we know, made a contract with Hiram, king of Tyre, for the service of Tyrian artificers; and Phœnicians exercised great influence on the decoration of the temple of Jehovah at Jerusalem—even more than the Egyptians. "Everywhere on the Ark of the Covenant, on the old Tabernacle, and on the Temple of Solomon, we find the practice, which was characteristic of this people, of covering the walls with gold sheeting."[3] Aram dealt with the Phœnicians for their various works of art, their carbuncles, corals and rubies, their purple dyes and embroidered linen. The influence of Phœnician art is everywhere seen, and its superiority acknowledged, throughout the Iliad and Odyssey. Many precious works are spoken of as Sidonian, and always with high appreciation of the superior skill employed in their creation.[4]

---

[1] *Mem. de l'Institut Nat.* vol. xxxv. p. 29.
[2] *Revue d'Études Grecques,* vol. vii. p. 117 (1894). See Appendix XIV.
[3] K. O. Müller, translated by Leitch, 1847.
[4] Il. xxiii. 743: "A mixing bowl of silver chased . . . It was by far the best in all the earth, for artificers of Sidon wrought it cunningly." *Cf.* vi. 290, 291; Od. iv. 614; xv. 118.

The Women of Homer

The Phœnicians contributed the products of their looms to the artistic dress of the Achaians; and the work of the Sidonians is mentioned with the highest praise.[1] When Hector bids his mother make offerings to mitigate the wrath of Athene, Hekabe "goes to her fragrant chamber, where were her embroidered robes, the work of Sidonian women, whom godlike Alexander had brought from Sidon." The Sidonian slave of the king of Syria is said to be ἀγλαὰ ἔργ' εἰδυῖα (skilled in bright handiwork).

The home industry of Greece was no doubt quickened by importations from the East in general, and *not only* from Phœnicia. With their natural intelligence, the Achaians soon began to imitate and to rival the works which they imported. The linen garments from Eastern countries appealed to the natural love of the Ionians for bright colours, of which linen was more susceptible than wool. We read of Helen "wrapped in her radiant heanos," which was no doubt of linen. All the Homeric heroines, Andromache, Helen, Penelope, and Arētē, the immortal nymphs Calypso and Circe, and even the great goddess Athene herself, are all skilful embroiderers or weavers. We read of the πέπλοι παμφίλοι οὕς κάμεν αὐτή, "the robes of curious needlework which Athene herself had made." Penelope, too, works for years at a φᾶρος, "fine of woof and very wide," which she intends to be a winding-sheet for Laertes, the aged father of Odysseus.[2] Of Arete, the wife of Alkinoos, it is said that, with her fifty handmaidens,[3] "she wove the webs and turned the yarns; ... and the soft olive

---

[1] Od. vi. 290.   [2] Od. xxiv. 147.   [3] Od. vii. 103.

The Art of Caria and Mæonia

oil drops off that linen (ὀθονέων), so closely is it woven, for the Phæacian women are the most cunning at the loom, for Athene gave them notable wisdom at all fair handiwork and cunning wit."

Nor is it only the art of needlework that the Achaians are seen to cultivate. We read in the Odyssey of Laerkes the χρυσοχόος (goldsmith), who gilds the horns of the sacrificial ox.[1] The work of the Carians and Mæonians is also noted with high praise. The blood-stained shapely thigh of Menelaos is compared to the work of some woman of Mæonia or Caria, "who staineth ivory with purple to make a cheek-piece for horses; and it is laid up in the treasure chamber, though many a horseman prayeth to wear it; but it is laid up to be a king's boast, an adornment for his horse, and a glory for his charioteer."[2]

There is no mention in Homer's Epics of *purple* robes for women. But probably this colour is indicated in a passage of the Hymn to Venus[3] (φαεινότερος πυρὸς αὐγῆς), "more brilliant than the gleam of fire." Eos (Aurora) alone in Homer has saffron robes[4] (κροκόπεπλος), a colour which the Greeks adopted from Semitic nations.

When speaking of the works of art of the pre-Homeric period found in Mykenai, Tiryns, and other ancient sites, Helbig divides them into two classes, and says that those which are of finer design and execution are imported, while the inferior works are merely copies

---

[1] Od. iii. 425. *Cf.* Od. vii. 92; Il. v. 110.
[2] Il. iv. 146. [3] v. 86.
[4] Il. viii. 1; xix. 1. But *cf.* Hesiod, Theog. 273, 358; and Alcman, 74.

made in Greece itself. The source of these more valuable imported works of art, he thinks, is almost exclusively Phœnicia, and says, in so many words, that "what we now call *l'art Mycenien* should be called *l'art l'hénicien.*"

This is, we think, too great a reaction from the unmerited neglect and contempt with which "*les malheureux Phéniciens*" were treated by the last generation of scholars. There can be little doubt that the Phœnicians contributed largely to the objects of art and luxury which were exported from Asia to Greece, and especially to the seats of the great Achaian chiefs—Argos, Mykenai, and Tiryns ; but not exclusively. Assyria, Egypt, Caria, Mæonia, and the Ionian Islands also sent the productions of their own artists, which were for the most part brought to Greece by Phœnician traders.

MINERVA MEDICI.

CHAPTER VII

SOME HOMERIC WOMEN

WE know in our own acquaintance the counterpart of the wise and stern Athene, the unapproachable virgin, mighty in battle, yet skilled in all female handiwork. We know the virgin huntress Artemis, scorner of men—for Homer knows nothing of her weakness for Endymion. We know poor Hekabe, *all* mother, as fierce against the slayer of her darling Hector as a tigress against the huntsman who has robbed her of her cubs. We know Andromache, the loving wife and tender mother, the sad ill-fated spouse of the gallant patriot Hector, the noble gentleman *sans peur et sans reproche*. We have our faithful Penelopes, faithful during long long absence to not too faithful husbands like Odysseus. We have our lovely, laughter-loving Aphrodites, with their powerful spells and baleful wiles. We know, alas! our Helens, with beauty enough to set the world ablaze; whom, though we cannot altogether excuse, we are fain to love and pity. And, above all, we still have in many a country home our true Nausicaas, our stately peerless maidens, fresh, sweet, and innocent, joyous, brave, and true.

The Women of Homer

HERA.

We know our Heras too, proud, vain, treacherous, cruel and vindictive, full of gibes and scoffs, fretful, cantankerous, and quarrelsome. Hera was daughter of Kronos (Saturn) and Rhea, and therefore sister of Zeus, of whom she was also the consort. Her epithets are πότνια (revered), λευκώλενος (white-armed), βοῶπις (ox-eyed), χρυσόθρονος (golden-throned), &c. Her emblem was the peacock, whose tail represented the starry firmament.[1] In cosmogony she was considered as the Air.[2] As consort of Zeus, she was looked on as the patroness of marriage, and was called τελεία, from τέλος (the end or accomplishment), a name given to marriage as the acme of life; whence married couples were called τέλειοι (the perfected).

When the Trojan Paris, in his judgment of the comparative beauty of the three mightiest goddesses, gave the apple to Aphrodite, he brought on his country and himself the undying hatred of the rejected competitors, Hera and Athene, whose vengeance was hardly purged away by the fires of fallen Troy. Hera swears " never to help the Trojans from the evil day, not even when all Troy shall burn in the burning of fierce fires."[3] As supreme goddess and queen of heaven her bearing is royal and majestic, but her beauty would be greater had she grace and charm.[4] She lords it over all the

---

[1] Eurip. Helena, 1108.
[2] Hesychius, v. ἦρι, p. 1648 : ἦρα τὸν ἀέρα καὶ Ἔραν. Plato jokes about this in Cratylus, p. 404 e.
[3] Il. xx. 315.
[4] Il. xxi. 421.

Zeus and Hera

other gods,[1] with the exception of Athene and her omnipotent Consort; and even him she opposes and thwarts by her artifice and guile. Her power is immense; she hastens the setting of Helios, the sun, against his will and before his time, that the Achaians may be sheltered by the shades of night from the stress of battle:[2] "Then Hera, the ox-eyed queen, sent down the unwearying sun to be gone unwillingly unto the streams of ocean." Her pride is overweening, and she thinks herself the peer of Zeus himself.[3] "I also," she tells him, "am a god, and my lineage is even as thine; and Kronos, the crooked counsellor, begat me to the place of honour, in double wise, by birthright and because I am thy spouse."[4] On these grounds she claims to treat with her omnipotent lord—who by a word could have expelled her from Olympos and consigned her to the depths of Tartaros—on equal terms. How cunning is her hypocritical pretence of moderation and concession! "Therefore," she says, "let us in these things yield to one another, I to thee and thou to me; and let the other immortal gods follow us." Zeus, therefore, has no little difficulty in controlling her. He tells her plainly "there is nothing more unabashed than thou."[5] And again, when reproving Ares, he says: "Thy mother Hera's spirit is intolerable, even Hera; her can I scarcely rule with words."[6]

As her august husband Zeus favours the Trojans at the request of Thetis, he incurs the deadly wrath and

---

[1] Yet the chryselephantine statue of Hera by Polykleitos was surrounded by the Graces and the Hours.—Pausan. 2. 17.
[2] Il. xviii. 242.   [3] Il. iv. 58.   [4] Il. iv. 59–62.
[5] Il. viii. 483.   [6] Il. v. 890.

persistent opposition of his jealous spouse. After promising to honour Achilles by the overthrow of Agamemnon and the Achaians, Zeus is in great trepidation lest Hera should hear of his interview with Thetis. The cloud-gatherer is sore troubled. "Verily," he says to the suppliant goddess, "it is a sorry matter if thou wilt set me at variance with Hera. . . . Even now she upbraideth me ever amid the Immortals, and saith that I aid the Trojans."[1] But Hera quickly hears of the meeting with the silver-footed goddess, and pours out her jealous wrath on her unhappy husband: "Now, who among the gods, thou crafty of mind, hath devised counsel of thee? It is ever thy good pleasure to hold aloof from me."[2] Zeus loses patience, and thus makes her standpoint clear to her: "Abide thou in silence," he says to the ox-eyed queen, "and hearken to my bidding, lest all the gods of Olympos keep not off from thee my visitation when I put forth my hands unapproachable against thee." And again: "For thine anger reck I not; not though thou go to the nethermost bounds of the earth and sea, where sit Iapetos and Kronos, and have no joy in the beams of Hyperion, the sun-god, neither in any breeze."[3]

By her intrigues she creates a very formidable conspiracy of the gods against their king and father. Achilles suggests to Thetis that in her supplication she should remind Zeus that she alone of the Immortals saved him, the lord of the storm-cloud, from destruction, when all the other Olympians would have bound him, "even Hera, and Poseidon, and Pallas Athene." "Then

---

[1] Il. i. 116.   [2] Il. i. 540.   [3] Il. viii. 477.

Zeus, Hera, and Thetis

didst thou enter in and loose him from his bonds, having speedily summoned to high Olympos him of the hundred hands, whom the gods call Briareus, but all men Ægæon, who seated himself by Kronion's side, rejoicing in his triumph; and the blessed gods feared him and bound not Zeus."[1]

On another occasion she tries to rouse Poseidon to fight against her husband. "Did we but will," she says, "we that are confederates of the Danaans, to drive the Trojans back, and withhold far-seeing Zeus, then would he vex himself that he should sit there alone on Ida." She is utterly regardless of the wishes and feelings of her husband, as she plainly showed in the case of Sarpedon, over whose fate Zeus mourns so bitterly. He would fain have saved his dearly-beloved son, but Hera insists on the fulfilment of his destiny. Zeus consoles himself by ordering Apollo to rescue his dead body from the Achaians, and to have it conveyed by the brothers Death and Sleep to his house in Lycia.

Against the weaker gods, who side with the Trojans, she rages with vulgar abuse and even blows.[2] Artemis has reproached her brother Apollo for shunning conflict with Poseidon. Hera hears her, and reviles her with taunting words: "'How now, shameless dog! art thou fain to set thyself against me? Hard were it for thee to match my might, bow-bearer though thou art; since against women Zeus made thee a lion, and giveth thee to slay whom thou wilt. . . . But if thou wilt, try war, that thou mayst know well how far stronger am I than thou;' she said, and with her left hand caught both

[1] Il. i. 396.   [2] Il. xxi. 470.

The Women of Homer

Artemis' hands, and with her right hand took the bow from off her shoulders, and therewith, smiling, beat her on the ears, as she turned this way and that; and the swift arrows fell out of the quiver. And, weeping, the goddess fled like a dove that before a falcon flieth to a hollow rock."[1] Although she wearies Heaven and Earth in her efforts to give victory and glory to the Argives, her love for them is far feebler than her spiteful rancour against Priam and all his race. In reply to her outbreak of fury against them, Zeus addresses her with taunting words: "Good lady, how have Priam and his sons done thee such great wrong, that thou wouldst sack the citadel of Ilion? Perchance wert thou to enter the gates and devour Priam and his sons *raw*, and all the Trojans, then mightest thou assuage thy wrath. Remember this, when I am of eager mind to lay waste a city dear to thee; hinder thou nothing of my anger, as I yield to thee with soul unwilling."

She replies: "Three cities are the dearest to me, Argos, Sparta, and Mykenai; these lay thou waste; nor will I stand forth for them, nor do I grudge thee them."[2] So undying is the wrath *spretæ formæ*.

Finding that she cannot completely control her omnipotent husband, either by her own force or by the aid of other mutinous deities, she has recourse to woman's guile: "Now Hera of the golden throne beheld Zeus sitting on the topmost crest of many-fountained Ida, and *to her heart he was hateful*. Then she took thought, the ox-eyed lady Hera, how she might beguile the mind of ægis-bearing Zeus. And this seemed to her the best

[1] Il. xxi. 488.   [2] Il. i. 452.

Hera arrays Herself to beguile Zeus

counsel, to fare to Ida, when she had well adorned herself. . . . And she set forth to her bower that her dear son Hephaistos had fashioned. . . . There did she enter in, and closed the shining doors. With ambrosia first did she cleanse every stain from her winsome body, and anointed herself with olive oil, ambrosial, soft, and of a sweet savour. If it were but shaken on the bronze-floored mansion of Zeus, the savour thereof went right through earth and heaven. Therewith she anointed her body, and she combed her hair, and with her hands plaited her glossy tresses, fair and ambrosial, flowing from her immortal head. Then she clad herself in a fragrant robe (ἑανὸν) that Athene wrought delicately for her, and therein set many things delicately made, and fastened it over her breast with clasps of gold. And she girdled herself with a girdle arrayed with a hundred tassels, and set earrings in her pierced ears, earrings of three drops and glistening; therefrom shone grace abundantly. And with a veil (κρήδεμνον) over all, the peerless goddess veiled herself, a fair new veil, bright as the sun, and beneath her shining feet she bound the goodly sandals."[1]

Thus prepared for conquest, she seeks the aid of Aphrodite, whom she deceives by an artful tale. "I am going," she said, "to the limits of the bountiful earth and Okeanos, father of the gods, and Mother Tethys, who reared me in their halls. . . . Them am I going to visit, and their endless strife will I loose." For this pretended purpose she asks Aphrodite to lend her her famous cestus.[2] "Give me now love and desire, wherewith

[1] Il. xiv. 157.   [2] Il. xiv. 158, 190.

The Women of Homer

thou dost overcome all the Immortals and mortal men; give me thy girdle, wherein are love and desire and loving converse,[1] that steals the wits even of the wise."

Aphrodite, of course, complies with her request, and Hera carries off the precious girdle of grace. But the wily queen is not yet satisfied. She must have the aid of another mighty potentate. Rushing down from the peak of Olympos, "she sped over the hills of the Thracian horsemen, even over the topmost crests, nor grazed the ground with her feet; and from Mount Athos she fared across the foaming sea, and came to Lemnos. There she met Sleep, the brother of Death, and clasped his hand and called him by his name. 'Sleep, lord of all gods and men, . . . lull me now, I pray thee, the shining eyes of Zeus, so soon as I have laid me down beside him. . . . And I will give thee a golden throne, the work of Hephaistos, mine own child, who shall fashion it skilfully, and I will set beneath it a footstool for thy shining feet.'"[2]

Sleep is terrified at the suggestion. Any other god, he says, he would gladly lull in slumber—but Zeus! He reminds Hera how once before, at her request, he had drowned the Thunderer in sleep, that she might wreak her vengeance on Herakles, the mighty son of Zeus, as he returned from the first sack of Troy. "When Zeus awoke," said the trembling Hypnos, "he was full of wrath, and dashed the gods about his mansion, and me

---

[1] Il. xiv. 216: Ὀαριστὺς πάρφασις, intimate whisperings—the *lenes susurri* of Horace.

[2] Il. xiv. 226.

Hera bribes Sleep

he would have cast from Olympos to perish in the deep, if Night, that subdues gods and men, had not saved me ... for Zeus is in awe of doing aught displeasing to swift Night."[1]

Hera, however, persists, and offers an irresistible bribe: "Come now, and I will give thee one of the youngest of the Graces to wed, and to be called thy wife, even Pasithea, that ever thou longest for all thy days."[2]

There was no withstanding that, and Sleep, having made her swear by the Styx and all the gods below Tartaros to keep her promise, consents to dare the audacious deed. Then they went together to Ida, "to Lekton, where first they left the sea." Sleep halts before meeting the eyes of Zeus, and hides in the branches of a pine, in the shape of a bird, the *chalkis* or *kymindis*.[3] Hera goes on to the lofty Gargaros, the highest crest of Mount Ida, "and Zeus the cloud-gatherer beheld her."[4]

The rancorous queen attains her object: Zeus falls a victim to her charms, and is lulled to sleep; the Trojans are defeated with great slaughter, and Hector himself is wounded. Yet even when Zeus is most enamoured, he treats his artful spouse with scant respect. Most unseasonably he chooses this opportunity to recount to her, in what has been happily called his "Leporello list," the names of his many loves: "Never once as thus did the love of goddess or woman so mightily o'erflow

---

[1] Il. xiv. 260.   [2] Il. xiv. 266.
[3] Bewick says it was the night-jar. Other ornithologists see in it a kind of swift.   [4] Il. xiv. 290.

and conquer my heart; not when I loved the wife of Ixion (Dia), nor Danae of the fair ankles, nor the daughter of Phoinix, nor Semele, nor Alkmene, nor Demeter, nor Leto, as now I love thee."[1] Even this long list is not complete, as it does not include Leda, Themis, Eurynome, Mnemosyne, Europa, Io, Ægina, Kallisto, Antiope, and others.

But terrible was the awakening of Zeus: "He leapt up and stood and beheld the Trojans and Achaians, those in flight, and these driving them from the rear, and among them the prince Poseidon. And Hector he saw lying on the plain, gasping with difficult breath, and vomiting blood." Then he turns upon Hera: "Oh, thou ill to deal with, Hera! verily it is thy crafty wile that has made noble Hector cease from the fight. Nay but I know not whether thou mayst not be the first to reap the fruits of thy cruel treason, and I beat thee with stripes. Dost thou not remember, when thou wert hung from on high, and from thy feet I suspended two anvils, and round thy hands fastened a golden bond that might not be broken? And thou didst hang in the clear air and the clouds, and the gods were wroth in high Olympos, but they could not come round and unloose thee."[2]

And the lady Hera shuddered at the remembrance, and pacified him by falsely swearing, "by the high heavens and the falling water of the Styx," that "not by her will did earth-shaking Poseidon trouble the Trojans and Hector."

Again the omnipotent ruler of heaven and earth is

[1] Il. xiv. 313.   [2] Il. xv. 5.

Hera's Craft prevails

cajoled by his wily consort. He smiles and says: "Of a truth, if thou, O ox-eyed Hera, wouldst hereafter abide of one mind with me, then would Poseidon quickly turn his mind otherwise, after thy heart and mine." The craft of woman, as usual, prevails over the might of man.

CHAPTER VIII

ATHENE

IN the Theogony, Athene represents light and warmth independent of the sun.[1] Hesiod relates that Æther and Hemera proceeded from the darkness of chaos before the Titans existed, from a pair of whom Helios, Selene, and Eos sprang. Just as in Genesis light is created before the sun and moon, Αἰθήρ,[2] the higher, brilliant, fiery æther, is distinguished from the ἀήρ or lower air. And from αιθ came the name of the goddess Ἀθήνη.

As springing from the brain of Zeus, she is almost his equal, and often assumes his functions. She has the nearest seat to Zeus,[3] and thrones between him and Hera. In the Capitoline Temple at Rome her cell was on the right of Jove, and Juno's on the left. She alone knows where the keys of the room are kept in which the lightning was concealed,[4] and Zeus lends it to her to slay the Locrian Ajax.[5]

The virgin daughter of ægis-bearing Zeus differs widely from Hera, though closely allied with her for the destruction of Troy; for she too had been passed

---

[1] She is αἰθέρα καὶ Διὸς αὐγάς.   [2] From αἴθειν, to blaze.
[3] Plutarch, Symp. 1, 2; Æsch. Eum. 730–813; Soph. K. Œd. 163.
[4] *Schol. ad Iliad*, xx. 102.   [5] Eurip. Troad. 8.

ATHENE IN CAPITOLINE MUSEUM.

Character of Athene

over by Paris, when he awarded the prize of beauty to Aphrodite. Her commonest epithet is γλαυκῶπις[1] (grey-eyed, glowing-eyed), but she had many others, as πότνια (mistress, queen), ἐρυσίπτολις (protectress of cities), λαοσσόος (nation-stirring), πολύβουλος (rich in counsel), μεγάθυμος (magnanimous), ἠΰκομος (fair-haired), ἀτρυτώνη (unwearied), ἀλαλκομενηΐς (of Alkomenai, or protectress), ληΐτις (the dispenser of booty), ἀγελεία (the driver of spoil), &c. She sprang full grown and full armed from the head of Zeus.[2] She is, therefore, the goddess of reflection, prudence and wise counsel, of intellect and the highest culture. She delighted in the ἔργα τερπνὰ σωφροσύνης[3] (the delightful works of wisdom), and was herself accomplished in all the arts of life. She directs and encourages all mental activity and skilful handicraft, and even the clever shipwright works by her inspiration. As the votary and protectress of Science, whose breast must be undisturbed by the tumult of the passions, she is represented as a chaste virgin, of a manly and serious disposition.[4] As Athene ἐργάνη (operosa, Horace) "the worker," she was worshipped by πᾶς ὁ χειρῶναξ λεώς[5] (the whole labouring population). There was a temple of Athene ἐργάνη on the Acropolis of Athens. According to Apollodorus, the Trojan Palladion held a lance in the right hand and a spindle in the left.[6] Her symbol was the cock, as combining

---

[1] Cæsius; like the shining eyes of cats and lions: γλαύξ, the night-owl; glowing-eyed.
[2] Hesiod. Theog. 886; Pindar, Ol. vii. 62.
[3] Theocritus, 15–18.
[4] "Ἄρσην καὶ θῆλυς," Orphic Hym. xxxi. 10 (Hom. Hym. ix. 3).
[5] Soph. Fragm.   [6] 3. 12, 2.

The Women of Homer

industry and courage.¹ She presided over law and medicine, and Pericles erected a statue to her as Hygieia; the Minerva Medica of the Romans was also celebrated.²

She is the goddess of war,³ born in full armour with lance in hand. When she goes forth to battle she arrays herself in awe-inspiring fashion : "She casts down her woven vesture (πέπλον) many-coloured, which she herself had wrought, and dons the tunic of almighty Zeus."⁴ About her shoulders she casts the tasselled (θυσανόεσσα) ægis,⁵ which even the thunderbolt of Zeus cannot penetrate, wherein is panic (φόβος) "as a crown all round about," and strife (ἔρις), and chilly rout (ἰωκή), and the awful head of the monster Gorgo.⁶

As goddess of war she is superior to Ares himself, who rushes blindly on without forethought or deliberation, and is therefore often worsted. She is always victorious, because her courage and activity are directed by prudence and wisdom; and she only aims at the possible with adequate means and preparation. She meets the terrible Ares in single combat, hurls at him a mighty landmark, "huge and black and rough," and stretches him seven roods long upon the ground.⁷

She is the protectress of cities (ἐρυσίπτολις), as being the chief seats of intelligence and enterprise; and even the Trojans, whom she hates, appeal to her, in that capacity, to have pity on their city and their wives and

---

¹ Plut. Symp. 3, 6. ² Plin. 34. 19, 80.
³ 'Αρεία. There was a statue to Athene ἀρεία by Pheidias at Platæa.—Pausan. 2. 4.
⁴ Il. viii. 387. ⁵ Il. xxi. 402. ⁶ Il. v. 740.
⁷ Il. xxi. 403. Eustathius says : 'Εμφρόνως πολεμίζειν νικητικόν.

Athene and Poseidon compete for Athens

little children. Of course in vain.[1] She was the ever-watchful protectress of Athens, and the most popular legend connected with Athene is that in which she contends with Poseidon for the possession of that city. The council of the gods made their decision depend on the relative value of the gifts which the two deities should bestow on man. Poseidon then created the horse, and Athene the olive tree, and the prize was awarded to her. This contest, as is well known, formed the subject of the sculptures in the western pediment of the Parthenon at Athens, the work of Pheidias, the poor remains of which are the great glory of the British Museum.

She loves the strong and brave, the men of action and resource. She is ever at hand to aid and counsel the Achaian heroes, to heal their wounds and raise their spirits. She assisted Herakles in his terrible labours, and especially when he dragged Cerberus, the three-headed hound of loathed Hades, from Erebos to the light of day.[2] She comes down from heaven to check the wrath of Achilles when he is about to slay Agamemnon.[3] When Diomed is wounded by the archer Pandaros, she takes away the mist from his eyes, that he may distinguish between gods and men, and warns him to avoid all conflict with the blessed gods, excepting Aphrodite, for whom, as winner of the fatal apple, she has an especial hatred.

When Aphrodite leads the wounded Ares from the field, Athene speeds after her, and smites her with her heavy hand upon the breast, crying exultingly, "So be it to all who give the Trojans aid."[4] When Menelaos is

[1] Il. xv. 413. [2] Il. viii. 367. [3] Il. i. 194. [4] Il. xxi. 423.

The Women of Homer

defending the corpse of Patroklos from the Trojan onslaught, "she puts force into his shoulders and knees, and into his breast the boldness of a fly, that, albeit driven away from the skin of man, is still eager to bite; and sweet to it is the blood of mankind."[1]

Achilles is one of her favourites, and when he is weeping bitterly over his dead friend Patroklos, and refuses food, she descends from heaven like a falcon, "wide-winged and shrill-voiced," and distils nectar and pleasant ambrosia into his breast, that grievous hunger might not assail him.[2]

In his terrible conflict with the river-gods Simoeis and Skamandros,[3] Athene succours him in the last extremity, when Hera was obliged to invoke the aid of the fire-god Hephaistos to scorch with his fiery blasts the mighty rivers. And last of all she aids him, by force and atrocious craft, to slay the noble Hector, the only hope and bulwark of sacred Troy.[4]

But much as she delights in heroes and mighty deeds of war, her chiefest favour is bestowed on men of subtle skill, and even of crafty intrigue.

Odysseus, "rich in counsel," the "man of many devices," is the object of her especial care. She boasts that she is herself renowned among the gods "for wit and wile." When the Phæacians landed him in his own country, while still asleep, he does not recognise his home. Athene comes to him in the guise of a young man, and tells him that he is indeed once more in Ithaca. Then Odysseus spake unto her winged words,[5]

[1] Il. xvii. 570.   [2] Il. xix. 353.   [3] Il. xxi. 264, 328.
[4] Il. xxii. 227, 297.   [5] Od. xiii. 254.

Athene loves and guards Odysseus

"yet he did not speak the truth, for he had a crafty wit ever ready in his breast." He tells her a long story—how he had slain Orsilochos, who would have despoiled him of his Trojan booty; had then embarked in a ship of the Sidonians, and been left by them on his native shore.

The goddess, instead of being vexed at his duplicity, now assumes the semblance of a woman—smiles, and caresses him with her hand.[1] "Crafty," she says, "and knavish must he be who would outdo thee in all manner of guile, even if it were a god that encountered thee. Hardy man, subtle of wit, of guile insatiate;—so thou wast not, even in thine own country, to cease from thy slights and knavish words, which thou lovest from the bottom of thy heart. Thou art of all men the first in counsel and in discourse, and I, in the company of the gods, win renown for my wit and wile. Yet thou knewest not me, Pallas Athene, daughter of Zeus, who am always by thee, and guard thee in all adventures."[2]

And indeed throughout the Odyssey the great goddess seems to have little else to do but to act as guardian angel to Odysseus. But for her persistent watchfulness he would never have reached his home, or have regained his sovereignty when there.

After losing all his company in the den of the Cyclopes, in the passage between Scylla and Charybdis, in the encounter with the Læstrygones, in the isle of Helios Hyperion, and in the storms which the angry Poseidon raises against him, he is cast naked and alone on the banks of the river of Phæacia. "There of a truth

[1] Od. xiii. 285.   [2] Od. xiii. 290.

The Women of Homer

would the luckless Odysseus have perished, beyond that which was ordained, had not grey-eyed Athene given him sure counsel."

It was she who put it into the mind of the sleeping maiden Nausicaa, daughter of Alkinoos, king of Phæacia, to go with her maidens to wash her clothes at the very spot where Odysseus was crouching among the dry leaves in the adjacent wood. Having finished their work, the maidens begin to play at ball. Nausicaa misses her aim, and the ball rolls into the river. The cry they raise at the loss rouses Odysseus from his lair. All flee in terror but Nausicaa. She, by the influence of Athene, is moved with pity for his sad condition, and provides him with food and raiment. Athene then sheds grace about his head and shoulders, and wins for him the admiration and the favour of the lovely princess.

Athene by these means secures him a favourable reception at the court of Alkinoos and Queen Arētē, who provide him with a swift ship to bear him to his home, laden with costly presents.[1] Nor does she leave him now that he is once more in the halls of his fathers, for the struggle with the insolent suitors—a contest hopeless without her aid—has yet to be waged.

As Odysseus cannot yet safely show himself in his palace in his true shape, Athene, like a good fairy, changes his form and dress according to the exigencies of the case. Sometimes she arrays him in all the splendour of youth and beauty and costly apparel; at others in the guise of a loathsome beggar. "Come now," she says, "thy

---

[1] Od. xxii. 20.

She metamorphoses Laertes

fair skin will I wither, and make waste thy yellow hair, and wrap thee in a foul garment, such as one would shudder to see a man therein."[1] Every step he takes is under her wise guidance. For his sake she is equally helpful to his son Telemachos, whom she accompanies on his perilous journey to Pylos and Sparta. She plots with father and son for the destruction of the rapacious suitors. In the very crisis of the fight, when they are facing fearful odds, with only the faithful swineherd Eumaios and the goatherd to back them, Athene stands beside him in the shape of Mentor and rebukes him for his want of confidence and courage.[2] "Odysseus, thou hast no more steadfast might and prowess as when for nine whole years thou didst battle with the Trojans for high-born, white-armed Helen. . . . How then, now that thou art come to thine own house and possessions, dost thou bewail the need of courage to stand before the suitors?"[3] And again, at the affecting recognition between Odysseus and his aged father Laertes: "Athene drew nigh, and made greater the limbs of the aged shepherd of the people; taller she made him than before, and mightier to behold, so that his dear son marvelled at him, beholding him like to the deathless gods in presence."[4] And lastly, when Eupeithes,[5] weeping over the body of Antinoos, his son, the chief of the suitors, rouses the Ithacans to take vengeance on his slayers, Athene once more gives victory to her favourite hero.

To face their numerous assailants stood Odysseus,

---

[1] Od. xiii. 399.   [2] Od. xxiv. 496.   [3] Od. xxii. 223.
[4] Od. xxiv. 371.   [5] Od. xxiv. 420.

The Women of Homer

Telemachos, the swineherd and the goatherd, the six sons of Dolios, with their father and Laertes, grey-bearded though they were, and "warriors only through stress of need." So full of the spirit breathed into him by Athene is Laertes, that when he hears the bold answer of Telemachos to Odysseus, who exhorts his son to show himself worthy of his high lineage, he greatly rejoices,

ODYSSEUS AND THE SEIRENS.
Reproduced, by permission of the Publishers, from " The Journal of Hellenic Studies," vol. xiii.

saying: "What a day has dawned for me, kind gods! Yea, and a glad man am I! for my son and my son's son are vying with one another in valour."[1] Then grey-eyed Athene stood beside the old warrior and spake: "O son of Arkesios, that art far the dearest of all my friends, pray first to the grey-eyed Maid, and to Father

[1] Od. xxiv. 513.

Happy Termination of Odysseus' Trials

Zeus, then swing thy long spear and hurl it straightway. Therewith she breathed great strength into his aged frame, and he smote Eupeithes through his casque, and he fell with a crash to the ground. Odysseus and his followers then fell on the front rank of the enemy and smote them with sword and spear."

But Athene intervenes again, and stays the impending slaughter: "Son of Laertes, seed of Zeus, Odysseus of many devices, refrain now, and stay the strife of even-handed war, lest perchance the son of Kronos be angry with thee, even Zeus of the far-borne voice."[1] Herewith the civil war and the long wanderings and trials of the patient Odysseus are brought to a happy termination. By the guardian care of Pallas Athene he is restored to his kingdom, his home, his faithful wife and son, and reigns in peace and safety.

[1] Od. xxiv. 542.

CHAPTER IX

APHRODITE

APHRODITE was one of the chief female goddesses of the Semites, whose cult was brought by Phœnicians to Cyprus. She was called "the Cyprian" by the Greeks, because she was born and lived there. Her first temple was at Askalon, and she was especially worshipped in Paphos, Amathus, and Idalion, in Cyprus.[1] She had temples in the remotest ages in Egypt, Chaldæa, and Phœnicia; but there are no traces of her temples in Mykenai, Tiryns, or Hissarlik. In later times temples were raised to her in Greece, under Oriental influences.

As she came by water, she is represented as rising from the sea, where she is immediately joined by Eros and Himeros (Love and Desire).[2] According to the Homeric hymn she was received with embraces on the seashore by the golden-filleted Hours, clothed by them in ambrosial garments, and conducted to the Immortals.

Homer does not adopt the theory of her foreign origin or her rising from the sea, but her connexion with the ocean was long remembered in later literature. The Knidians called the celebrated statue which Praxiteles made for them "Aphrodite Euploia" (giving a fair voyage), and on sarcophagi and gems she is followed

[1] Herodotus, i. 105.   [2] Hesiod, Theog. 201.

The Queen of Love and Beauty

by Tritons and Nereids. On coins of Corinth her chariot is drawn by Hippocamps. So Ovid—

"In mare nimirum jus habet orta mari."[1]

Festivals of Aphrodite and Poseidon were celebrated at Ægina for sixteen days; and the two deities were worshipped together in Arcadia, Messene, and Ægion.

In the Epics she is the daughter of Zeus and Dione,[2] and the wife of Hephaistos, the divine artificer, to whom she proves a faithless and undutiful wife. She is beloved by Ares, to whom she bore Harmonios, and, according to Hesiod, Deimos and Phobos; by Hermes, to whom she bore Hermaphroditos; by Dionysos, the father of Priapos; and by Anchises, the father of Æneas, the great founder of Rome.

HEAD OF VENUS.

She is the queen of love and beauty.[3] Her epithets in Homer and other Greek poets are—καλυκῶπις (roseate), καλλιπάρηος (fair-cheeked), καλλίκομος (fair-haired), ἐυπλόκαμος (fair-tressed), καλλίσφυρος (fair-ankled), λευκώλενος (white-armed), ῥοδόπηχυς (with rosy elbows), ῥοδοδάκτυλος

---

[1] Her. 16. 24.   [2] Il. v. 370.
[3] Αἰδοίην χρυσοστέφανον καλὴν Ἀφροδίτην!
Χαῖρ' ἑλικοβλέφαρε γλυκυμείλιχε.—Hom. Hym. in Ven.

The Women of Homer

(rosy-fingered), ἑλικοβλέφαρος (quick-glancing), φιλομμειδής (laughter-loving), ἡδὺ γελοιήσασα (sweetly smiling), γλυκυμείλιχος (sweetly winning), ἐυπέπλος (with beautiful robe), χρυσέη (golden), χρυσοστέφανος (golden-crowned), ἰοστέφανος (violet-crowned), ἑλκεσίπεπλος (robe-trailing), ἐυζώνος (well-girdled), and many more. Her favourite birds are doves and sparrows, from their tenderness and fertility.

Her entrancing beauty is enhanced by the most exquisite apparel. Her garments shine far brighter than the fire or the moon; her gold-garlanded hair breathes ambrosial fragrance round her. Her rich garments are made by the Graces themselves, who, with the Hours, are her constant attendants, and arrange for her their lovely dances. Her whole being is the expression of passionate, longing love, with which, at will, she inspires all the Immortals and mortal men.

Yet with all her beauty, her ineffable loveliness, sweetness and grace, her radiant smile and bewitching laugh, she is evidently no favourite of Homer, and the vivid image he portrays interests us only by its physical charms. She is not the

"Æneadum genetrix, hominum Divomque voluptas,[1]
Alma Venus! cœli subter labentia signa,
Quæ mare navigerum, quæ terras frugiferentis
Concelebras."

"Great mother of Æneas' race, thou joy of gods and men,
Beneath the shining orbs that roll beyond our human ken,
Thy spirit, Venus, fills the world in every hour of birth,
Throughout the sail-swept ocean waves, and all the teeming earth." —H. A. P.

[1] Lucretius, De Rer. Nat. Bk. I. v. 1.

Venus Urania and πάνδημος

But rather the *sæva mater Cupidinum* (the ruthless mother of the Cupids) of Horace.

Of course there is a serious side of Aphrodite, which appears more clearly in later literature. In the settlements of the Phœnicians in Sicily—Eryx and Egesta—there were temples of Aphrodite Urania (the heavenly), whose influence inspired a pure love, far removed from carnal desire.[1] The priestesses of the Aphrodite Urania must be virgins.[2] Under her feet Pheidias placed the tortoise, as emblem of home-staying, domestic love. It is under the inspiration of this Aphrodite that Plato rises to the highest flight of the soul.

VENUS.

As she appears in Homer, however, there is nothing heroic or grand about her but her form. She is the divine Olympian courtesan—frivolous, voluptuous, self-indulgent—not the Venus Urania, but almost the Venus πάνδημος, the vulgar Venus, patroness of wantonness and lubricity. Her much-abused husband Hephaistos describes her well,

[1] Ἐπὶ Ἔρωτι καθαρῷ καὶ ἀπαλληγμένῳ πόθου σώματος.
—*Cf.* Xenoph. Symp. 8, 9; Thucyd. 612.
[2] Pausan. ii. 10. 4.

and with surprising moderation, when, after her scandalous intrigue with Ares, he tells her father Zeus that his daughter is "fair indeed, but without discretion."[1] Like women of the same nature and character, she is generally sweet-tempered, kind, caressing and flattering. When the daughters of Pandaros are bereft of father and mother,[2] "the fair Aphrodite cherished them with curds and sweet honey and delicious wine," and begged of Zeus "that a glad marriage might be accomplished for the orphaned maidens"—"but the spirits of the storm carried them away." She was the patroness of marriage, for whose ties she showed so little respect.

Yet she could be harsh enough when her wishes were opposed. Paris, the least heroic of all the Homeric heroes, was her especial favourite. She loved him as her devoted worshipper, and for his goodly favour and brilliant accomplishments; but above all, she loved him for awarding to her the prize of beauty, won, as he was, by her promise to give him the fairest of mortal women.[3]

When Paris is defeated by Menelaos in single combat, and is being dragged along the ground to death, Aphrodite intervenes,[4] "snatches him up very easily, as a goddess may, covers him with thick darkness, and sets him down in his fragrant vaulted chamber." She then summons the unwilling Helen, who at first positively refuses to go with her, and tells Aphrodite to go to him herself. "Go and sit thou by his side, and depart from

---

[1] Od. viii. 320: οὐκ ἐχέθυμος.   [2] Od. xx. 68.
[3] In the famous judgment of Paris. *Vide* Eurip. Iphig. in Aul. 178, 575, 1292; Prop. ii. 2, 14; Ovid, Her. xvii. 15.   [4] Il. iii. 380.

the way of the gods . . . and still vex thyself for his sake, and guard him till he make thee his wife, or perchance his slave."[1] Strange language to be addressed to the daughter of Zeus, the all-powerful goddess of beauty and love! Then the goddess turns upon her victim in furious wrath: "Provoke me not, rash woman, lest in mine anger I desert thee, and hate thee as now I love thee beyond measure . . . and so thou perish in evil wise."[2]

Though self-willed and tyrannical to those unhappy ones who had fallen a prey to her seductions, she is weak and cowardly when met by superior strength. She loves Aineias, too, her son by the mortal Anchises. When Diomed is about to slay him, "she winds her white arms about her beloved son, and spreads before his face a fold of her radiant peplos, to be a shield from the darts of the Achaians."[3] Then Tydides, at the instigation of Hera, dares to attack the Cyprian queen, as she bore her dear son out of the battle, "for he knew that she was a coward goddess . . . no Athene, nor Enyo, waster of cities. So the great-hearted son of Tydeus pursued her through the throng, and thrust at her with his keen spear, and wounded the skin of her weak hand. Straight through the ambrosial vesture, that the Graces themselves had woven, pierced the spear into the flesh above the springing of the palm." Then with a loud cry she lets fall her son, and leaves his fate to chance.[4]

Ares carries her out of the battle in his chariot, and she flies to Olympos and falls on the knees of Dione,

---

[1] Il. iii. 404. [2] Il. iii. 413.
[3] Il. v. 315.   [4] Il. v. 330.

The Women of Homer

her mother, to whom she relates at length the outrage she had suffered at the hands of the impious Diomed. But Dione gives her cold comfort,[1] telling her that she was by no means the first of the blessed gods who had been wounded by a mortal hero ; and how Ares himself had been imprisoned by Otos and Ephialtes ; how Hera, the great queen of heaven, had been pierced in the right breast by a three-barbed arrow from the bow of

ATHENA, HERA, AND APHRODITE.

Amphitryon's son (Herakles) ; and how even Hades, the awful ruler of the infernal regions, was smitten by the same mortal hero, and fled to Olympos with the dart in his shoulder, "pierced through with anguish." "But,"[2] she adds, "the heart of Tydeus' son knoweth not this, that he is surely not long-lived that fighteth with immortals, nor ever do his children prattle on his knees at his returning from war and terrible fray." Hera and

[1] Il. v. 334.   [2] Il. v. 406.

Her Place in the Olympian Court

Athene, sitting near, mock the weeping Aphrodite with bitter sarcasm,[1] while her almighty father Zeus smiles and calls her to him: "Not unto thee, my child, are given the works of war; follow thou after the loving tasks of wedlock, and to all these things shall fleet Ares and Athene look." Yet, in a pretty epigram, she is represented as in full armour[2]—

> "Who has arrayed thee, laughter-loving, honey-sweet Cyprian, in warlike arms?
> To thee the pæan was dear, and golden-haired Hymenæus."

To which she answers, laughing—

> "If I conquer nude, what shall I not do when I take up arms?"

In spite of her irresistible all-pervading power over the hearts and senses of gods and men, she holds but a secondary place in the Olympian family and court. Father Zeus and mother Dione treat her, as we see, as a silly child. She is an object of ridicule, as well as hatred, to Hera and Athene, and the latter chases her from the field when she comes to the assistance of Ares, and fells her to the ground "with her stout fist."[3]

And lastly, to complete the evil picture of the lovely queen, she is made the principal actor in the scandalous scene in the eighth book of the Odyssey, in which she and Ares are caught in a bronze net by her injured husband Hephaistos, and exposed to the inextinguishable laughter of the blessed gods. "The lady god-

---

[1] Il. v. 419.
[2] *Jacobi de Epig. Græc.* i. 46.   Pausanius mentions several armed statues of Aphrodite, iii. 23.   See Appendix XV.   [3] Il. xxi. 423.

The Women of Homer

desses," we are glad to learn, "abode each within her house for shame." The whole passage, the only one in the Homeric Epics which can be fairly called vulgar or immoral, is so alien in spirit and style to the rest of the poems, that we feel justified in regarding it as an interpolation of a later and more vicious age.

It is a singular fact that her position in the later poets and in art is far more honourable than in Homer. In Pindar she is the wife of Ares,[1] and among the twelve gods she and Ares are placed together, as they are also on the Francois vase.[2] In the double temple at Argos there was a *xoanon* of Aphrodite in the east entrance, and of Ares in the west. In the temple of Ares at Athens, in which stood his statue by Alkamenes, there were two statues of Aphrodite.[3] Perhaps the best examples of these two deities combined are on coins of Corinth.[4]

ARTEMIS—DIANA.

The daughter of Zeus and Leto, and sister of Apollo, born in the island of Ortygia or Delos; the symbol of maidenhood and chastity.[5] Keats, thinking of the story of the "ever-sleeping" Endymion, is not willing to let her altogether escape the pangs of love—

> "Though the playful rout
> Of Cupids shun thee, too divine thou art,
> Too keen in beauty, for thy silver prow
> Not to have dipt in Love's most gentle stream."

---

[1] Pyth. iv. 87; Æschyl. Suppl. 6, 39.
[2] R. Rochette, Peint. p. 261, n. 4: and p. 268, n.   [3] Pausan. 1. 8, 5.
[4] Pausan. 2. 4, 7.   [5] Eustathius ad Od. v. 123.

DIANE À LA BICHE.

Artemis the Huntress

Her epithets are ἁγνὴ (holy, pure), εὐπλόκαμος (fair-tressed), χρυσόθρονος (golden-throned), κελαδεινὴ (noisy, swift-rushing, loud-voiced), ἀγροτερή (the huntress), ἰοχέαιρα (the arrow-pourer, archer), χρυσηλάκατος (with spindle of gold), εὔσκοπος (keen-sighted),[1] ἐλαφήβολος (stag-slayer). Her name is probably derived from ἀρτεμὴς (untouched).

All her tastes are manly, and her principal vocation is the chase of bears and stags, in pursuit of which she is ever ranging forest and mountain, attended by the twenty nymphs "that hold the steep hill-tops, the river springs, and the grassy water-meadows." Of majestic stature and exceeding beauty, she surpasses them all in height, in strength, activity and courage, and rises pre-eminent among them, a very sylvan queen. She instructed her favourites in archery, and among them Skamandros, the mighty hunter.[2]

She favours the Trojans, but plays a very minor part in the fierce struggle before Troy. When she does venture on the warpath, she is no match for Hera or Athene; and when she stirs up her brother Apollo against Poseidon with bitter reproaches, it goes ill with her, as we have seen, at the hands of Hera, who cuffs her, breaks her bow, and spills her arrows.[3] Her mother Leto gathers them up, and Artemis, like Aphrodite, goes to Olympos to complain to Zeus. She seats herself upon his knee, "while round her her divine vesture quivered." "Who," he asks, gently laughing, "dear child, hath thus dealt with thee?" And the fair-

---
[1] Il. xxi. 511; xvi. 183; v. 53.
[2] Il. v. 51.
[3] Il. xxi. 503.

The Women of Homer

crowned goddess of the echoing chase replies : " It was thy wife that buffeted me, my father, the white-armed Hera, from whom strife and contention come upon the Immortals." Zeus does nothing !

When wearied of the chase, the swift huntress goes to Delphi, where she delights to dance with the Muses and the Graces.

All gentle, painless deaths of women are attributed to her, as those of men to Apollo. We often read of women being slain " by the visitation of her gentle shafts "[1]—not in anger, but in love. Penelope, in her dire distress at the importunity of the insolent suitors, breathes a prayer to Artemis : " Oh ! that pure Artemis would give me so soft a death, even now, that I might no more waste my life in sorrow of heart, longing for the manifold excellence of my dear lord."[2]

But her golden shafts were not always the messengers of peace-bringing love to weary souls. It was in wrath that she slew Orion, the lover of the rosy-fingered Dawn (Eos), and Laodameia, the daughter of Bellerophon,[3] and the children of unhappy Niobe; for that Niobe matched herself against Artemis' mother, the fair-cheeked Leto, saying that " the goddess bare but twain, but she many children."[4]

As she had the power of sending plague and death, like her brother Apollo, she is called θεὰ ἀπόλλουσα, but also θεὰ σώτειρα, from her power of healing, which she exercised in the case of Aineias.[5] And although her principal occupation was the slaughter of wild beasts,

---

[1] Il. xxiv. 759 : ἀγανοῖς βελέεσσι.   [2] Od. xviii. 202.
[3] Il. vi. 205, 428 ; Od. xv. 477.   [4] Il. xxiv. 606.   [5] Il. v. 447.

Selene and Endymion

whence her epithet ἐλαφηβόλος (stag-slayer), she was regarded as the patroness of the young, and Æschylus calls her the protectress of young sucking animals.

As Luna the Moon, with whom she was identified, she was perhaps the most generally worshipped of all the heavenly powers,[1] and in Greece especially by the Arcadians and Thessalians. The importance attached to the changes of the moon by the Jews, and the influence on the weather and on man and beast attributed to them, even in the present day, are too well known to need comment here. Some of the tribes of Africa are said to worship the moon without the sun.[2] Even the rigidly monotheistical Osmanlis offer prayers to the rising moon. At Athens, also, men prayed to the new moon, either on the Acropolis or at home.[3]

Selene, afterwards identified with Artemis (though not vowed to virginity like Artemis, for she had fifty children), is connected with Endymion of Latmos, on the beautiful white range of rocks of which Selene visited the ever-sleeping youth, that she might kiss him while he was unconscious of the favour. There was a saying that he who sleeps with a goddess cannot live, a rule certainly not of universal application—witness Peleus, Anchises, Odysseus, and others.

The legend was a favourite theme of the poets.[4] Sappho sings of Selene's visit to the ever-sleeping one in his cave (adyton) in Latmos, from which he never moves. In the Theogony, Selene, like the Dawn (Eos),

---

[1] Pliny calls her cult *terris familiarissimum*.
[2] *Zoega de Obel.* p. 243, n. 4.   [3] Demosth. Aristogeiton, i., sec. 99.
[4] Theocr. iii. 49; Ovid, Her. 15, 89.

is the sister of Helios, as Artemis of Apollo.[1] The Scholiast Æschylus calls her the daughter of Helios, because she derives her light from him.

The forms under which Artemis appears in different countries and periods are extremely various and different in character. What, for example, can be more unlike the forest-ranging virgin huntress Artemis, than the breast-covered Diana of the Ephesians?

Artemis appears in Homer as the sister and female counterpart of Apollo; and we find them together — the one at the east, rising, and the other at the west, setting — in the eastern pediment of the Parthenon in the British Museum.

Hecate, who was sometimes regarded as one of the "persons" of the triform goddess, is not mentioned in Homer. She was worshipped in Athens under the name Μουνυχία (reigning alone by night — *sola noctu dominans*), and was called the Munychian Hecate in the Orphic Hymn.[2] The tenth month was named after her by the Athenians, and they held a festival, called Munychia, in her honour at the time of the full moon.[3]

---

[1] Hymn to Helios, 31, 6; Eurip. Phœn. 179.
[2] Argonautica, 933; Pausan. i. 1, 4.   [3] Plut. Glor. Athen. 7.

CHAPTER X

THE DEMI-GODDESSES OR NYMPHS—CALYPSO, CIRCE, THETIS

THESE inferior Immortals are chiefly notable in the Epics for the important part they play in the lives of Odysseus and Achilles.

Calypso, daughter of Atlas, dwelt in the island of Ogygia, on which Odysseus was wrecked after escaping, with the loss of half his crew, from Scylla and Charybdis. This island "lies far off in the sea; there dwells the crafty Calypso of the braided tresses, an awful goddess of mortal speech, nor is any, either of the gods or men, conversant with her."[1]

Of course many futile attempts have been made to identify this island, and Kallimachos was probably the first to fix upon the island of Gaulos (Gozo). Homer calls it "the navel of the sea" (ὄμφαλὸς θαλάσσης), and says that Odysseus was sailing eight days and nights from Charybdis before he reached it. We have seen above how little dependence can be placed on Homeric distances, and we cannot but agree with Eratosthenes, the greatest of ancient geographers, that the geography of the Epics was entirely the creation of the poet's fancy.

Her chief epithet in the Odyssey is δῖα θεάων, but she

[1] Od. xii. 449, and vii. 245.

The Women of Homer

is also "fair-haired" and "crafty." In the Homeric Hymn she is called ἱμερόεσσα (desirable, charming). This strange and lonely goddess conceived a warm attachment for Odysseus, entertained him royally (as he says, against his will) for seven long years, and only let him go at the express command of Zeus.

Hermes,[1] the bearer of the message, having reached that far-off isle, "rose from the violet-blue sea to get him up into the land, till he came to a great cave wherein dwelt the nymph of the braided tresses, and he found her within. And on the hearth there was a great fire burning, and from afar was smelt the fragrance of cleft cedar and sandal-wood, blazing through the isle. And the Nymph within was singing with a sweet voice as she fared to and fro before the loom and wove with a shuttle of gold. And round about the cave there was a wood blossoming, alder and poplar and sweet-smelling cypress. And therein all long-winged birds had their places of rest, owls and falcons and chattering sea-crows, which have their business in the waters. And lo! there about the hollow cave trailed a gadding garden-vine, all rich with clusters. And the wells of four streams, set orderly, were running with clear waters hard by one another, turned each to a separate course. Moreover, all around soft meadows of violets and parsley blossomed, and even a deathless god who came there might wonder at the sight and be glad at heart."

The fair goddess first, as in duty bound, set before Hermes the entertainment of strangers; and as he was a deathless god, she spread for him a table with ambrosia,

[1] Od. v. 43, 56.

Odysseus and Calypso

and mixed the ruddy nectar. And after he had comforted his soul with food, he answered her question :[1] "'Twas Zeus that bade me come hither, by no will of mine ; nay, who of his free-will would speed over such a wondrous space of brine, whereby is no city of mortals that do sacrifice to the gods and offer choice hecatombs ? ... And now Zeus biddeth thee send Odysseus hence with what speed thou mayest, for it is not ordained that he die away from his friends, but to come to his high-roofed home and his own country."[2]

The nymph shuddered as she heard the stern decree, and bitterly complains of the jealousy of the gods ; but she makes no resistance. "Him," she says, "have I loved and cherished, and I said that I would make him to know not death and age for ever. Yet, forasmuch as it is in nowise possible to go beyond or make void the purpose of Zeus, let him away over the barren sea. But I will give him no despatch, not I, for I have no ships by me with oars. ... Yet will I be forward to put this in his mind, and will hide nought, that all unharmed he may come to his own country."[3]

"Then she went to the sea, and found the great-hearted Odysseus sitting on the shore, and the tears were never wiped from his eyes, and his sweet life was ebbing away as he mourned for his return. ... And in the daytime he would sit on the rocks, straining his soul with tears and groans and griefs, and through his tears he would look wistfully over the barren sea."[4]

She tells him how to build his raft, and furnishes him

---

[1] Od. v. 99.   [2] Od. v. 116.
[3] Od. v. 135. [4] Od. v. 158.

with timber and tools, and gives him provisions and raiment, and promises to send a fair breeze. His suspicious nature finds it difficult to believe in so much generous kindness from one whom he was deserting. Instead of a profusion of gratitude, he only expresses doubts of her sincerity and fears of her real intentions. " Herein, goddess, thou hast plainly some other thoughts, and in nowise my furtherance, for that thou biddest me cross in a raft a great gulf of the sea, so dread and difficult, the which not even the swift gallant ships pass over rejoicing in the breeze of Zeus. Nor would I against thy will go aboard a raft, unless thou wilt deign, O goddess, to swear a great oath not to plan any hidden guile."[1]

Instead of being angry at his undeserved mistrust, the fair goddess smiled, caressed him with her hand, and spake, showing a certain admiration of his crafty ways. " Knavish thou art, and no weakling in wit."[2] Then she swears by earth and heaven and the water of the Styx, that she will not plan any guile to his hurt; and she adds, with a certain pathos, "for I too have a righteous mind, and my heart within me is not of iron, but pitiful even as thine." They then return to the cave and take their meal he of "meat for men," she of nectar and ambrosia. Then Calypso, the fair goddess, spake : "So it is indeed thy wish to start this moment for thy home. Didst thou know what a measure of suffering thou art ordained to undergo or ever thou reach thine own country, here, even here, thou wouldst abide with me, and wouldst never taste of death, though thou longest to see thy wife, for

[1] Od. v. 171.   [2] Od. v. 183.

Calypso's Generosity

whom thou hast a desire day by day. Not, in sooth, that I allow me to be worse than her in form or fashion; for it is in nowise meet that mortal women should match them with Immortals in shape and comeliness."[1] And Odysseus, rich in counsel, answers her: "Be not wroth with me, goddess and queen. Myself, I know it well, how wise Penelope is meaner to look upon than thou, in comeliness and stature. And she is mortal, and thou knowest not age or death. Yet even so, I long, day by day, to face homeward and see the day of my returning; yea, and if some god shall wreck me in the wine-dark deep, even so will I endure, with a heart patient of affliction. For already have I suffered much, and toiled in perils of waves and wars; let this be added to the tale of those."

As soon as the rosy-fingered Dawn shone forth, "Odysseus put on a mantle and a doublet, and the Nymph clad her in a great shining robe, light of woof and gracious, and about her waist she cast a fair golden girdle, and a veil withal upon her head."[2] She shows him where the tall trees grow, alder and poplar and pine, and leaves him to his work. But she comes again and brings him a web of cloth for sails, which he fashioned very skilfully. In four days the raft is finished, and on the fifth the fair goddess, when she had bathed him and clad him in fragrant attire, sent him on his way from the island, and caused a warm and gentle wind to blow. She instructs him how to steer his raft by keeping ever on the left of the Wain, "which alone hath no part in the baths of ocean."

[1] Od. v. 201. [2] Od. v. 230.

The Women of Homer

There is no pathetic leave-taking, no expression of gratitude from Odysseus for her long and loving care, and the lavish generosity with which she aided him to leave her for the arms of another. Odysseus, rejoicing, sets his sails, which *she* had furnished, to the favouring breeze, which *she* had sent, and the lonely goddess returns to her solitude, having lost the only being she loved, "for none, either of gods or mortals, were conversant with her." We see no more of the fair Calypso.

KIRKE (CIRCE).

Circe of Aia is the enchantress and magician of the Homeric epic, answering to the witch of our Northern fairy tales, except that the latter is generally a frightful old woman, while the former is a lovely nymph.

Circe of the braided tresses[1] was the daughter of Helios and Perse, the daughter of Okeanos, and sister of the "wise and terrible" Æetes, the father of the well-known sorceress and infanticide, Medea. Homer calls her, like Calypso, an "awful goddess of mortal speech,"[2] and applies to her the epithet of δολόεσσα (crafty). The later poets and mythographers, both Greek and Roman, and especially the latter, occupy themselves very much with Circe, and apply to her very numerous epithets, almost all of which are evil. To Virgil, Horace, Tibullus, Ovid, Claudian, &c., she is *vitrea, meretrix, docta* (in a bad sense), *Titanis, venefica, callida, insidiosa*.

In almost all instances, the post-Homeric writers

---
[1] Od. x. 136.   [2] Od. x. 136: δεινὴ θεὸς αὐδήεσσα.

Odysseus and Circe

seem to delight in degrading the characters created by Homer to a lower level than he had assigned to them. Thus Helen, in many respects so noble and lovable, becomes a worthless wanton; Penelope, an adulteress; and Hekabe, a savage infanticide, a female dog, &c.

Odysseus, after losing eleven of his twelve ships

CIRCE.

Reproduced, by permission of the Publishers, from "The Journal of Hellenic Studies," vol. xiii.

among the savage Læstrygonians, escapes to the island Æææ, the abode of this much-dreaded goddess. Having landed, he ascends a hill, from which he sees smoke rising from a dwelling in the coppice below. While returning to his ship, a tall antlered stag crosses his very path, which he smote with his brazen shaft, and bore as a welcome prize to his famished companions.

The Women of Homer

So the rest of the day was spent in feasting on abundant flesh and sweet wine. As soon as the rosy-fingered Dawn shone forth, he orders a gathering of his men, and tells them how he had seen the smoke rising from a dwelling in the woodland below. The men, as usual, wept copiously, but, as he said, "no avail came of their weeping." He then divides them into two companies, taking the command of one himself, and assigning the other to Eurylochus. To decide which should undertake the perilous enterprise to the halls of Circe; they cast lots in a brazen-fitted helmet, and the lot of proud Eurylochus leapt out. So he and two-and-twenty of the crew went on their way "all weeping."[1]

They soon found the halls of Circe in the forest glades, built of polished stone, from which there was a clear prospect. "And all around the palace wolves of the hills and lions were roaming, whom she herself had bewitched with evil drugs."[2] Being wild beasts only in form, they naturally did not hurt the newcomers, but fawned on them; but nevertheless they were affrighted when they saw the strange and terrible creatures.

Having arrived at the gate, they heard the goddess "singing in a sweet voice as she fared to and fro before the great web imperishable, such as is the handiwork of goddesses, fine of woof and full of grace and splendour."[3] On their summons she came forth, and opened the shining doors, and they all went in "in their heedlessness." Eurylochus[4] alone held back, fearing some treachery.

[1] Od. x. 203. [2] Od. x. 212.
[3] Od. x. 221. [4] Od x. 232.

Hermes gives Odysseus an Antidote

The fair goddess "entertains them with a mess of cheese and barley-meal, yellow honey and Pramnian wine, with which she mixed harmful drugs. Then she smote them with a wand, and shut them up in the styes of the swine, changed in all respects except their minds." "Thus were they penned weeping, and Circe flung them acorns and mast and fruit of the cornel-tree to eat."[1]

Eurylochus returns to Odysseus with the evil tidings. It was long ere he could compose himself sufficiently to tell his sad tale, which when Odysseus had at last extorted from him, he girt on his sword and took his bow, and ordered the weeping Eurylochus to lead him to the fatal spot. Eurylochus, completely overmastered by his fears, begs him not to take him thither against his will, and Odysseus contemptuously allows him to remain behind. "As for thee, Eurylochus,[2] thou mayest abide here eating and drinking by the black hollow ship; but I will go forth, for a strong constraint is laid on me."

In spite of his many ugly qualities, we must allow that Odysseus was a true leader of men, always ready to face danger in defence of his followers.

As he was passing through the sacred glades on his apparently hopeless enterprise,[3] Hermes of the golden wand met him in the guise of a youth, "with the first down upon his lip, the time when youth is most gracious." Hermes tells him what had befallen his men, and that in all likelihood he himself would never return, but abide there with the others. "But," he adds, "I will set thee free from thy distress, and bring thee

---

[1] Od. x. 241.   [2] Od. x. 271.   [3] Od. x. 275.

deliverance." He then gives him the flower *moly*,[1] which would render vain all the magic power of Circe's drugs. He further tells him exactly how to deal with her and subdue her to his will: "When it shall be that Circe smites thee with her long wand, then draw thy sharp sword and spring upon her, as one eager to slay her."[2]

Odysseus proceeded on his way with darkly troubled heart, and halted in the portals of the fair-tressed goddess. At his loud summons she comes forth with smiling welcome, seats him on a goodly carven chair, and gives him a footstool—a sure mark of honour. Then she gives him the poisoned cup, and strikes him with her wand, saying: "Go thy way now to the stye, and couch thee there with the rest of thy company."[3]

The antidote preserves him. He springs on Circe, sword in hand, as if he would slay her. With a great cry, she slips down and clasps his knees in the utmost astonishment, and wails for mercy. "There lives no man else that is proof against this charm. . . . But thou, methinks, hast a mind within thee that may not be enchanted. Verily thou art Odysseus, whom the slayer of Argos full often told me was to come hither on his way from Troy."[4]

Like Calypso, she falls in love with this renowned hero, and becomes completely subservient to his will. True to his prudent and suspicious character, he rejects all her offers until she has sworn the mighty, irre-

---

[1] Theophrastus (Hist Plant. ix. 15, 17) understands it to mean *Allium nigrum Gouan*, a kind of garlick with black root and white flower.
[2] Od. x. 293.   [3] Od. x. 320.   [4] Od. x. 327.

Odysseus' Companions restored

vocable oath, which binds the most powerful as well as the wiliest of the gods.[1] She then, according to custom, bathes him; and after the bath the handmaid drew a polished table to their side, and a grave dame bare wheaten bread, and laid dainties on the board, "giving freely of such things as she had." But Odysseus sat silent without touching the food. Circe, seeing him thus afflicted, asks him the cause of his silence and distress. "Wherefore dost thou sit there like a speechless man, consuming thine own soul? . . . Thou hast no cause to fear some further guile, for I have sworn thee a strong oath not to harm thee."[2] He answers, "O Circe, what righteous man would have the heart to taste meat and drink ere he had redeemed his company? If in good faith thou biddest me eat and drink, then let them go free, that my eyes may behold my dear companions." Circe at once consents. She opened the door of the stye, and drave them forth in the shape of swine of nine years old, and they all stood before her.[3] And she went through the midst of them, anointing each one of them with another charm. "And lo! from their limbs the bristles dropped wherewith the venom had clothed them. And they became men again, younger than before and goodlier far, and taller to behold." And they all knew Odysseus again, and "took his hands, and wistful was the lament that sank into their souls, and the roof around rang wondrously. And even the goddess was moved with compassion."

Circe then exhorts him to go back to his swift ship, and return with his dear companions. He finds them

[1] Od. x. 345. [2] Od. x. 382. [3] Od. x. 388.

lamenting piteously, and, as usual, *shedding big tears,* Yet they were overjoyed to see him : " Yea, and to their spirit it was as though they had already got to their dear country, and the very city of rugged Ithaca, where they were born and reared."[1] Odysseus then invites them to go to the palace of Circe, and to see their fellows, where they eat and drink in the sacred dwelling of the goddess, "for they have continual store."[2] All consent but the timid Eurylochus, who tries to hold them back. Odysseus was enraged by his mutinous conduct, and would have slain him, but the others stayed him on every side with soothing words. They proposed to leave Eurylochus behind to guard the hollow ship, but he too followed with them, "for he feared his lord's terrible rebuke."

Meanwhile the goddess bathed the others with all care, anointed them with olive oil, and cast thick mantles and doublets about them. And when they saw the rest of their company face to face, they wept and mourned, and the house resounded.[3] Circe then counsels them to remain with her till their spirit should return to them again, as when first they left their own home in rugged Ithaca, "for now," she said, "ye are wasted and faint in heart, ever mindful of your sore wandering, nor has your heart been ever merry, for very grievous hath been your trial."[4] "So spake she, and our lordly spirit consented thereto. So there we sat, day by day, for the full circle of a year, feasting on abundant flesh and sweet wine."[5]

[1] Od. x. 414.   [2] Od. x. 422.   [3] Od. x. 453.
[4] Od. x. 463.   [5] Od. x. 467.

Odysseus' Journey to Hades

At last, on the return of the long days of summer, his followers exhort him once more to think of his return to his own dear country.[1] He therefore supplicates the fair goddess to fulfil her promise to send him on his homeward way. Grieved as she was to part with him, she consents, for he had thoroughly won her heart; and she now, with unselfish zeal, loyally bends her mind to the fulfilment of his wishes.[2] But she warns him that it is absolutely necessary to his salvation that he should journey to the dwelling of Hades and dread Persephone, and seek the shade of Theban Teiresias, the blind soothsayer; to him, she said, Persephone had given judgment, even in his death, that he alone should have understanding; "but the other souls sweep shadow-like around."[3]

Odysseus is terrified at the prospect of this new and terrible adventure. He sat up in his bed and wept, "and his soul had no more care to live and to see the sunlight."[4] But when he had had his fill of weeping and grovelling, he asks her: "And who, Circe, will guide us on this way? for no man ever yet sailed to hell in a black ship."

Circe is fully equal to the occasion, and gives him the most exact and detailed instructions for his voyage, and tells him what offerings to make. She exhorts him to take especial care to conciliate, with many prayers, "the strengthless heads of the dead," and to promise them that, on his return to Ithaca, he would offer to them a barren heifer, the best he had, and fill the pyre with

---

[1] Od. x. 483. [2] Od. x. 490.
[3] Od. x. 494. [4] Od. x. 496.

The Women of Homer

treasure; and would sacrifice apart, to Teiresias alone, a black sheep without spot, the fairest of his flock.[1]

Odysseus then imparted the dread news to his companions, who sat them down, even where they were, and made lament and tore their hair. "Howbeit, no help came of their weeping."[2]

Arrived at the appointed spot in Hades, where the river Pyriphlegethon flows into Acheron, and likewise Cocytus, a branch of the Styx, he digs a trench and fills it with the blood of the victims sacrificed to the "lordly dead." The spirits throng round him in their eagerness to drink the blood, but he suffered no one to approach the trench, not even his dear mother Anticleia,[3] until he had had word of Teiresias, on whom all his hopes depended. At last the sage draws near, and bids him hold off from the ditch, and draw back the sharp sword by which he kept the other shades off, that he might drink the blood "and tell him sooth."

Teiresias tells him that he will not pass unheeded by the Shaker of the Earth, "who hath laid up wrath in his heart against thee for rage at the blinding of his dear son."[4] He also warns him against landing on the sacred island of the sun-god Helios; telling him that if he lands there, and does injury to the god's sacred cattle, he will atone for it by the loss of all his men; yet that he himself should escape, and return in evil plight, with the loss of his ship and all his company, on board the ship of strangers. But after all his troubles, Teiresias prophesies that he should reach his

[1] Od. x. 521. [2] Od. x. 566.
[3] Od. xi. 84. [4] Od. xi. 101.

NEREID ON THE SEA-BULL.

Teiresias prophesies Smooth Things

home. "And thine own death shall come upon thee from the sea—a gentle death, which shall end thee foredone with smooth old age, and the folk shall dwell happily around thee."[1]

I have dwelt on the adventures of Odysseus at greater length than the scope of a work on the *women* of Homer appears to warrant, because I wish to show what a very prominent part the women play in the wondrous tale *of Homer*. In every crisis of Odysseus' fate it is a goddess, a nymph, or a woman who comes to save him. The great goddess Athene, the immortal nymphs Calypso, Circe, and Ino-Leucothea, the queenly Arētē, and above all the peerless maiden Nausicaa, appear successively, in the very nick of time, to save him from impending disaster and death. These details, too, serve to illustrate the peculiar character and functions of the demi-goddesses or nymphs. We see them acting as messengers of the greater deities, as mediators between them and mortal men, and generally as compassionate, loving, and beneficent friends of the helpless and distressed.

THETIS.

Daughter of Nereus and Doris, and grand-daughter of Poseidon, whence she is called "Neptunine" by Catullus.[2]

As one of the highest order of marine deities, she lived with her father Nereus in the depths of the

---
[1] Od. xi. 134.
[2] 64, 28: "Tene Thetis tenuit pulcherrima Neptunine?"

ocean.¹ There, attended by her sister nymphs, she sported and danced by the ever fresh-flowing streams.² Her epithets are ηὔκομος and εὐπλοκαμος (fair-haired, fair-tressed), and τανύπεπλος (long-robed), and ἀργυρόπεζα (silver-footed). She played a great part in Greek mythology, and in the Iliad as the unhappy mother of the short-lived Achilles. She is remarkable for her sympathetic kindness to the unfortunate in their distresses, and for her devoted love to her son. She received Dionysos, "and took him to her bosom," when he plunged beneath the salt sea wave, after he had fled from the murderous tyrant Lykourgos.³ The wine-god, in token of his gratitude, gave her a two-handled golden urn, the work of Hephaistos.⁴ She also received Hephaistos himself, when he was cast out of heaven. She was reared by Hera, and her great beauty and high distinction of character attracted Zeus himself and Poseidon, who both sought her hand in marriage.⁵ But when Themis prophesied that Thetis' son would be greater than his father they desisted, and determined that she should marry a mortal, that no god might suffer from his son.

The husband fixed on was Peleus, a favourite of the gods, with whom she was forced into a marriage degrading to her as a goddess, sorely against her own

---

[1] Hesiod. Theog. 244 ; Il. i. 58 ; xviii. 35 ; xxiv. 82.
[2] Eurip. Ion. 1099 ; Aristoph. Acharn. 882.
[3] Il. vi. 135.   [4] Od. 24, 75 ; Tsetz. ad Lycophron. 273.
[5] Pindar, Isthm. 8. 18, 70; Ovid. Met. xi. 225 :

> "Namque senex Thetidi Proteus, Dea dixerat undæ
> Concipe ; mater eris juvenis, qui fortibus actis.
> Acta patris vincet, majorque vocabitur illo."

Ovid. xv. 856 ; Æsch. Prom. 767.

Wedding of Thetis and Peleus

will. But Cheiron, the wise Centaur, instructs his friend Peleus how to bring her into subjection—no easy task, for Thetis, like many other marine deities, had the power of transforming herself into any shape she pleased.[1] But all her efforts were in vain, for Peleus, forewarned, held her fast till she returned to her proper shape.

The wedding of Peleus and his victim was attended by all the gods, and Apollo and the Muses sang the bridal song.[2]

When she had given birth to her illustrious son Achilles, Nereus prophesies to her that his life, though glorious, would be short. All the sea deities, Proteus,[3] Nereus, Ino, Thetis herself, and others, possessed the power of prophecy, which seems to have been connected in the mind of the Greeks with water.

Her whole soul is devoted to her son; her only thought how to render his short span of life glorious and happy.

When the heralds took away his loved Briseis, Achilles wept, and sat aloof from his comrades on the beach of the grey sea. He stretched forth his hands and prayed earnestly to his dear mother: "Mother! seeing thou didst of a truth bear me to so brief a life, honour, at the least, ought the Olympian to have granted me . . . but now doth he not honour me, no, not a whit."

---

[1] Pindar. Nem. iii. 60; Pausan. v. 185.

[2] Il. xxiv. 62. Stories of her changes are given in Pindar, Nem. iii. 60; and in Apollodorus, iii. 13, sec. 5.

[3] Proteus, when bound by Menelaos, assumes the form of a snake, a pard, a huge wild boar, of fire and running water, and of a tall and flowering tree.—Od. iv. 453.

The Women of Homer

His lady mother heard him, as she sat in the sea-depths by her aged sire. With speed she rose from the grey sea, like a mist, and sat before the face of her weeping son, and stroked him with her hand. "My child," she said, "why weepest thou? Speak it forth, that both may know it."

He then relates to her all that had happened—how the Far-darter had sent a plague upon the Greeks because Agamemnon had kept the daughter of his favoured priest Chryses as a slave; and how, when the chiefs of the Greeks compelled him to restore Chryseis to her aged father, and the plague was stayed, Agamemnon had robbed him by force of Briseis, whom the Greeks had given him as his prize. He urges his mother to use all her influence with Zeus, and to remind him of the day when all the gods—even Hera, Poseidon, and Pallas—would have bound him, and she alone came to his aid, and summoned the hundred-handed Briareus to his side, and thus saved him from shameful wreck. "Do thou clasp his knees, if perchance he will give succour to the Trojans, and hem the Achaians among their ships' sterns, giving them over to slaughter, ... that even the wide-ruling Agamemnon may perceive his blindness, in that he honoured not at all the best of the Achaians."[1]

Thetis forgets not her dear son's charge. "Ah me, my child!" she wails, "why reared I thee, cursed in my motherhood?... Lo, now thou art made short-lived alike and lamentable beyond all men. But now I will go myself to snow-clad Olympos."[2] At early morn she

[1] Il. i. 397.
[2] Il. i. 495.

Thetis supplicates Zeus for her Son

mounts up to heaven and high Olympos, where she finds the mighty Son of Kronos seated alone upon the highest peak. He listens to her fervent prayer, but sat long time in silence. Then with still more desperate eagerness she clung to his knees, until he at last gave way, reluctantly indeed, for he was afraid of Hera's sharp reproaches, and said: "Come now, I will bow my head to thee, for that is the surest token among the Immortals." "He nodded his dark brow, and the ambrosial locks waved from the king's immortal head, and great Olympos quaked."[1]

He is, of course, severely cross-examined by his jealous consort, and can only quiet her by threats. "Lady," he says, "ever art thou imagining, nor can I escape thee. . . . But abide thou in silence, and hearken to my bidding, lest all the gods in Olympos keep not off from thee my visitation, when I put forth my hands unapproachable against thee."[2]

Thetis does not disguise from her dear son that he is destined to an early doom, which he could only escape by forfeiting his fair fame. "For thus,"[3] he tells the Achaian chiefs who come with earnest prayers and rich presents from Agamemnon, hoping to mitigate his wrath —"for thus my goddess-mother telleth me, Thetis the silver-footed, that twain fates are bearing me to the issue of death. If I abide here and besiege the Trojan city, then my returning home is taken from me, but my fame shall be imperishable; but if I go home to my dear native land, my high fame is taken from me, but my life

---

[1] Il. i. 529. [2] Il. i. 556. [3] Il. ix. 410.

The Women of Homer

shall endure long while." The *hero*, of course, could not hesitate.

When his dearest friend, the good Patroklos, is slain by Hector, "then terribly moaned Achilles,[1] and with both hands he took dark dust and poured it over his head, and defiled his comely face, and tore and marred his hair."[2] His lady mother, ever watchful, heard him in the depth of the sea, as she sat by her aged sire. "At her bitter cry all the goddesses flocked around her—the daughters of Nereus, Glauke and Thaleia, and Kymodoke, Nesæa and Speio, and Thoe, and ox-eyed Halië, and Kymothoe, and Aktaie, and Limnoreia, and Melite, and Iaira, Amphithoë, and Agave, and Doto and Proto, and Pherusa, and Dynamene and Dexamene, and Amphinome, and Kallianeira, Doris and Panope, and noble Galateia, and Nemertes, and Apsendes, and Kallianassa, and Klymene, and Ianeira, and Ianassa, and Maira, and Oreithuia, and fair-tressed Amatheia, and other Nereids.[3] With these the bright cave was filled, and they all beat together on their breasts, and Thetis led the lament." She tells them how her son, the chief of heroes, had shot up "like a young branch," and she had reared him "as a plant in a very fruitful field." "I will go to him," she says, "that I may look upon my dear child."

She rose from the sea with her attendant nymphs, and went up upon the shore, where lay the ships of the Myrmidones.[4] She stood beside her darling child, and with a shrill cry clasped his head, and asked the cause of his bitter lamentation. "One thing," she says, "at least

[1] Il. xviii. 35. [2] Il. xviii. 23.
[3] Il. xviii. 42. [4] Il. xviii. 68.

Thetis procures New Armour from Hephaistos

hath been accomplished of Zeus, that the sons of the Achaians should be pent up in their ships for lack of thee."

"True, mother," he answers; "but what delight have I therein since my dear comrade Patroklos is dead, whom I honoured as it were my very self. Him have I lost, and Hector, that slew him, hath stripped from him the armour, great and fair, a wonder to behold, that the gods gave to Peleus—a splendid gift—on the day when they laid thee in the bed of a mortal man. Would thou hadst abode among the deathless daughters of the sea, and Peleus had wedded a mortal bride." And he adds: "My soul biddeth me no longer live, if Hector be not first smitten by my spear."

Then Thetis, shedding tears, answers him: "Short-lived, I ween, must thou be then, my child, by what thou sayest, for straightway after Hector is death appointed unto thee."[1]

She cannot save him, for he has but one thought, one desire—to avenge his beloved comrade.

She then turns her thoughts to the best means of aiding him in his purpose. His splendid armour, the glorious gift of the gods to his father Peleus, now adorned the back of the noble Hector. She charged her son not to go forth to the battle until she returned; and to her sister-nymphs she said: "Go ye down to the wide bosom of the deep, and tell the Ancient One of the sea that I am going to high Olympos, to Hephaistos of noble skill, if haply he will give unto my son noble armour shining gloriously."

[1] Il. xviii. 94.

The Women of Homer

The silver-footed goddess sped quickly to the house of Hephaistos, "imperishable, star-like ... a house of bronze, wrought by the crook-footed god himself."[1] She found him forging twenty magic tripods, which he set on golden wheels, that they might move automatically to the assembly of the gods, and again return to his house.

Thetis is received by Charis "of the shining chaplet, whom the renowned god had wedded." Charis summons her husband, and he comes gladly, for he owed a great debt of gratitude to the silver-footed one. "Verily," he says, "a dread and honoured guest is she that is within, seeing that she delivered me when great pain came upon me from my great fall, through the ill-will of my shameless mother Hera, who would fain have hid me away, for that I was lame. Then had I suffered anguish of heart, had not Thetis and Eurynome taken me to their bosom ... wherefore behoveth it me verily in all wise to repay fair-tressed Thetis for the saving of my life."

He then wiped away the soil of his labour, and donned his doublet; and there were handmaidens of gold that moved to help their lord, "the semblance of living maids. In them is understanding at their hearts, in them are voice and strength, and they have skill from the immortal gods."

He then approaches Thetis, clasps her hand, and asks the reason of her coming. "Speak what thou hast at heart; my soul is fain to accomplish it, if accomplish it I can."

Thetis then relates to him all that had befallen her short-lived son—the death of Patroklos, and the loss of

[1] Il. xviii. 367 *et seq.*

The Famous Shield of Achilles

his armour—and begs the artist-god to make him "shield and helmet, and goodly greaves, and cuirass."[1]

Hephaistos gladly accedes to her wishes, and promises goodly armour, "such as all men afterward shall marvel at, whosoever may behold."

Of that splendid work of the divine artificer, celebrated through all ages, and discussed in a thousand volumes, we cannot speak here at any length. We shall only notice the one scene that comes within our scope—the marriage festival.

"He fashioned two fair cities of mortal men. In the one were espousals and marriage feasts, and beneath the blaze of torches they were leading the brides from their chambers through the city, and loud arose the bridal song. And young men were whirling in the dance, and among them flutes and viols sounded high."[2]

"Also did the glorious lame god devise a dancing-place, like unto that which once, in wide Knosos, Daidalos wrought for Ariadne of the lovely tresses. There were youths dancing, and maidens of costly wooing. . . . And now would they run round with deft feet exceeding lightly, . . . and now, anon, in lines to meet each other. And a great company stood round the lovely dance. . . . So, when he had finished all the armour, he laid it before the mother of Achilles. Then she, like a falcon, sprang down snowy Olympos bearing from Hephaistos the glittering arms."

When the saffron-robed Morn arose from the streams of ocean, Thetis came to the ship, bearing the gifts of the god, and laid them before her son. "Awe fell on

[1] Il. xviii. 456. [2] Il. xviii. 491.

The Women of Homer

the Myrmidones, nor dare any gaze thereon. But when Achilles looked on them his eyes blazed terribly, as it were a flame beneath their lids."[1]

Achilles is greatly troubled lest the body of his dear comrade should see corruption, and become the prey of flies, of which the Greeks had an abiding horror. But his mother comforts him, and promises to ward from him "the cruel tribes of flies; . . . and she shed ambrosia and red nectar on Patroklos through his nostrils, that his flesh might abide the same."

When next we see the silver-footed goddess, she is joining with the Myrmidones in the funeral lament over the body of Patroklos. Achilles led the mourning, and "Thetis stirred among them the desire of wailing."

When Hector has fallen beneath the mighty hand of Achilles, aided by the foul treachery of Athene, Zeus, who dearly loved the noble Trojan hero, is anxious to save his corpse from the dogs and birds, and to give it the honourable burial which Hector had vainly asked of Achilles. "Hector," said the mighty son of Kronos to the pitiless Hera, "was dearest to the gods of all the mortals in Ilios; at least he was to *me*, for in nowise failed he in the gifts I love."

He bethinks him of Thetis, for whom he had an especial love, hoping that she could best prevail on her son to accept a splendid ransom at the hands of Priam. He sent for Iris, and bids her seek out Thetis and bear his message.[2] Iris,[3] the "wing-footed," "storm-

---

[1] Il. xix. 1.
[2] Iris, who appears so often in the Iliad as the swift messenger of the gods, is not mentioned in the Odyssey.   [3] Il. xxiv. 77.

Iris, the Golden-Winged Messenger

footed," "golden-winged" Messenger of the gods,[1] sped forth upon her errand, and, between Samothrace and rocky Imbros, leapt into the black sea, and the waters closed above her with a noise. She found Thetis in a hollow cave, sitting in the midst of the other sea-goddesses, wailing for the fate of her noble son. The silver-footed one is greatly disturbed by the message of Zeus. "I shrink," she says, "from mingling among the Immortals, for I have countless woes of heart; yet go I will, nor shall his word be in vain, whatsoever he saith."

Then the noble goddess took to her a dark-hued robe, "no blacker raiment was there found than that," and followed Iris through the surging waves to the shore, whence they sped up to heaven. There the sad goddess sat down beside Father Zeus, "and Athene gave her place, and even Hera set a fair golden cup in her hand, and cheered her with words."

Zeus unfolds to her his purpose, and bids her tell her mighty son that the gods are wroth with him for refusing to give back the body of Hector.[2] Thetis obeys, and speeds darting from the peaks of Olympos. She found Achilles in his hut, still making grievous moan. She seats herself beside him, strokes his hand and soothes him, and delivers the message of the Thunderer. Thetis, of course, obeys, though she knows that the message will be unwelcome to her son.[3] She sat her down close beside him, and wailed over his and her own misery. "Not long," she said, "shalt thou be left alive to me; already death and forceful fate are standing

---

[1] Ποδήνεμος, αελλόπος, χρυσόπτερος. Il. viii. 398; xxiii. 198; v. 353, 368.
[2] Il. xxiv. 3.   [3] Il. xxiv. 126.

nigh thee. But hearken unto me, for I am the messenger of Zeus. Restore Hector and take ransom for the dead." Achilles at once complies. "So be it; whoso bringeth ransom, let him take back the dead." Iris meanwhile was despatched to Priam, to bid him go alone to the hut of Achilles, bearing a splendid ransom.

As the Iliad ends with the death and obsequies of Hector, we are not allowed to witness the sufferings of poor Thetis, when her dear son undergoes the doom so long foretold and prepared for him by the Fates.

The worship of Thetis and the Nereids was continued in historical times. The whole Pegasæan Bay was regarded as belonging to them, and the region of Pthia was called Thetideion, after the goddess.[1]

[1] Eurip. Androm. 16–20; Strabo, 9, p. 431.

CHAPTER XI

ANDROMACHE

THERE is not in all literature a more exquisite picture of a gentle, modest, and affectionate woman than that of Andromache, the loving spouse of the noble Hector, and mother of the little Astyanax. She has all the delicacy, sweetness and refinement, the heart and soul devotion to her husband and her child, which we only expect to find in periods of the best and highest civilisation. Her tenderness and tears, her sad and undeserved fate, fill us with an unwonted pathos, and we feel angry with the gods for laying such a weight of misery on such a tender and innocent soul. We see her only twice in the Iliad, and yet how fully we seem to know her, and how warmly we love her!

Andromache was born in Thebe, under woody Plakos, in the house of Eëtion, her father,[1] the king of Kilikia, from which "glorious Hector of the glancing helmet" led her forth, "having given bride-gifts untold."[2]

After a conference with the penitent Helen—who admires and loves him as much as she really despises the weak and worthless Paris—Hector goes on to seek his dear wife in his "well-founded house." He found

[1] Il. vi. 395; viii. 187.   [2] Il. xxii. 472.

The Women of Homer

her not there, but with her fair-robed maidens and the boy Astyanax on the towers, weeping and wailing bitterly. When he had passed through the great city and was come to the Skaian gate, "his dear-won wife[1] came running to meet him, even Andromache, daughter of great-hearted Eëtion; so she met him now, and with her went the handmaid, bearing in her bosom the little child, Hector's loved son, like unto a beautiful star." And Hector,[2] smiling, gazed silently at his boy, while Andromache stood weeping at his side, and clasped his hand in hers, and called him by his name: "O my dear lord, thy courage will destroy thee; neither hast thou any pity for thy infant boy, nor wretched me, that soon shall be thy widow. . . . But it were better for me to go down to the grave if I lose thee, for never more will any comfort be mine when thou, even thou, hast met thy fate. Moreover, I have no father, nor lady mother. My father was slain by the goodly Achilles, for he

ANDROMACHE.

Reproduced, by permission of the Publishers, from "The Journal of Hellenic Studies," vol. ix.

[1] Il. vi. 393: πολύδωρος.   [2] Il. vi. 404.

The Parting of Hector and Andromache

wasted the populous city of the Kilikians, even high-gated Thebe, and slew Eëtion; yet he despoiled him not, for his soul had shame of that, but he burnt him in his inlaid armour, and raised a barrow over him, and all about were elm trees, planted by the mountain nymphs, daughters of ægis-bearing Zeus. And the seven brothers that were mine . . . all these the fleet-footed, goodly Achilles slew amid their kine of trailing gait, and white-fleeced sheep. And my mother, that was queen beneath woody Plakos, he brought hither with the other spoils, but afterward took a ransom untold to set her free; but in her father's halls she was smitten by the archer Artemis. Nay, Hector, thou art to me father and lady mother, yea, and brother, even as thou art my blooming husband. Come now, have pity, and abide here upon the tower, lest thou make thy child an orphan, and me a widow."

Hector answers as only the brave warrior and the patriot should or could: "I do take thought of all these things, my wife, but I have very sore shame of the Trojans, and Trojan dames with trailing robes, if, like a coward, I shrink away from battle. Moreover, mine own soul forbiddeth me, for I have learnt ever to be valiant, and fight in the forefront of the Trojans. . . . Surely I know this in my heart and soul. The day shall come for holy Ilios to be laid low, and the folk of Priam of the goodly ashen spear. Yet doth the anguish of the Trojans hereafter not so much trouble me, neither Hekabe's, neither King Priam's, neither my brethren's . . . as doth *thine* anguish in the day when some mail-clad Achaian shall lead thee away weeping,

The Women of Homer

and rob thee of the light of freedom. So shalt thou abide in Argos, and ply the loom at another woman's bidding, and bear water from fount Messeis or Hypereia, being grievously entreated. And then shall one say, that beholdeth thee weep: 'This is the wife of Hector, that was foremost in the battle of the horse-taming Trojans, when men fought about Ilios.'"[1]

So spake glorious Hector, and stretched out his arm to his boy. But the child shrank, crying, to the bosom of his fair-girdled nurse, dismayed at his dear father's aspect, and in dread of the bronze and horse-hair crest, that he saw nodding fiercely from the helmet's top. "Then his dear father laughed aloud, and his lady mother; forthwith glorious Hector took the helmet from his head and laid it, all gleaming, on the ground. Then kissed he his dear son, and dandled him in his arms, and prayed to Zeus and all the gods: 'O Zeus, and all ye gods, vouchsafe that this my son may likewise prove, even as I, pre-eminent amid the Trojans, and as valiant in might, and be a great king in Ilios. Then may men say of him, " Far greater is he than his father," as he returneth home from battle.'"[2]

---

[1] Il. vi. 440. See his address to his followers (Il. xv. 494), "But fight, in your firm companies, at the ships, and whosoever of you be smitten by dart or blow, and meeteth death and fate, so let him die. It is no dishonourable thing for him to fall fighting for his country, but his wife and his children after him are safe, and his house unharmed."

"'Ἀλλὰ μάχεσθε ἐπὶ νηυσὶ διαμπερὲς ὃς δὲ μὲν ὑμέων
Βλήμενος ἠὲ τυπεὶς θάνατον καὶ πότμον ἐπίσπῃ
Τεθνάτω. ὅυ οἱ ἀεικὲς ἀμυμένῳ περὶ πάτρης
Τεθνάμεν. ἀλλ' ἄλοχος τε σόη καὶ νήπια τέκνα
Καὶ κλῆρος καὶ οἶκος ἀκήρατος·"

[2] Il. vi. 470.

The αἰδώς of Andromache

"So spake he, and laid his son in his dear wife's arms, and she took him to her fragrant bosom. And her husband had pity as he looked on her, and caressed her with his hand, and called her by her name. Dear one ! I pray thee be not over sorrowful ; no man against my fate can hurl me to Hades. . . . But go thou to thine house, and see to thine own tasks, the loom and the distaff, and bid thy maidens ply their work; but for war shall men provide, and I in chief of all men that abide in Ilios."[1] Then the noble pair separate, never to meet again in life !

Even in that dread hour we see that Andromache preserves the moderation (αἰδώς)[2] of the Greek woman. Of course, she could not but pray him to abide within the impregnable walls of holy Ilios, and not to go forth to certain death, for the fate of all three hung upon his decision. But she must have known in her heart of hearts that a Hector could not yield to her prayer. Had he done so he would no longer have been *her* Hector, nor the great ensample of honour to her boy. After the natural inevitable outpouring of her despair, she quietly returns home with her little son, to attend, according to her lord and master's bidding, to *her* tasks, as he was doing to his own. We hear and see nothing more of the afflicted wife and mother until her worst fears are more than realised, and the dread cry rings through the doomed city—" The noble Hector is slain !" She was weaving a double purple web, and

---

[1] Il. vi. 483.
[2] Ζηνὶ σύνθακος θρόνων αἰδώς.—Soph. O.C. 1268.
  (Αἰδώς, assessor of the throne of Zeus.)

embroidering it with flowers. Her maidens, under her direction, were setting a great tripod on the fire, that Hector might have a warm bath when he came from the bloody field—"Fond heart! and was all unaware how, far from all washings, bright-eyed Athene had slain him by the hand of Achilles."[1]

Suddenly she hears the shrieks of her noble mother-in-law Hekabe from the battlements, and her limbs reeled, and the shuttle fell from her hands to the earth. Then she bids two of her maidens to follow her to the towers, where she stood still and gazed, and saw her adored husband dragged through the dust by swift horses towards the hollow ships. "Then darkness shrouded her eyes, she fell backward, and gasped forth her spirit."[2]

Recovering from her swoon, "she tore from her head the bright attire, frontlet (ἄμπυκα) and net (κεκρύφαλον) and woven band (πλεκτὴν ἀναδέσμην), and the precious veil (κρήδεμνον), which golden Aphrodite had given her when Hector of the glancing helmet led her forth from the palace of Eëtion." Then, wailing with deep sobs, she cried: "O Hector, woe is me! to one fate, then, were we both born, thou in Troy, in the house of Priam, and I in Thebe, under woody Plakos, in the house of Eëtion, who reared me from a little one. Ah! would he had not begotten me! Now, thou to the house of Hades, beneath the secret places of the earth, departest, and me, in bitter mourning, thou leavest a widow in thy halls; and thy son is but an infant child, son of unhappy parents, thee and me. Nor

[1] Il. xxii. 440.   [2] Il. xxii. 466.

The Wail of Andromache over Hector

shalt thou profit him, Hector, since thou art dead, neither he thee."

Once again we meet with the bereaved Andromache, at the funeral rites of Hector, after his body had been ransomed from Achilles by the aged Priam. Among the white-armed Trojan women, Andromache, in right of her precedence as wife of Hector, led the lamentation, while in her hands she held his head. "Husband, thou art gone young from life, and leavest me a widow in thine halls. And the child is yet but a little one; nor, methinks, shall he grow up to manhood; for ere then shall this city be utterly destroyed. For thou art verily perished who didst watch over it and guard it, and keep safe its noble wives and infant little ones. These soon shall be voyaging in the hollow ships, yea, and I too with them; and thou, my child, shalt either go with me unto a place where thou shalt toil at unseemly tasks, labouring before the face of some harsh lord; or else some Achaian will take thee by the arm and hurl thee from the battlements,[1] for that he is wroth because Hector slew his brother, or father, or son. For no light hand had thy father in the grievous fray. Therefore the folk lament him throughout the city, and woe unspeakable and mourning hast thou left to thy parents, Hector, but with me chiefliest shall grievous pain abide. For neither didst thou stretch forth thy hands from a bed when thou wert dying, neither didst thou speak to me some memorable word that I might have thought on evermore, as my tears fall night and day."[2]

---

[1] According to later tradition, this was done at the suggestion of **Odysseus** or **Neoptolemos**.   [2] Il. xxiv. 723.

The Women of Homer

Andromache is an exception to the general rule that the women of Homer reappear in a degraded form in the Tragedians. In the Troades (642) of Euripides she is still the model wife; and she tells Hermione that "not beauty alone, but virtues, delight the wise." Of Andromache's fate Homer tells us nothing, but he has foreshadowed it for us, and we may easily imagine it. The "Captive Andromache" is the subject of a beautiful and touching picture by the late lamented Lord Leighton, and is fresh in the memory of all.

HELEN.

Helen, daughter of Zeus and Leda, sister of Kastor and Polydeukes. Her epithets in Homer are — Διὸς ἐκγεγαυῖα (sprung from Zeus), Ἀργείη (Argive), Διὰ γυναικῶν (noblest of women), Ἐυπατέρεια (nobly-born), καλλιπάρῃος (fair-cheeked), λευχώλενος (white-armed), ἠΰκομος (fair-haired), τανύπεπλος (with flowing peplos), ῥιγεδανή (whose name one shudders at).[1]

Helen was chosen by Aphrodite as the most brilliant reward for the preference shown to her by Paris in his judgment of the three goddesses. Considering the fearful evils to the Trojans resulting from her transgression and her presence in their city, the toleration shown to her by them is very remarkable. She is called the ἄκοιτις (lawful wife) of Paris. She calls Hector her

[1] Almost the only disparaging epithet in Homer, except those which she applies to herself, is this, uttered by Achilles.

Helen's Entrancing Beauty

δαήρ¹ (brother-in-law), and she ranks third among the noble Trojan dames, after Hekabe and Andromache.

Although she was the apparent cause of the war, so fatal to both Greeks and Trojans, she is generally spoken of with sympathy and compassion. Even Priam, who had most to lose by the war—his sons and daughters, his royal rank, and vast possessions—addresses her in affectionate terms. When she appears on the walls, he says, "Come hither, dear child, and sit by me, that thou mayst behold thy former husband, kinsfolk, and friends. I hold *thee* not to blame; nay, I hold the gods to blame, who brought on us this dolorous war of the Achaians."² Hector, too, that true gentleman, always treats her with kindness and respect. Even the pattern of all faithful wives, Penelope, excuses her, and attributes her action to a hostile god.³

Of her entrancing beauty it is impossible to speak in adequate terms. It has been the favourite dream and theme of countless generations of men, but no writer has raised our conception of it to such a height as Homer himself. His method is simple, but singularly effective. He does not, like modern poets and novelists, give details of her various charms. We know not whether she was dark or fair, her eyes blue, black, or grey. He does not attempt to describe her charms, but he shows us their *effect*, and every one is left to find his own Helen in his own surroundings. We doubt whether even her portrait by Zeuxis, "evolved, of course, from his inner consciousness," would have satisfied us.

[1] Il. vi. 144.   [2] Il. iii. 161.   [3] Od. xx. 222.

The Women of Homer

Who ever saw a satisfactory portrait of the Scottish Helen—Mary Stuart, Queen of Scots?

The aged Priam and the sages of Troy[1] are sitting on the battlements by the Skaian gate. They have ceased from battle from old age, but are still good orators. They are sunning themselves on the tower "like grasshoppers on a tree in the forest, uttering their lily-like voice." There was probably not one of them who had not lost son, brother, or kinsman in this bloody war—not one who did not foresee the fall of holy Troy, his native city, and the captivity of his wife and children. And yet, such was the almost demoniac influence of her dazzling and bewildering beauty, that they can see nothing for the moment but the radiant loveliness of the woman before them. As they saw Helen coming to the tower, followed by her two handmaids, Aithre and ox-eyed Klymene, "they softly spake winged words one to another."

"Small blame is it that Trojans and well-greaved Achaians should, *for such a woman*, long time suffer hardships; marvellously like to the immortal goddesses is she to look upon."[2]

Reason, of course, quickly resumes its sway, and they add: "But even so—such a woman as she is—let her depart in the black ships, and not leave destruction to us and to our children."

Though Helen could not but be conscious of the extraordinary fascination which she exercised on all who saw her, there is nothing triumphant or coquettish in her bearing. On the contrary, she addresses the aged

---

[1] Il. iii. 144.   [2] Il. iii. 154.

Helen's Penitence

Priam with a very touching humility. "Reverend art thou to me, and dread, dear father of my lord. Would that sore death had been my pleasure when I followed thy son hither, and left my home and my kinsfolk, and my daughter in her girlhood, and the lovely companions of my own age. That was not to be, therefore I pine with weeping."[1]

We see that she had long discovered the utter

HARPY TOMB IN THE BRITISH MUSEUM.

worthlessness of her brilliant lover, whom she sees to be devoid of all sense of wrong or shame. Her admiration—or was it love?—for the noble Hector is a sign of the correctness of her judgment and the essential goodness of her heart. When the great hero goes to seek Paris in Helen's chamber, and urges him to take

[1] Il. iii. 172.

his proper part in a war in which the people were perishing about the city for his unworthy sake, he has a brief conference with Helen, whom he treats with the gentlest courtesy. "My brother," she says, "mine, that am a dog, mischievous and abominable, would that on the day when my mother bare me an evil storm-wind had caught me away to a mountain or a billow of the loud-resounding sea! . . . Would that I had been mated with a better man, that felt dishonour and the multitude of men's reproaches! As for him, neither hath he a sound heart now, nor ever will have. But come thou and sit upon this bench, my brother, since thy heart chiefly trouble has encompassed for the sake of me that am a dog, and for Alexandros' sin."[1] She has fully recognised what a fatal gift beauty may be. Compare Eurip. Hel. 27 and 304:—

"Τοὐμὸν δὲ κάλλος, ἐι καλὸν τὸ δυστυχές."

"My beauty, for what is beauteous oft
Is most unhappy."

Hector answers her with kindly words: "Bid me not sit, Helen, of thy love, for my heart is set to succour the men of Troy. . . . But do thou rouse this fellow, while I go into my house to behold my dear wife and my infant boy, for I know not whether I shall ever return to them again."[2]

In the last book of the Iliad we find her among the Trojan women at the official solemn wailing by the lofty pyre on which lay the body of the noble Hector. When his wife, Andromache, and his mother, Hekabe,

---

[1] Il. iii. 343. [2] Il. iii. 59.

Helen's Lament over Hector

had exercised their right of precedence, then, in the third place, Helen led the sore lament. "Hector, of all my brethren in Troy by far the dearest to my heart! Truly my lord is godlike Alexandros, who brought me hither to Troyland. Would that I had died ere then. For this now is the twentieth year since I came thence, but never yet heard I an evil or despiteful word from thee. Nay, if haply any other upbraided me in the palace halls, whether brother or sister, or brother's fair-robed wife, or mother—but thy father was ever kind to me, as if he were mine own—then wouldst thou soothe them by the gentleness of thy spirit, and by thy kindly words. Therefore bewail I thee with anguish of heart, and my hapless self with thee; for no more is any left in Troyland to be kind to me, but all men shudder at me."[1]

Homer, of course, tells us nothing of the fate of Helen between the death of Hector and the fall of Troy. After that event, no doubt, she was at once delivered up to her lawful husband, Menelaos. He, with a wise charity, knowing that she was the victim of Aphrodite and the Fates, receives her back with all love and honour, and in the Odyssey we find her reinstated in her former home in Sparta. For the meeting of Menelaos and Helen, see Hel. 622 :—

> "*Men.* Fate now is kind; once more I hold my wife,
> Daughter of Jove and Leda."

Menelaos is represented to us as a man of mild, benevolent, and cautious temper, inferior to some of

[1] Il. xxiv. 762.

The Women of Homer

the foremost Achaians in enterprise and daring, but not without courage and endurance, and always mindful of his duty. He prudently declined to fight alone against Hector, saying: "None of the Danaans should be wroth with me, though he beholdeth me giving way to Hector, since he warreth with gods upon his side."[1] Yet his soul is thoroughly roused by the ungrateful outrage committed by Paris, his guest, on his home and hearth, and is ready to do and dare all things to get Helen back. "Yea," he cried over the body of Peisandros, whom he had slain, "ye shall not lack reproof and shame ... ye hounds of evil, having no fear in your hearts of the strong wrath of loud-thundering Zeus, the god of guest and host ... O ye that wantonly carried away my wedded wife *when ye were entertained by her!*"[2]

He does not make Helen the object of his curses, but evidently takes the same tolerant view of her misfortunes as Priam, Hector, and others. It was not only her radiant beauty that rendered her a desirable consort for him. She was the daughter of Zeus, and the Egyptian Proteus prophesied to him a safe return to his country on that account. "Thou, Menelaos, son of Zeus, art not ordained to die and meet thy fate in Argos ... for thou hast Helen to wife, and therefore men deem thee the son of Zeus."[3]

His return home had been perilous and full of adventure. He roamed over Cyprus, Phœnicia, and Egypt, and visited the Æthiopians, Sidonians, and Libyans, whose lambs are horned from their birth, and

[1] Il. xvii. 99.   [2] Il. xiii. 621.   [3] Od. iv. 561.

Helen entertains Telemachos

their ewes yean thrice a year.[1] After a woeful wandering of more than seven years he reached his home, bringing with him his rich Trojan booty and other spoil, and, no doubt, Helen herself, the precious prize of a ten years' bloody war.

When Telemachos goes to Sparta in search of his lost father, Odysseus, he is received with the utmost kindness and hospitality by Menelaos and Helen in their splendid palace. As the son of Odysseus enters the lofty mansion, he expresses his astonishment and delight to his companion, Peisistratos: "Son of Nestor, delight of my heart, mark the flashing of bronze through the echoing halls, the lustre of gold and of amber, of silver and of ivory! Such, methinks, is the court of Olympian Zeus within, for the world of things that are there; wonder comes upon me as I look upon it!"

Menelaos, who overhears him, modestly declines to compete with Zeus, "whose mansions and treasures are everlasting," but evidently thinks that no mortal man can vie with him in splendour.

While Menelaos is pondering these things in his mind and in his heart, "Helen comes forth from her high-roofed, fragrant chamber, like Artemis of the golden arrows."[3] She is attended by three maidens, of whom Adrastë places for her her well-wrought chair, Alcippë bears a rug of soft wool, and Phylo a silver basket, which Alcandrë, the wife of Polybos of Thebes in Egypt, had given to Helen. Alcandrë also gave her a golden distaff, and a silver basket with wheels beneath, "and the rims thereof were of gold. And beneath was

[1] Od. iv. 85.   [2] Od. xiv. 71.   [3] Od. iv. 120.

a footstool for her shining feet." It is thus, in royal state, that we see her again, and we find in her a clever, kind-hearted, lovely, and lovable woman.

She is immediately struck by the likeness of Telemachos to his father, and addresses her husband: "Menelaos, fosterling of Zeus, never have I seen a man so like another . . . as this man is like the son of the great-hearted Odysseus—Telemachos, whom he left, a new-born babe, when for the sake of me, the shameless one, the Achaians came beneath Troy."[1]

Then Menelaos recalls, in sad words, the friendly converse he had held with Odysseus before Troy, "from whom," he says, "nought would have parted me in friendship and in joy, ere the black cloud of death overshadowed us."[2]

"So spake he, and stirred in all the desire of lamentation. Helen wept, the daughter of Zeus, and Telemachos wept, and Menelaos, the son of Atreus, nor did the son of Nestor keep tearless eyes."

But the prudent Menelaos admonishes them: "Let us now cease from weeping, and once more bethink us of our supper."

The beauteous Helen, now a stately matron, finds a still more powerful sedative of their sorrow. "Helen, daughter of Zeus, turned to new thoughts. She cast a drug[3] into the wine whereof they drank—a drug to lull all pain and anger, and to bring forgetfulness of every sorrow. Whoso should drink that draught, on that day he would let no tear fall down his cheeks, not though his mother and his father died, not though

[1] Od. iv. 141.   [2] Od. iv. 183.   [3] Νηπενθής.

Helen's Soothing Drug

men slew his brother or dear son with the sword before his face ... medicines of such virtue and so helpful had the daughter of Zeus, which Polydamna, the wife of Thou, had given her, a woman of Egypt, where Earth, the grain-giver, yields herbs in greatest plenty, many that are healing, and many baleful."[1]

Helen then exhorts them to sit down and feast, and take joy in the telling of tales; and she herself leads off with an account of the daring exploit of Odysseus, when he entered Troy in the guise of a beggar.[2] She recognised him when she was about to bathe him and anoint him with oil, but promised not to betray him.

When Telemachos takes leave on his departure, she shows him a quite motherly affection, and loads him with costly gifts. "She stood by the coffers in the treasury, wherein her robes of curious needlework were laid, which she herself had wrought. And the divine lady lifted one and brought it out, the widest and most beautifully wrought of all, and it shone like a star.[3] 'Lo, I give thee this gift, dear child, a memorial of the hands of Helen, for thy wife to wear, against the day of thy desire, even of thy marriage. Meanwhile let it lie by thy mother in her chamber.'"

As Telemachos was leaving the palace, an eagle with a great white goose in its claws flew forth at his right hand, drew near him, and flew off to the right across the horses. Menelaos was puzzled by the portent, and pondered thereon how he should interpret it. But Helen assumes at once the functions of an augur. "Hear *me*," she said, "and I will prophesy as the

[1] Od. iv. 220.   [2] Od. iv. 249.   [3] Od. xv. 104.

The Women of Homer

Immortals put it into my heart. Even as yonder eagle came down from the hill and snatched away the goose, so shall Odysseus return home after much trial and long wanderings, and take vengeance on the suitors."[1] And Telemachos answers, "May Zeus the Thunderer ordain it so. Then would I worship thee, even in Ithaca, as it were a god."

HELEN PURSUED BY MENELAOS.

And here we see our last of the divine Helen. We leave her in the greatest prosperity, indulging her sweet, kindly nature in speeding the parting guest, whom she had so royally entertained, with bright augury for the future. We leave her, loved and honoured by her husband and her people, as though she had never known sin and its attendant sorrows. Her unrivalled

[1] Od. xv. 172.

Mr. Gladstone on Helen

beauty, already celebrated through the world for some three thousand years, her consummate elegance of form and movement, her keen appreciation of all that was good and noble in her surroundings, her gratitude for sympathy and kindness, and, above all, her sweet, penitential remorse for her past transgression, render her one of the most interesting and charming figures in ancient history.[1]

It is not only the sages of the Old World whose imagination has been excited to fever heat by the Homeric Helen. How often has the dull *Studirzimmer* of aged German scholars been brightened by her presence! And in our own country we see the effect of her charms in the writings of Mr. Gladstone, an ardent Homerologist.[2] Speaking of Helen, he says: "No one forming his estimation of Helen could fall into the gross error of looking upon her as a type of a depraved character." And yet this "gross error" *was* committed by Virgil.[3] In some rather suspected lines Æneas calls her—

"Trojæ et patriæ communis Erinnys."

"Curse to the land that had housed her, and curse
　to the land of her birth."

and would have slain her in his wrath, but is checked by his mother, Venus—

---

[1] *Cf.* the *Encomium Helenæ* of Isocrates, 61; and the *Epithalamium* of Theocritus.
[2] *Juventus Mundi*, p. 593.   [3] *Æneid*, ii. 573.

The Women of Homer

"Non tibi Tyndaridis facies invisa Lacenæ,
 Culpatusve Paris; Divom inclementia, Divom!
 Has evertit opes."

"'Tis not the beauty of Helen, the Spartan woman abhorred,
 Nor the reviled one Paris; 'tis Heaven's fierce anger alone,
 Levels in dust this kingdom, and lays low Troy from her throne."[1]

And what is more surprising, in recent times, is that the same unfavourable view of her is taken by that refined and elegant scholar, Colonel Mure, who says that "she is the female counterpart of Paris; both are unprincipled votaries of sensual enjoyment." She fares still worse at the hands of the Cyclic poets, who make her an adulteress under her husband's roof. In the Hekabe of Euripides,[2] too, she is cursed by Hekabe. Compare Eurip. Androm. 103:—

"Οὐ γάμον ἀλλὰ τιν' ἄταν."

"A pest, and not a bride, to Ilium's towers
 The mischief-working Helen Paris bore."

Mr. Gladstone sums up his estimate of Helen in almost exaggerated panegyric. "Her self-abasement," he says, "and self-renouncing humility come nearer, perhaps, than any other heathen example, to the type of Christian penitence"!

---

[1] Lord Bowen's Translation.   [2] Hekabe, 440.

CHAPTER XII

HELEN—*continued*

A GREAT deal of what seems to us very futile discussion has been raised, both in ancient and modern times, respecting the extraordinary duration of Helen's beauty. Lucian,[1] in his cynical way, says that she was by no means so fair as was generally imagined. He makes Gallus (the Cock) say that he had seen her more than once; that "she was *tolerably* fair, and long-necked enough to pass for the daughter of a swan; that she was then an old woman, not much younger than old Hekabe. How could it be otherwise," he adds, "since she was carried off in her younger days by Theseus, and lived with him at Aphidna?" Bayle,[2] in his *Diction. Critique*, calculates that she must have been at

PARIS LEADING HELEN AWAY.

[1] Gallus, 17.   [2] Art. "Helene,"

The Women of Homer

least fifty when she went with Paris to Troy. Modern writers have tried to account for the phenomenon by referring to Sarah,[1] in Egypt, who was sixty-five when Pharaoh took her "for her beauty's sake," to Ninon de l'Enclos, and others.

Such writers seem to look on Homer as a writer of trustworthy biography. But he is, above all things, a poet, a romancer. If it lay in the scope of his tale, in the interest of his poem, to make Helen as lovely as ever at fifty or sixty, he certainly would not hesitate for a moment to do so. And besides the omnipotence of the poet, there is the omnipotence of the gods, who throughout the Epics bestow youth and comeliness on whom they will. Moreover, Helen was the daughter of Zeus !

We have endeavoured to represent the figure of Helen as it was moulded by the hand of Homer. As we have seen, very different views of her character and actions were taken by later writers. Round her form, as Homer drew it, have gathered legendary incrustations which destroy its fair proportions and mar its beauty. We should fail to say how many hypothetical deductions from the narrative of Homer have taken rank as trustworthy traditions of long bygone ages. Among the most curious of these is one which relates to the famous web which Helen was weaving when Iris was sent to summon her to see the duel between her husband and her lover.[2] "In the hall she found Helen weaving a great purple web of double woof, and embroidering

---

[1] I. Mos. xii. 4.
[2] Il. iii. 125: "Speciosa spectacula pandit."

Defence of Helen's Character

thereon many battles of horse-taming Trojans and mail-clad Achaians, that they had endured for her sake at the hands of Ares."

Now we read in the Scholia of Venice on this passage, that from the scenes embroidered on this web, the divine Homer took the greater part of his history of the Trojan war, " as saith Aristarchus ὁ Ὁμηρικός."[1]

While, on the one hand, we have seen how badly Helen fared at the hands of some post-Homeric writers, we observe, on the other, the eagerness with which many later authors strove to exonerate her from all sin whatever.[2]

Much is made of the expression in Homer, ἁρπάξας[3] (having snatched thee), used by Paris. Stesichorus of Himera (632 B.C.), in his Palinodia, declares that Helen did not elope to Troy, but that Paris only carried off an εἴδωλον (a counterfeit image),[4] and this idea is partly adopted by Euripides.[5] Herodotus[6] tells us that the

---

[1] See Appendix XVI.
[2] Four Encomia were written on Helen, by Gorgias, Polycrates, Isocrates, and Anaximenes.
[3] Il. iii. 344.   [4] See Appendix XVII.
[5] Electra, 1283. *Cf.* Helena, 582 and 670:—

"Οὐκ ἦλθον εἰς γῆν Τρωαδ' ἀλλ' εἰδωλον ἦν."

"*I* never went to Troy; my image went."

Helena, 33:—

"δίδωσι δ' οὐκ ἔμ' ἀλλ' ὁμοιώσας ἐμοὶ
Εἴδωλον ἔμπνουν οὐρανοῦ ξυνθαισ' ἀπὸ."

" But Juno, for her slighted form,
Indignant, frustrates his fond hope, and gives
Not me, but what resembling me, she formed,
A breathing image of ætherial air,
To royal Priam's son."

[6] Euterpe, 42.

The Women of Homer

Spartans always maintained the chastity of Helen, to whom they erected a temple at Therapnæ, where matrons prayed for beauty for their daughters. Dion Chrysostom, addressing the inhabitants of Ilium, tries to prove that Troy had never been taken by the Greeks, and that Helen was the legitimate wife of Paris.

PENELOPE

For centuries the well-known type of the devoted wife, faithful through long years of uncertainty as to the fate of her husband Odysseus, though surrounded by high-born and persistent wooers.

Penelope was the daughter of Icarios and Periboea, and wife of "the wily Odysseus," who is said, contrary to the usual custom, to have obtained her hand with a large dowry and without bridal gifts. Her epithets are ἐχέφρων (sensible), περίφρων (careful), ἄπυστος (unheard of, retiring), and all her actions and words bespeak a thoughtful, prudent nature.

Homer has drawn her portrait with a loving as well as a skilful hand, and though she does not excite our interest in the same degree as an Andromache or a Helen, we regard her with esteem and admiration. Her position is difficult in the extreme. Odysseus, at his departure for the fatal war before Troy, being well aware of the perils he would have to undergo, exhorts her thus: "When thou seest thy son a bearded man, marry whom thou wilt, and leave thine own house."

In the Odyssey she is really under the tutelage

Penelope and her Suitors

(*mundium*) of her son Telemachos, and he is continually called upon by the suitors to exercise his lawful authority over her, and compel her to choose one of the Ithacan princes. "For all the noblest that are princes in the Isles, in Dulichium and Same and wooded Zacynthus, and as many as lord it in rocky Ithaca, all these," says Telemachos, "woo my mother and waste my house."[1] Specially mentioned of these are Eurymachos, "who outdid the others in gifts," and Ctesippos of Same, "a man of lawless heart, who trusted in his vast possessions."[2] These princes, "flown with insolence," hope to hasten her decision by entering the palace of Odysseus and living there at free quarters. She is, as it were, put up to auction, and it is agreed among the suitors that she is to go with the highest bidder. Their constant cry to Telemachos is: "Bid thy mother wed the man who gives the most gifts, and comes as the chosen of fate."[3] "Send away thy mother, and bid her be married to whomsoever her father commands, and whoso is well pleasing to her."[4]

Telemachos by no means denies that he has the right to dispose of his mother's hand. He knows, and on some occasions exercises, his power. Rather harshly, when she had gone down into the hall of the men, and begged the minstrel cease from chanting the sad tale of the Trojan war, he orders her "to go to her chamber and mind her own housewiferies, the loom and the distaff, and bid her handmaids ply their tasks."[5] "But speech," he adds, "shall be for men,

---

[1] Od. i. 245. [2] Od. xx. 286. [3] Od. xxi. 162.
[4] Od. ii. 112. [5] Od. i. 356.

The Women of Homer

for all, but for me in chief, for mine is the lordship in the house."

It is only his affection for his mother that prevents him from complying with what would seem to every Achaian a reasonable demand. To Agelaos, who emphatically repeats it, he says: "In nowise do I delay my mother's marriage; nay, I bid her be married to what man she will, and I offer gifts without number. But I do, indeed, feel shame to drive her forth from the hall, despite her will. God forbid that this should ever be."[1] And again to Antinoos: "It can in nowise be that I should thrust forth from the house, against her will, the woman that bare me and reared me."[2]

Nor has she any support, in her determination to remain true to the memory of her husband, in her father or brothers, who all exhort her to marry Eurymachos, "for he outdoes all the wooers in his presents." She herself is hopeless to escape her doom. She tells the disguised Odysseus, when her artifice with the web has been betrayed to the suitors: "Now I can neither escape the marriage nor devise any other counsel, and my parents are instant with me to marry, and my son chafes, while these men devour his livelihood."[3]

There is a tendency on the part of some writers to *dénigrer* the constancy of Penelope, and to accuse her of something like "flirting" with the suitors. Nothing can be more unjust. She stood alone before a host of adversaries. Arrayed against her were tra-

[1] Od. xx. 341. [2] Od. ii. 130. [3] Od. xix. 154.

Penelope's Artifice of the Web

dition, which imperatively pointed out to her, as a clear duty, to give herself to the wealthiest suitor; the parting injunction of her husband; the evident wish of her son; the advice of her father and brothers; and the persistent courtship of the suitors, who claimed her hand by a generally acknowledged right. Yet for twenty long years, without any tidings from her absent husband to encourage her, she resisted all these potent influences. When it seemed to all men certain that Odysseus had long been dead, and she had no excuse to make except her longing for "the perfect excellence" of the husband of her youth, who shall blame her for cajoling her persecutors with false hopes, and delaying, by the artifice of the web, the hated marriage for a few years longer? The suitors complain, saying, "She gives hopes to all, and makes promises to every man, and sends messages to them, but her mind is set on other things," *i.e.* on keeping her troth to the very last. Of course she *does* deceive them.

"Ye princely youths," she says, addressing the assembled wooers, "now that the goodly Odysseus is dead, do ye abide patiently, how eager soever to speed on this marriage, till I finish the robe." But one of her women, who knew all, betrayed her, and the suitors caught her in the act of unravelling by torchlight the work she had finished during the day.

That the suitors eagerly desired her for her beauty, her wisdom, and her skill in embroidery, is evident through the whole of the Odyssey. They compare her to Artemis or golden Aphrodite. Their hearts swell with joy at the sight of her. Eurymachos, the best of the

The Women of Homer

suitors, addresses her thus:[1] "Daughter of Icarios, if all the Achaians in Iasian Argos could behold thee, even a greater press of wooers would feast in thy halls, since

PENELOPE.

thou dost surpass all women in beauty and stature, and within in wisdom of mind."[2]

When Athene has bathed her face with beauty imperishable—such as that wherewith the fair-crowned

[1] Od. xix. 54.   [2] Od. ii. 116; xviii. 245.

The Beauty and Skill of Penelope

Cytherea is anointed when she goes to the lovely dance of the Graces [1]—and she goes down from her shining chamber to the hall, "their limbs are loosened," they are dazed and enchanted with love, and "each man uttered a prayer that he might be her husband." They place her above the most renowned heroines of antiquity—above Tyro, Alcmene, and "Mykene of the bright crown." [2]

But it was not only her great beauty and manifold accomplishments that made her a desirable consort. Now that Odysseus was no more, and Telemachos too young to wield his father's sceptre over the chiefs of Ithaca and the Isles, the husband of Penelope might reasonably hope to succeed to the γέρας, the suzerainty over the other princes which had been enjoyed by Odysseus himself.

After Odysseus had slain Antinoos with the first arrow from his terrible bow, Eurymachos tries to lay all the blame on *him*. He tells Odysseus that Antinoos was the cause of all the wrongdoing of the suitors; "not," he adds, "so greatly longing for the marriage, nor needing it sore, but that he might himself be king over all the land of stablished Ithaca; and he was to have lain in wait for thy son to kill him." [3]

Penelope shows high courage, as well as prudence and patient endurance. She bravely defends Telemachos against the suitors, and sharply rebukes Telemachos himself for allowing his guest (Odysseus in disguise of a beggar) to be evil entreated in the halls. [4] "Antinoos," she says, "full of all insolence, deviser of mischief! and

---

[1] Od. xviii. 193. [2] Od. ii. 120.
[3] Od. xxii 49. [4] Od. xvi. 418.

The Women of Homer

yet they say that in the land of Ithaca thou art chiefest among thy peers in counsel and in speech! Nay, no such man dost thou show thyself. Fool! why indeed dost thou contrive death and doom for Telemachos, and hast no regard for suppliants who have Zeus to witness?" She reminds him that his father had been saved from the wrath of his own people by Odysseus, who received him as a suppliant. "His house thou now consumest unatoned for, and his wife thou wooest, and wouldst slay his son"!

But though she struggles with might and main against fearful odds, she knows and feels that she is doomed. "The night shall come," she says, "when a hateful marriage shall find me out—me most luckless, whose good hap Zeus has taken away."

When the artifice of the web had failed, she gives up all hope, all resistance. "She fetches her husband's mighty bow from the treasure-chamber, and sitting down, set the case upon her knees, and cried aloud and wept."[1] Then bringing forth the bow, she makes the following announcement, little knowing that it is Odysseus himself to whom she is confiding her resolve : "Now I am about to ordain for a trial the axes which he was wont to set up in his halls, twelve in all; and he would stand far apart, and shoot his arrow through all their rings ... Whoso then shall most easily string the bow and shoot through the rings of all twelve axes, with him will I go, and forsake this house, this honourable house, so very fair, and filled with all livelihood, which methinks I shall yet remember, aye in a dream."[2]

[1] Od. xxi. 51.   [2] Od. xix. 572.

Penelope's Despair

But though she reluctantly gives up the long, long, apparently hopeless struggle, and submits to fate, her love is unshaken. The memory of her lost husband is dearer to her than any of the lordly youths who seek her favour with gifts untold. She longs for death, as the only escape from marriage with another. "Would that the spirits of the storm would snatch me from the sight of men, or that fair-tressed Artemis would strike me with her gentle darts, that so, with a vision of Odysseus before my eyes, I might even pass beneath the gloomy earth, nor ever make a baser man's delight." [1]

Like another Niobe, her tears cease not day or night. "I will go," she says to Telemachos, "up to my chamber, and lay me in my bed, the place of my groanings, that is ever watered by my tears, since the day that Odysseus departed with the sons of Atreus for Ilios." [2]

We are surprised and somewhat disappointed by Odysseus's long delay in making himself known to his despairing wife. Athene herself, his guide and counsellor, rebukes him for his excessive caution. "Right gladly," she says, "would any other man, on his return from wandering, have hasted to behold his children and his wife in the halls. But thou hast no will to learn or to hear aught, till thou hast furthermore made trial of thy wife." [3]

Yet she approves of his caution in face of the danger from the suitors, and she aids him to conceal his identity by changing his person and dress to those of a loathsome beggar.

From the faithful swineherd Eumaios he learns the

[1] Od. xx. 77. [2] Od. xix. 594. [3] Od. xiii. 333.

The Women of Homer

state of affairs in his palace; and to him he first reveals himself. Then he makes himself known to his dear son, and the three together, with every precaution, "sow the seeds of evil for the suitors."

The swineherd, even before Odysseus had revealed himself, assures him of the constant, tearful devotion of his wife. He tells him how she receives every lying vagrant who may possibly bring news of her lost husband. "Whosoever comes straying to the land of Ithaca, goes to my mistress with words of guile. And she receives him kindly and lovingly, and inquires of all things, and the tears fall from her eyelids for weeping."[1]

The well-laid plans of the wily Odysseus, backed by the constant intervention of Athene, are completely successful, and the bloody tragedy of the slaughtered suitors is enacted. If any doubt could enter our minds of the entire freedom of Penelope from any *penchant* for any of her wooers, even for Amphinoos, "whose words more than all the rest were pleasing in her eyes," it must now be dispelled. When she hears of the ghastly massacre of the princes, of the hanging of the wicked maids, and the disgusting mutilation of the treacherous Melanthios, she summons Eurykleia and says: "Let us go, that I may see the wooers dead, and him that slew them."[2]

If Odysseus showed suspicious wariness on his return home, Penelope showed no less caution.[3] Right well did they deserve their epithets—he of $\pi o \lambda v \mu \eta \chi a v o \varsigma$ (of many devices), and she of $\dot{\epsilon} \chi \dot{\epsilon} \phi \rho \omega \nu$ (prudent, reserved).

[1] Od. xiv. 125.   [2] Od. xxiii. 83.   [3] Od. xxiii. 90.

Penelope's Excessive Caution

When she had come down from her chamber, to where her husband was, she debated in her mind whether she should sit apart and question him, or draw nigh and kiss his head and hands. Crossing the stone threshold, she sat down opposite to Odysseus in the light of the fire by the farther wall. Odysseus was sitting by the tall pillar, waiting to see whether his noble wife would speak to him. But she sat long in silence, for she knew him not, "for that he was clothed in vile raiment." Telemachos, astonished at her cold bearing, rebukes her: "Ill mother of ungentle heart, why turnest thou away from my father? ... No other woman in the world would thus harden her heart to stand aloof from her lord, who after much travail had come to her in the twentieth year. But thy heart is harder than stone."[1]

There was some excuse for her. Odysseus, no doubt, was greatly changed in twenty years of war and travail by land and sea. She is still in doubt. "If this is indeed he," she said, "we shall be ware of one another, for we have tokens that we twain know, secret from all others."[2]

Odysseus, seeing that she remained obdurate, postpones the interchange of mutual confidences. "Leave now," he says to Telemachos, "thy mother to make trial within the halls, for now I go filthy, and am clad in vile raiment; wherefore she has me in dishonour, and will not allow that I am he."[3]

He and Telemachos then consult together how best to meet the formidable attack of the friends of the slaughtered suitors, whom he himself calls the best of all the noble youths of Ithaca.[4]

[1] Od. xxiii. 97.   [2] Od. xxiii. 107.   [3] Od. xxiii. 113.   [4] Od. xxiii. 117.

The Women of Homer

Meanwhile the house-dame, Eurynome,[1] bathed the great-hearted Odysseus, and anointed him with olive oil, and cast about him a goodly mantle and a doublet. Moreover, "Athene shed great beauty from his head downwards, and made him greater and more mighty to behold, and from his head caused deep curling locks to flow like the hyacinth flower . . . even so did Athene shed grace about his head and shoulders, and forth from the bath he came in form like to the Immortals."[2]

Even now Penelope cannot lay aside her suspicion, and Odysseus, sorely grieved, reproaches her : "Strange lady, surely to thee, above all womankind, the Olympians have given a heart that cannot be softened."[3]

The wise Penelope replies : "Strange man! I have no proud thoughts, . . . but I know what manner of man thou wast when thou wentest forth from Ithaca on the long-oared galley."[4] She then bids Eurycleia to spread for him a bed outside the bridal chamber that he had built himself. Then Odysseus, in sore displeasure, exclaims : "Who has set my bed otherwise ? Hard would it be for any one, unless it were a god, to set it in another place. Of men there is no one living that could easily raise it, for a great marvel is wrought in the fashion of the bed, and it was I that made it. There was growing a bush of olive within the inner court, and the stem was as large as a pillar. Round this I built the chamber, with stones close set, and I roofed it over well, and added compacted doors well fitting. Next I sheared off all the light wood of the

[1] Od. xxiii. 154. [2] Od. xxiii. 155.
[3] Od. xxiii. 166. [4] Od. xxiii. 173.

ATHENE FARNESI.

The Secret of the Bed

thick-leaved olive, and rough-hewed the trunk upward from the root, and polished it with an adze, and so fashioned it into a bed-post. . . . Beginning from this head-post, I wrought at the bed till I had finished it, and made it fair with inlaid work of gold, and silver, and ivory; . . . and I would know, my lady, whether the bed be still in its place, or whether some man has cut away the stem of the olive tree, and set the bedstead otherwhere."[1]

Then at last she is convinced. "Her knees were loosened, and her heart melted within her, as she knew the sure tokens that Odysseus showed her. She broke into tears, ran straight up to him, cast her arms about him, and kissed his head"[2]—so welcome to her was the sight of her lord, and her white arms would never quite leave hold of his neck. "Be not thus angry with me because I did not welcome thee gladly, as I do now, when first I saw thee. For always my heart shuddered for fear lest some man should come and deceive me, for many there be that devise gainful schemes and evil."[3]

Herewith the perils of Odysseus, the sorrows of Penelope, are ended, and all is well as far as their relation to one another is concerned. He has still to meet the wrath of the friends of the dead suitors. This, as we have seen, was successfully accomplished by the help of Athene; and he can now look forward with hope to the fulfilment of the happy prophecy of Teiresias in Hades: "Thine own death shall come upon thee from the sea — a gentle death, which shall end

[1] Od. xxiii. 183.   [2] Od. xxxiii. 205.   [3] Od. xxiii. 213.

thee, foredone with smooth old age, and the folk shall dwell happily around thee."[1]

Such was Penelope—a woman of unusual strength of character, as shown in her long years of faithful devotion to her absent husband, and in her courageous resistance to the powerful influences which almost compelled her to resign her hopes and to accept a hateful marriage. Her caution, when Odysseus at last reveals himself, appears to us excessive; but when her doubts and fears are dispelled, she is full of tenderness and affection for the dear, sorely-missed husband of her youth. Well does she deserve the warm eulogy of Agamemnon's shade in Hades: "Ah! happy son of Laertes, Odysseus of many devices; yea, for a wife most excellent hast thou gotten, so good was the wisdom of steadfast Penelope, daughter of Icarios, that was duly mindful of her gentle lord. Wherefore the fame of her virtue shall never perish, but the Immortals will make a gracious song in the ears of men on earth to the fame of steadfast Penelope."[2]

The question naturally arises in our minds, Was Odysseus worthy of the devotion of so noble a woman? With many of his traits we of the North and West cannot sympathise; they are essentially Oriental. We prefer successful daring to successful fraud, and we look with dislike at the subtle wiles, the elaborate falsehoods, by which he carried out his crafty designs. His search for poison, in which to dip his arrows, is repugnant to us.

Nor can we help contrasting the lonely, tearful life

[1] Od. xi. 133. [2] Od. xxiv. 192.

Was Odysseus worthy of Penelope?

of Penelope, amidst importunate and plundering wooers and a ruined household, with his seven years' sojourn in the beautiful cave and the lovely gardens of the charming nymph Calypso, and his long rest in the splendid halls of the seductive sorceress, the *vitrea* Circe.

On the other hand, we cannot but recognise in him the high and noble qualities of undaunted courage and infinite resource—the skill to plan, the patience and the energy and valour to execute. In spite of his lingering, partly enforced perhaps—like another Tannhäuser in the Venusberg—in the enchanted grotto of Calypso, he loved his wife and country, and for them he left the arms of the lovely nymph, and refused the offer of immortal youth.[1] He knows how far superior is the lovely Nymph, "in form and fashion," to his mortal wife, whom he has not seen for twenty years; yet he is ready to risk all, to resign all, to face the anger of the gods and the treachery of men, for the mere chance of seeing her and his home again.

It is evident, too, that he had the power of winning the highest admiration and affection of both men and women. The women, indeed, are his devoted slaves. Not to mention Penelope—for the name of husband covers a multitude of sins—he is the favourite of Athene, he is loved by the demi-goddesses Calypso and Circe; his life is saved at a critical moment by the sea nymph Ino-Leucothea, who lends him her magic veil (κρήδεμνον), on which he floats safely to shore; and—greatest triumph of all—he is the first to stir the maiden heart of the lovely and innocent Nausicaa.

[1] Od. v. 136: Θήσειν ἀθάνατον καὶ ἀγήραον ἤματα πάντα.

The Women of Homer

Nor was it only by women that he was admired and loved. He ranks among the highest of the Achaian princes; he is the first to be consulted in any great emergency—the first to be employed in any hazardous enterprise. Menelaos mourns his loss like that of a brother. When Telemachos comes to his court, Menelaos, speaking of Telemachos, says to Peisistratos: "So now, in good truth, there has come unto my house the son of a friend indeed, who for my sake endured many trials. And I thought to welcome him on his coming, more nobly than all the other Argives; if but Olympian Zeus of the far-borne voice had vouchsafed us a return over the sea in our swift ships. . . . And in Argos I would have given him a city to dwell in, and stablished for him a house, and brought him forth from Ithaca, with his substance and his son, and all his people. . . . Then ofttimes would we have held converse here, and nought would have parted us in our friendship and our joys, ere the black cloud of death overshadowed us. Howsoever, the god himself must have been jealous thereof, who from that hapless man alone cut off his returning."[1]

[1] Od. iv. 168.

CHAPTER XIII

HEKABE

DAUGHTER of Dymas, king of Phrygia, wife of Priam, mother of the great Hector and Paris and seventeen other sons and daughters. The only epithet applied to her by Homer is ἠπιόδωρος (bountiful). She is almost exclusively the *mother*, pious, tender-hearted, and loving, yet a very tigress in defence of her children;[1] far more careful of the life than of the honour of her husband and her favourite son, the glorious Hector.

When Hector thinks it his duty to himself and his country to meet the terrible Achilles, she does all that she can, and far more than she ought, to turn him from his high resolve. If anything could have prevailed against his sense of honour, it would have been her piteous entreaties: "Then his mother wailed tearfully, loosening the folds of her robe, while with the other hand she bared her breast, and through her tears spake unto him winged words: 'Hector, my child! have regard unto this bosom, and pity me if ever I gave thee consolation of my breast. Think of it, dear child, and from this side of the wall drive back the foe, nor stand in front to meet him. He is merciless; if he slay thee,

[1] Il. xxiv. 212.

The Women of Homer

it will not be on a bed that I, and thy wife, wooed with many gifts, shall bewail thee, my own dear child; but far away from us, by the ships of the Argives, will the swift dogs devour thee.'"[1]

With tears and prayers she goes to the temple of Athene, "the guardian of cities," bearing splendid embroidered robes, the work of Sidonian women. These she gives to the priestess, the fair-cheeked Theano, who lays them on the knees of the fair-haired Athene, begging her in piteous terms to have mercy on the city, and on the Trojans' wives and little children; "but Pallas Athene denied the prayer."[2] When he is slain, her passionate grief knows no bounds; "she tore her hair and cast far from her her shining veil ($κρήδεμνον$), and cried aloud with an exceeding bitter cry."[3]

Life seems no longer dear to her: "My child, woe is me! Wherefore should I live in my pain, now thou art dead, who night and day wert my boast through the city, and a blessing to all, both men and women of Troy, who hailed thee as a god; for verily an exceeding glory to them wert thou in thy life."[4]

And again, at the official wailing over Hector's recovered corpse, she leads the loud lament: "Hector, of all my children far dearest to my heart, verily while thou wert alive, dear wert thou to the gods, and even in thy doom of death have they had a care for thee."[5]

When Priam nobly resolves to go to the tent of the fierce slayer of his son, and by a magnificent ransom to redeem him from lying unburied—a fate which seemed

[1] Il. xxii. 82.   [2] Il. vi. 293.   [3] Il. xxii 406.
[4] Il. xxii. 431.   [5] Il. xxiv. 747.

Hekabe's Weakness and Despair

to the Achaians more terrible than death itself—she does all that she can to deter him from the noble effort. "If it be my fate," he says, "to die by the ships of the mail-clad Achaians, so would I have it; let Achilles kill me with all speed, when once I have taken my son in my arms and given my sorrow vent."[1]

Hekabe treats him like a madman. "Woe is me," she cries, "whither is gone thy mind, whereby aforetime thou wert famous among strangers and among them thou rulest? How art thou fain to go alone to the ships of the Achaians, to meet the eyes of the man who hath slain full many of thy brave sons?"[2] Much as she loved her noble son, she can make no effort: "Let us sit in the hall, and make lament afar off. Even thus did forceful Fate erst spin for Hector with her thread at his beginning, when I bare him, even I, that he should glut the dogs far from his parents."[3]

We learn nothing, of course, from Homer of the subsequent fate of Hekabe. According to later writers she was made captive and slave by the Greeks after the fall of Troy. Euripides makes her witness of the sacrifice of her daughter Polyxena to the shade of Achilles,[4] and of the murder of her youngest son Polydoros by Polymestor, king of the Thracian Chersonesus, on whom she took a terrible vengeance. Polymestor, whose eyes she put out after slaying his two sons, prophesies that she should be metamorphosed into a she-dog, and should leap into the sea at Cynosema. According to Ovid this prophecy was fulfilled in Thrace, the inhabi-

[1] Il. xxiv. 224.   [2] Il. xxiv. 201.   [3] Il. xxiv. 210.
[4] Eurip. Hekabe, 40 and 1050; Virg. Æn. iii. 49; Ovid, Met. xiii. 443.

tants of which stoned her; but she was turned into a dog, and in this form howled through the country for a long time.¹

NAUSICAA

Of all the beautiful creations of Homer's genius, there is perhaps none so attractive, so charming, as the sweet, gentle, innocent, yet high-spirited and courageous Nausicaa. She was the daughter of the powerful and high-minded Alcinoos, ruler of the island of Scheria, which Homer describes with so much love. Her mother was Arētē, daughter of Rhexenor, whom Alcinoos took to wife, "and honoured as no other woman in the world is honoured."² "Thus she hath, and hath ever had, all worship heartily from her dear children, and from her lord Alcinoos, and from all the folk, who look on her as a goddess."

KEY TO NOBLE MAIDENS.

Nausicaa describes the blessed land in which she lives to Odysseus, whom, as we shall see, she rescued from a lingering death by starvation.³ "That mortal breathes not who shall come with war to the land of

---

¹ Ovid, Met. 423, 570; Juvenal x. sed—
"Torva canino
Latravit rictu, quæ post hunc vixerat uxor."
² Od. vii. 64.　　　　　　　　　　　　³ Vide *infra*.

TRAIN OF NOBLE MAIDENS.
(*From the Parthenon Frieze.*)

The Palace of King Alcinoos

the Phæacians, for they are very dear to the gods. Far apart we live, in the wash of the waves, the outermost of men, and no other mortals are conversant with us."[1]

For this reason, the Phæacians cared not for bow and quiver, but for masts and oars and gallant barques, and "their ships are as swift as the flight of a bird, or as thought." Nor do they need pilots[2] or rudders, after the manner of other ships, but "the barques themselves understand the thoughts and interests of men; they know the cities and fat fields of every folk, and swiftly they traverse the gulf of the salt sea, shrouded in mist and cloud, and never do they go in fear of wreck or ruin."

The palace of Alcinoos was worthy of the land, and of a monarch endowed with wisdom by the gods. "For there was a gleam as of the sun or moon through the high-roofed hall of the great-hearted Alcinoos. Brazen were the walls which ran this way and that from the threshold to the inmost chambers, and round them was a frieze of blue, and golden were the doors that closed in the good house. Silver were the door-posts that were set on the brazen threshold, and silver the lintel thereupon, and the hook of the door was of gold. And on either side stood golden hounds and silver, which Hephaistos wrought by his skill, to guard the palace, being free from death and age all their days. And within there were seats arranged this way and that against the wall, and thereon were spread light coverings, beautiful and

[1] Od. vi. 200.   [2] Od. viii. 557.

The Women of Homer

finely woven, the handiwork of women. There the Phæacian chieftains were wont to sit eating and drinking, for they had continual store. Yea, and there were youths fashioned in gold, standing on firm-set bases, with flaming torches in their hands, giving light through the night to the feasters in the palace. And Alcinoos had fifty handmaids in the house, and some grind the yellow grain on the millstone, and others weave webs and turn the yarn, as they sit, restless as the leaves of the tall poplar-tree. For as the Phæacian men are skilful beyond all others in driving a ship, so are the women the most cunning at the loom, for Athene hath given them notable wisdom in all fair handiwork and cunning wit."[1]

We have also a description of the gardens in which the childhood of the lovely Nausicaa was passed. "Without the courtyard, hard by the door, is a great garden of four ploughgates,[2] and a hedge runs round on either side. And there grow tall trees, blossoming—pear-trees, and pomegranates, and apple-trees, with bright fruit, and sweet figs and olives in their bloom. The fruit of these trees never perisheth, never faileth, winter or summer. Evermore the west wind brings some fruits to birth and ripens others; pear upon pear wax old, and apple on apple; yea, and cluster on cluster of the grape, and fig upon fig. There, too, hath he a fruitful vineyard planted. . . . There, too, skirting the farthest line, are all manner of garden beds, planted trimly, that are fresh continually; and therein are two fountains of water, whereof one

---

[1] Od. vii. 84.   [2] Γύαι, as much as a man can plough in a day.

The Gardens of Alcinoos

scatters his streams all about the garden, and the other runs over against it, beneath the threshold of the courtyard, and issues by the lofty house ; and thence did the townsfolk draw water. These were the splendid gifts of the gods in the palace of Alcinoos."[1]

As we read of the splendours of Alcinoos' mansion, with its brazen walls, its costly furniture, and its golden vessels, we might fancy ourselves in the gorgeous palace of some Assyrian or Phœnician despot, which it resembles in its conventional style and brilliant colouring. The gold and silver dogs remind us of the Egyptian Sphinx, the Chaldæan bulls and lions, the colossal Assyrian beasts with human heads. The golden torchbearers are reminiscences of the architectural figures of Oriental art, and do not by any means imply the existence of the art of independent sculpture in the heroic age of Greece. Homer makes no mention of statues proper. The idol of Athene in Troy was not a statue, but a mere idol,[2] like the shapeless, black, wooden Virgin Mary, which fell down from heaven. Nor are there any traces of temples before the Dorian migration ; nor do we find remains of them at Mykenai, Tiryns, or Hissarlik. The gods were worshipped at altars reared in the midst of woods. The stone threshold of Phœbos Apollo in rocky Pytho is twice mentioned in Homer.[3] We do indeed read of a temple of Athene in Troy, to which Homer has given a somewhat Oriental colouring. The temples of a later age on Greek soil were all of Oriental origin.

[1] Od. vii. 102.   [2] Helbig, Epos, 336, 371.
[3] Il. ix. 404 ; Od. viii. 79.

The Women of Homer

Such were the surroundings in which Nausicaa was reared under wise and affectionate parents, in comfort, and even splendour, rejoicing in the free life of the country, conscious of the favour and protection of the gods, whom she was accustomed to see as guests in her father's house.

Nausicaa plays a most important and decisive part in the life of Odysseus, as he in hers. She is employed by Athene to save him from impending death, and to set him well on his way towards his longed-for home.

The fair Calypso, as we know, had furnished him with the means of constructing a raft, which she stocked with food and wine and "all manner of dainties," and sent forth a warm and gentle wind to blow. For ten and seven days he traversed the deep, with his eyes ever fixed on the constellation of the Wain, and keeping it to the left, according to the instructions of Calypso; and "on the eighteenth day appeared the shadowy hills of the land of the Phæacians."[1]

But his inveterate foe the god Poseidon,[2] whom he had offended by blinding the son of the god, the mighty Cyclops, beheld him from the mountains of the Solymi. "He gathered the clouds and troubled the waters, grasping his trident in his hands. And he roused all storms of all manner of winds, and shrouded in clouds the land and the sea, and down sped night from heaven." Then were his knees loosened, his heart melted, and he longed for death. "Thrice blessed," he cries, "are those Danaans, yea, four times blessed, who perished on a time in wide Troy. . . . Would to God that I too

[1] Od. v. 277. [2] Od. v. 282.

The Magic Veil of Ino-Leucothea

had died, . . . when the press of Trojans cast their bronze-shod spears upon me, fighting for the body of the son of Peleus. Then should I have gotten my dues of burial, and the Achaians would have spread my fame."[1]

In this extremity he is seen by Ino-Leucothea "of the fair ankles," daughter of Kadmos, who in times past was a maiden of mortal speech, but now in the depths of the salt sea had gotten her share of worship from the gods. Like all the goddesses and women whom he meets with, she takes pity on Odysseus. "Do as I tell thee," she says. "Cast off thy garments, and leave the raft to drift before the winds; but do thou swim, and strive to win a footing on the coast. Take this veil divine ($κρήδεμνον$) and wind it round thy breast; then there is no fear that thou suffer aught or perish. But when thou hast laid hold of the mainland, loose it from off thee and cast it into the wine-dark deep."[2]

Contrary to the injunctions of Ino - Leucothea, Odysseus clings to his raft, which, however, Poseidon quickly shatters, and leaves the wretched man sitting on a single plank. Then his guardian angel Athene again intervenes. "She binds up the courses of the other winds, and charged them all to cease and be still; but she roused the swift North wind, and brake the waves before him, that so he might avoid death and the Fates, and mingle with the Phæacians."[3]

Yet for two days and two nights more he was wandering in the swell of the sea, and much his heart

[1] Od. v. 305. [2] Od. v. 345. [3] Od. v. 382.

boded of death. But when at last the fair-tressed Dawn brought the light of the third day, the breeze fell, and there was a breathless calm."[1]

But his danger is not yet over. There was no landing-place from out of the grey waters. He rushes in and tries to clutch the jagged rock, but the backward wash leapt on him and cast him forth again into the deep. Once more he rose from the breakers and swam outside along the shore, ever looking landwards for a practicable landing-place. And fortune favoured him, for he soon came swimming over against the mouth of a fair-flowing river, smooth of rocks, and protected from the wind. And Odysseus felt the river running, and prayed to the river-god in his heart: "Hear me, O king, whosoever thou art; unto thee am I come, as to one to whom prayer is made. . . . Yea, reverend even to the deathless gods is that man who comes as a wanderer, as now I come to thy stream and to thy knees, after much travail. Pity me, O king, for I call myself thy suppliant."[2] The divine river heard him, and withheld his waves, and made the water smooth before him, and brought him safely to the mouth of the river.

But he lands in evil case. "His knees bowed and his stout hands fell, for his brave spirit was quelled by the brine. His flesh was all swollen, and the sea water gushed up through his mouth and nostrils." There he lay swooning, without breath or speech.[3]

Recovering from his swoon, he still sees fresh trouble and death before him. "If I watch in the river-bed

[1] Od. v. 388.   [2] Od. v. 445.   [3] Od. v. 454.

Odysseus lands near a River of Phæacia

through the careful night, I fear that the bitter frost and fresh dew may overcome me. If I climb the hillside to the shady wood, and take rest in the thickets, though, perchance, the cold and weariness may leave me, and sweet sleep come over me, I fear lest I fall a prey to the beasts."[1]

"But he went into the wood, and crept beneath twin bushes of olive, through which the force of the wet wind never blew, ... so closely were the branches intertwined—and heaped together a broad couch of fallen leaves, and laid himself in the midst thereof, and flung over himself the fallen leaves. And Athene shed sweet sleep upon his eyes, that it might release him from his weary travail."[2] There he lay, the patient, goodly Odysseus, foredone with toil and weariness.

Meanwhile Athene does not forget him. She went to the palace of the high-hearted Alcinoos,[3] and entered the rich-wrought bower wherein was sleeping a maiden, "like to the gods in form and comeliness," Nausicaa, the daughter of the king. Beside her, on either hand of the pillars of the door, were two handmaids, "dowered with beauty by the Graces," and the shining doors were shut. Fleet as the breath of the wind the goddess swept towards the couch of the maiden, and spake to her in the semblance of the daughter of Dymas, a girl of like age with Nausicaa, who had found favour in her sight. "Nausicaa, how hath thy mother so heedless a maiden to her daughter? Lo! thou hast shining raiment that lies uncared for, and thy marriage day is near at hand, when thou thyself must go beautifully clad, and

---

[1] Od. v. 465. [2] Od. v. 476. [3] Od. vi. 13.

The Women of Homer

have garments to give to them who shall lead thee to the house of the bridegroom. . . . But come, let us arise and go a-washing with the break of day, and I will follow to be thy mate in the toil, that thou mayest get thee ready, since truly thou art not long to be a maiden. Lo! they are already wooing thee, the noblest youths of all the Phæacians. So come, beseech thy noble father to furnish thee with mules and a wain, to carry the men's raiment, and the robes and the shining coverlets."[1]

As soon as the rosy-fingered, throned Dawn had awakened the lovely Nausicaa she goes to her father, and asks for the mules and the wain, "that she might take the goodly raiment to the river; for," she said, "it is seemly that thou thyself, when among the princes in council, shouldst have fresh raiment to wear. Also there are five dear sons of thine in the halls . . . always eager for new-washed garments to go to the dances."[2] "This she said because she was ashamed to speak of glad marriage, but *he saw all.*"

Having stored the wain with food and wine, and soft olive oil which her mother gave her in a golden cruse, that she and her maids might anoint themselves after the bath, she climbed into her seat, took the whip and the shining reins, and touched the mules to start them. "She was not alone, for her attendant maidens followed with her."[3]

When they had come to the beautiful stream, they took the clothes from the wain, bore them to the black water, "and briskly trod them down in the trenches in

[1] Od. vi. 26. [2] Od. vi. 66. [3] Od. vi. 85.

Nausicaa and her Maidens play at Ball

busy rivalry."[1] When they had spread them on the shore, where the sea had washed the pebbles clean, they bathed and anointed themselves with olive oil, and then took their mid-day meal on the river's bank. Then the princess and her maidens fell to playing at ball, casting away their tires (κρήδεμνα); and the white-armed Nausicaa began the song:[2] "And as Artemis, the archer, moves down the mountain slopes of Taygetus or Erymanthus, taking her pastime in the chase of boars and deer, and with her the wild wood nymphs, the daughters of Zeus, disport themselves, while high over all she rears her head and brows, even so the girl unwed outshone her maiden company."

Meanwhile Athene is preparing the awakening of Odysseus, that he may see the lovely girl who is to save him from a cruel death. During the ball-play Nausicaa threw the ball with great force at one of her companions, but missed her, and it rolled away into the eddying current. The cry over the lost ball roused Odysseus from his leafy couch. "How shrill a cry of maidens rings around me, of the Nymphs that hold the steep hill-tops, and the river springs, and the grassy water-meadows! It must be that I am near men of human speech."[3]

Tormented by hunger, and nearly at the limit of endurance, he sees that he is now at the very crisis of his fate. Holding the leafy branch of a tree before him, he issues from the wood "like a lion of the hills," such need had come upon him. But when the maidens caught sight of this strange and terrible figure, wasted by hunger

---

[1] Od. vi. 92.   [2] Od. vi. 102.   [3] Od. vi. 122.

The Women of Homer

and all marred by the salt sea-foam, they fled cowering here and there about the jutting spits of the shore. The noble daughter of Alcinoos alone stood firm, for Athene gave her courage of heart, and took all trembling from her limbs, and she halted and stood over against Odysseus.[1]

Then the afflicted hero addresses her in a speech which is a very model of refined and persuasive eloquence. "I supplicate thee, O queen, whether thou art some goddess or a mortal! If thou art a goddess, to Artemis, then, I liken thee for beauty of stature and shapeliness; but if thou art of the daughters of men, thrice blessed are thy father, and thy lady mother, and thy brethren. Surely their hearts ever glow with gladness each time they see thee entering the dance, so fair a flower of maidens. But he is of heart the most blessed beyond all others who shall prevail with gifts of wooing, and lead thee to his home. Never have mine eyes beheld such an one among mortals; great awe comes upon me as I look on thee! Yet in Delos once I saw as goodly a thing, a young sapling of a palm-tree springing by the altar of Apollo. . . . Never yet there grew so goodly a shoot from ground; even in such wise do I wonder at thee, lady, and am astonied, and do greatly fear to touch thy knees, though grievous sorrow is upon me. . . . But, queen, have pity on me, for of the people who hold this city and land I know no one. Show me the town; give me an old garment, if thou hadst when thou camest hither a wrap for the linen. And may the gods grant thee all thy heart's desire, a husband and a home, and a mind

[1] Od. vi. 141.

Odysseus' Prayer to Nausicaa

at one with his—a good gift, for there is nothing mightier and nobler than when man and wife are of one heart and mind in the house, a grief to their foes, and to their friends great joy, *but their own hearts know it best.*" [1]

Nausicaa, touched by his prayer—as what woman would not be?—does more than he has asked. She calls aloud to her fair-tressed, frightened maidens: "Halt, my maidens; whither flee ye at the sight of a man? Ye surely do not take him for an enemy? ... This man is doubtless some helpless one ... whom we must kindly entreat, for all strangers and suppliants are from Zeus. ... So give the stranger meat and drink, and bathe him in the river." [2]

But goodly Odysseus bids the maidens stand apart while he bathes himself. After the bath Athene makes him greater and more mighty to behold ... and shed grace about his head and shoulders. "Then to the shore of the sea went Odysseus apart, and sat down glowing in beauty and grace, and the princess marvelled at him." [3]

We now see the first budding of love in her pure and as yet untroubled heart, which, with true Homeric *naïveté*, she half-jokingly confesses to her fair-tressed companions: "Listen, my white-armed maidens, and I will say somewhat. Not without the will of all the gods has this man come among the godlike Phæacians. Erewhile he seemed to me uncomely, but now he is like the gods that keep the wide heavens. Would that such a one might be called my husband, dwelling here. ... But come, my maidens, give the stranger meat and drink." [4]

---

[1] Od. vi. 149. [2] Od. vi. 198.
[3] Od. vi. 237. [4] Od. vi. 239.

The Women of Homer

Having arranged the clean linen in the wain,[1] and climbed into the seat, she gives Odysseus directions to follow her to the palace of her father. With maidenly caution and reserve, she tells him to follow the wain with her maidens as quickly as possible, as long as they were in the open fields. But when they arrived at the city, then he was to sit down in the poplar grove of Athene, near the road; "for," she said, "I would avoid the ungracious speech of the baser sort of people, and there are too many insolent folk who might meet me and say: 'Who is this that goes with Nausicaa, this tall and goodly stranger? Where found she him? Her husband he will be, her very own. Either she has taken in some shipwrecked wanderer of strange men, or some god has come in answer to her instant prayer. From heaven has he descended, and will have her to wife for evermore . . . for, verily, she holds in no regard the Phæacians here in the land, the many men and noble who are her wooers.' Thus will they speak, and it would be a shame to me."[2]

Her very caution betrays the nascent inclination of her breast; and the comments of the people which she imagines—that, after all, show high appreciation of her immeasurable superiority — imply that her heart, untouched by any of her noble countrymen, was beating with a new sensation in favour of the goodly Odysseus.

She further instructs him[3] how to gain the favour of her parents, and especially of her mother Arētē, the queen. "When thou art within the shadow of the halls and the court, pass quickly through the great chamber

---

[1] Od. vi. 251.   [2] Od. vi. 276.   [3] Od. vi. 303.

Odysseus supplicates the Queen Arētē

till thou comest to my mother. Her chair is leaned against a pillar, and her maidens sit behind her. And there my father's throne leans close to hers, wherein he sits and drinks his wine like an Immortal. Pass by him and cast thy hands about my mother's knees. . . . If but *her* heart be kindly disposed toward thee, there is hope that thou shalt see thy friends, and come to thy well-built house and to thine own country."[1]

When Odysseus rose from his seat in the sacred grove of Athene, the goddess herself met him in the guise of a maiden carrying a pitcher of water. Odysseus asks the way to the palace, and the goddess, that he may meet with no hindrance from the town-folk, who love not strangers, shrouded him in a thick mist until he came into the presence of Alcinoos and Arētē. Then the wondrous mist melted from off him, and silence fell on all within the house, and they marvelled as they beheld him. He clasps the knees of Arētē, and prefers his prayer for her happiness and for her aid in sending him safely to his home. He then sat down in the ashes of the sacred hearth, and the ancient lord Echeneos[2] pleaded his cause before the royal pair. Thereupon Alcinoos raises him from the hearth, sets him on a shining chair, and directs the servants to provide him with food and drink and all that he required. "If," he said, "he is some deathless god come down from heaven, then is this some new device wherewith the gods encompass us. For heretofore the gods appear openly amongst us when we offer glorious hecatombs, and they feast by our side, sitting at the same board.

---
[1] Od. vi. 305.   [2] Od. vii. 153.

The Women of Homer

And if ever a lonely wayfarer meets them they use no disguise, for we are near of kin to them."[1]

Odysseus disclaims divinity, and begs before all things for food and drink; "for nothing," he says, "is more shameless than a ravening stomach. Though one be worn and sorrowful it biddeth me eat and drink, and maketh me utterly forgetful of all my sufferings."[2] Then, in reply to the eager questioning of Queen Arētē, who recognises the garment which her daughter had given him, he relates his latest adventures.[3]

Alcinoos is so struck by the majestic bearing and the eloquent speech of the hero, that he almost echoes the words of Nausicaa to her maidens: "Would to Father Zeus, and Athene, and Apollo, that so goodly a man as thou, and like-minded with me, wouldst wed my daughter and be called my son, here abiding; so would I give thee house and wealth, if thou wouldst stay of thine own will."[4] He then promises to send him to Ithaca, and meantime entertains him with a rich banquet and the song of a divine minstrel.

Rather against his will—for sorrow was nearer his heart than sports—he is roused by the taunts of the Phæacian youths to show his strength and prowess. Without even laying aside his mantle, he caught up a huge stone—far heavier than the others threw—and sent it hurtling beyond all the marks. Nausicaa, with the whole court, were witnesses of his triumph. He then challenges all comers to wrestle and to box, in proud consciousness of superiority. "I avow myself far

[1] Od. vii. 199.
[2] Od. vii. 216.
[3] Od. vii. 240.
[4] Od. vii. 311.

Dance, and the Song of Demodocos

more excellent than all besides of the mortals who are now upon the earth."[1]

Of course no one accepts the challenge, and Alcinoos alone makes answer: "We[2] are no perfect boxers nor wrestlers, but speedy runners and the best of seamen, and dear to us is the banquet and the dance, and changes of raiment, and the warm bath, and love and sleep."[3]

The king then sends for the minstrel Demodocos and the best dancers. "And Demodocos gat him into the midst, and round him stood boys in the first bloom, skilled in the dance, and they smote the good floor with their feet. And Odysseus gazed at the twinklings of the feet, and marvelled in spirit."[4]

The song of Demodocos, though the worst part of it (v. 333-343)—the shameless avowal of Hermes—is justly suspected, is certainly in entire consonance with the character which Alcinoos gives of his people, and well suited to their luxurious and hedonist tastes. He sang of the loves of Ares and Aphrodite.

Odysseus gives a full description of his marvellous adventures, and both king and queen are transported with admiration. The white-armed Arētē spake: "What think ye, Phæacians, of this man for comeliness, and stature, and wisdom of heart?"[5] And Alcinoos chimes in: "Beauty crowns thy words, and wisdom is within

---

[1] Od. viii. 221.   [2] Od. viii. 246.
[3] "Nos numerus sumus, et fruges consumere nati,
   Sponsi Penelopes, nebulon.s, Alcinoique
   In cute curanda, plus æquo operata Juventus,
   Cui pulchrum fuit, in medios domire dies et."
                                    —Horace, Ep. i. 27.
[4] Od. viii. 265.   [5] Od. xi. 336.

The Women of Homer

thee."[1] He calls on all who hear him to bring costly presents. And thus laden with rich garments and costly works of art, they send him home in a splendid barque to his country and his long-suffering faithful wife.[2]

We have dwelt at too great length, perhaps, on the appearance and the actions of Odysseus, because of the love with which they inspired the maiden heart of the lovely Nausicaa. We have seen how little of the heroic there was in the character of her voluptuous countrymen to warm the imagination and touch the heart of so pure and noble a girl as Nausicaa. We learn incidentally that she remained indifferent to the suit of the gay young Phæacian nobles. But when Odysseus appears—the hero of a hundred battles, the bold mariner who has just emerged from long conflict with the angry sea-god—she falls in love with him at first sight. And the impression he made on her at their first strange meeting by the river side is deepened by all that she afterwards heard and saw of him—by his strength and manly beauty, his skill in games, his wondrous eloquence in the relation of his manifold sufferings and trials.[3] Yet when she learns that he is married and must go and leave her to her dreams, there is no frantic outbreak of disappointed love. She lived in a contracted sphere, in simple patriarchal surroundings, but in that narrow world her being was harmoniously perfect. Like all Homeric women, her inclinations were restrained by the αἰδώς,[4]

---

[1] Hor. Epist. 1. 27.   [2] Od. xiii. 4, 16.
[3] "She loved him for the dangers he had passed."
[4] Hesiod characterises the Age of Iron by saying that αἰδώς had fled the earth.

Nausicaa's Farewell to Odysseus

the self-respecting modesty, of the Greeks, and the sanctity of family customs and traditions. She was no heroine in the modern sense of the word, but a noble, unsophisticated girl of sweet, cheerful, and amiable nature, without that depth of sentiment, that tearing violence of passion, in which modern romance delights. She was no Iphigenia or Antigone, no Dido, painted in blood-red colours; and yet her image is stamped on our imaginations with the clearest lines, and the freshest, loveliest hues.

How characteristic is her farewell to Odysseus in its quiet simplicity, its modest self-restraint! When all is prepared for Odysseus' departure, Arētē bids her handmaids prepare the warm bath, and brings forth a beauteous coffer from the treasury, and bestows the gifts therein, precious raiment and gold, which the Phæacians had given him. Then he goes to the bath, and he saw the warm water and was glad, for he was not wont to be so cared for from the day that he left the house of the fair-tressed Calypso; "but all that while he had comfort continually as a god."[1]

After the maidens had bathed him, and anointed him with olive oil, and had cast a fair mantle and a doublet about him, he stepped forth, and went to sit with the chiefs at their wine. "And then Nausicaa, dowered with beauty by the gods,[2] stood by the door-post of the well-built hall, and marvelled at Odysseus, beholding him before her eyes; and she uttered her voice, and spake to him winged words: "Farewell, stranger; see that

---

[1] Od. viii. 450.
[2] Θεῶν ἀπὸ κάλλος ἐχουσα.

thou remember me in thy country on a day, for that to me first thou owest the price of life." [1]

Odysseus' answer is worthy of him and her : " Nausicaa, daughter of great-hearted Alcinoos, even so may Zeus the thunderer, the lord of Hera, grant me to reach my home, and see the day of my returning ; yea, thereon would I do thee worship as to a god all my days, for thou, lady, hast given me my life." [2]

We cannot believe that his heart remained untouched by so much beauty and sweetness, and by such vital services in the hour of his greatest peril. Yet he goes calmly to the royal banquet, and sends, in true Biblical fashion, a portion of the chine of a white-toothed boar, " with rich fat on either side," to the minstrel Demodocos ; for he said, " From all men on earth minstrels get their meed of honour and worship." And Nausicaa looks after the retreating form of him who alone had touched her heart, and retires quietly and sadly to her chamber, and we see her no more. She is placid and resigned, but she will not be so merry again at ball-play and dance, as before the meeting by the river. We are glad to know that she has now her place in the starry heavens as the "asteroid Nausicaa." [3]

There can be no better proof of the extraordinary fascination exercised in all ages on the minds of great poets by the episode of Nausicaa, than the fact that both Sophocles and Goethe wrote, or endeavoured to write, a drama of which she was the heroine.

The Ναυσίκαα or Πλύντρια of Sophocles is lost, with the exception of a few fragments. It was probably a

[1] Od. viii. 457.   [2] Od. viii. 464.   [3] Palisa Pola, 1879.

youthful work of the great poet, and we may be quite sure that he would treat the subject in a very different way from Homer, whose plot would seem much too tame for the author of "Œdipus," "Ajax," and "Antigone." One of the scenes is said to be the meeting of Odysseus and Nausicaa by the seashore, in which scene her maidens form the chorus. Casaubon and Lessing, on slight grounds, conjecture that it was a satyric drama; but Welcker, following a remark of Eustathius,[1] maintains that it was a tragedy, and certainly neither the character of Odysseus nor of Nausicaa seem to lend themselves to farce.

At the fall of the curtain Odysseus is seen standing on the shore in early morning, naked, and wasted by long fast and immersion in the water, pondering on his helpless condition, and not knowing what to do. At last he ascends a wooded hill, and prepares himself a couch among the leaves. He enlarges on past and present dangers and perplexities, as one wrecked on a strange and apparently uninhabited coast. He speaks in a natural wash-house, in front of which are the unfailing cisterns.[2] This grotto was between the river bank and the wood to which Odysseus betook himself just before the appearance of Nausicaa and her maidens. The audience know that Odysseus is sleeping on his bed of leaves, which is hidden by the trees. Nausicaa and her handmaids enter, and begin to talk of the wash and the secret reason for it—viz. the preparations for her "glad marriage." As they busily trample on the linen, a fine opportunity is

---
[1] Ad Il. iii. 54, 381; Welcker, Gr. Trag. II. Abth., Bonn, 1839.
[2] Πλυνοί ἐπηετανοί. These were not trenches, but a floor of stone with raised edges.—Od. vi. 86.

The Women of Homer

afforded for the chorus to chant a song of merry and mythical contents. During a pause in the washing the chorus execute a dance, in imitation of the trampling action. Nausicaa, perhaps, was absent during the work, looking out for a convenient drying-ground. When Nausicaa returns, the linen is laid out and they bathe and anoint themselves with the olive oil which Arētē had given them, and then take their meal. When they were satisfied with food they fell to playing ball,[1] casting away their tires, and the white-armed Nausicaa began the song.

Odysseus, as we know, was awakened by the cry of the maidens over the lost ball. He emerges from the wood, driven by fierce hunger, naked, gaunt, and terrible. It is a matter of life and death to him, and he must find help now or perish miserably. All flee at his approach but Nausicaa. He addresses her in moving words, and she pities and relieves him. The fragments do not enable us to realise the *dénouement* which Sophocles gives to the drama.

Sophocles also wrote "The Φαίακες," in which the life of Odysseus among the Phæacians is portrayed. He is also said to have written other plays, of which the plots were drawn from the Odyssey.

Goethe too contemplated the composition of a tragedy with Nausicaa as the central figure. He was not a great Greek scholar, in the usual sense of the word. He read his Homer in translations, and it was not until the year 1771, when he was more than twenty years old, that he could read Homer in the original language. Yet no

[1] See Appendix XVIII.

Goethe attempts to write a 'Nausicaa'

man was ever more thoroughly imbued with the spirit of classical antiquity; no one has ever handled the Homeric metre more happily than he, in the beautiful idyll "Hermann and Dorothea." And above all other songs of the Greek Muse he loved the Iliad and the Odyssey. In reference to his domestic epic, "Hermann and Dorothea," he says:

"Denn wer kämpfte mit Göttern, und wer mit dem *Einen?*
Doch Homeride zu sein, wenn auch der letzte, ist schön!"

"For who would fight with the gods, and who with the *One?*
Yet to be a follower of Homer, even the meanest, is fine!"

In April 1787 he visited Palermo in Sicily, and was shown the enchanting gardens in the neighbourhood of that city. "All this," he says (*i.e.* the sight of that most beautiful promontory in the world, and the dædal loveliness of the Sicilian vegetation), "recalled to my mind the island of the blessed Phæacians, the gardens of the king Alcinoos, and the sweet figure of the lovely Nausicaa." He went into the town and bought the Odyssey, and took it with him to read in these famous gardens; and there, he says, for the first time, did the scenes of that wondrous poem become a reality to him. It was there, at the foot of the Rosalienberg, that he brooded over the conception of a "Nausicaa," and even began to write the plan. In a letter to Schiller (iv. 102), Goethe says: "Uns Bewohner des Mittellands entzückt zwar die Odyssee, es ist aber nur der sittliche Theil des Gedichts, der eigentlich auf uns wirkt, dem ganzen beschreibenden Theile hilft unsere Imagination nur kümmerlich und unvollkommen nach. In welchem Glanze

The Women of Homer

aber dieses Gedicht vor mir erschien, als ich Gesänge desselben in Neapel und Sicilien las! Es war als wenn man ein eingeschlagenes Bild mit Firniss überzieht, wodurch es sogleich deutlich und in Harmonie erscheint."

But the luxuriant plant-life of the South awakened in him his old idea of the "Urpflanze"—the original plant from which all other plants were derived and developed. The fair vision of Nausicaa became dim; "the garden of Alcinoos vanished from his mind, and in its place rose the garden of the world."

Many years afterwards, in December 1817, he wrote to his friend Boisserée: "It vexes me afresh that I did not follow up my purpose of writing a 'Nausicaa.'" He thought that it would have been as good as his "Iphigenia" and his "Tasso." We may regret it too, but Goethe's Nausicaa would have been a very different person from Homer's. There can be no more instructive example of the difference between the spirit of the heroic age of Greece and that of our modern world, than the difference between these two figures, as we shall see more clearly in the following sketch.

He describes Nausicaa, of course, as a lovely, much-wooed maiden, as a young girl, free, frank, and cheerful, lovingly obedient to her parents; amiable, hospitable, and religious. She has hitherto been a stranger to the sentiment of love, and receives with entire indifference the homage of the noble Phæacian youths, but succumbs at once to the majestic stranger, who presents such a striking contrast to the effeminate, feasting, dancing, carpet youths by whom she is surrounded.

The impression which he made on her at first sight

Plot of Goethe's Unfinished Play

is deepened by the display of his mental and bodily powers, by his eloquence and skill in games. In one passage she tells Odysseus the circumstances in which she lived—the wealth of her father, and the glorious beauty of the island and the palace in which she lived—and hereby betrays her inceptive love.

The following is Goethe's sketch of the plot of the never-finished play.[1]

ACT I

The game of ball. The care she takes that Odysseus should not be seen in the town in her company is a sign of her rising inclination. In this scene a girl called Xanthe plays a conspicuous part; as does also another of Nausicaa's maidens, Tyche, the most active of the ball-players.

ACT II

Description of the palace of Alcinoos. The character of Nausicaa's suitors. Entrance of Odysseus.

ACT III

Is intended to set forth the interest and importance of Odysseus' adventures. "And I hope," says Goethe, "in relating the incidents of his long wanderings by sea and land, to produce something worthy of the art of poetry." During this relation Nausicaa's sympathy and excitement increase, and Odysseus' eloquence is warmed by her evident admiration.

ACT IV

Stung by the taunts of the young Phæacian nobles, Odysseus very reluctantly takes part in their games, and, to their astonishment and confusion, he hurls a huge stone far beyond the distance which they

---

[1] *Göthe-Forschungen*, von v. Waldemar, Freiherr v. Biedemann. Frankfurt, 1879.

had reached. He then challenges them to box and wrestle, a challenge which they prudently ignore. Nausicaa and the other women remain in the house, and give vent to their feelings of admiration of Odysseus' strength and skill. The display of his mental and physical superiority brings Nausicaa's feelings to a climax, and she compromises herself.

ACT V

Odysseus now announces the existence of his wife, which he has hitherto concealed, and his resolution to return to his home at once.

ACT VI

Nausicaa in despair commits suicide !

No doubt Goethe would have produced an admirable play, and a heroine more interesting to the nervous and excitable modern reader, than the calm, self-restrained maiden of Homer's Odyssey. Yet some, I think, will turn with a feeling of relief from the vista which Goethe opens to our eyes, of frantic passion, self-abandonment, and violent death, to the calm, gentle, self-respecting, though suffering figure of Homer's Nausicaa, and her pathetic parting words: "Farewell, stranger; see that thou remember me in thine own country on a day." The Nausicaa of Goethe affects our senses like a raging and destructive storm; that of Homer, like the fragrant breath of a flower garden on a bright May morning. To modern tastes a scene in Ibsen's play is more congenial. It shows how a recreant lover should be dealt with.

Ella Rentheim, speaking to her unfaithful lover, Borkman, says: "I am speaking of the crime for which there is no forgiveness. . . . *You are a murderer! You have committed the one mortal sin. You have killed the love-life in me.* The Bible speaks of a mysterious sin for which there is no forgiveness. I never understood what it could be; *but now I know. The great unpardonable sin is to murder the love-life in a human soul."*

As we contemplate the sweet image which Homer has drawn upon our hearts, we are astonished to remember how short a space she occupies in the beautiful Phæacian episode. Yet it brings her before us not only in the clearest outlines, but with the brightest and the fairest colours. She stands before us dowered with beauty by the Graces, religious,[1] helpful and loving to her parents, kind and hospitable to strangers, brave and cheerful, freely joining in the dance and song with her companions; so virginal that even her dreams are not of lovers, but of linen,[2] though keenly appreciative of heroic excellence, and capable of devoted love. Who can help loving this brave, sweet maiden? Who will not admire her dignified calmness under the bitterest disappointment that can befall a woman?

[1] Od. vi. 187.   [2] Od. vi. 27.

EXCURSUS

THERE is nothing more remarkable in the social history of Greece than the difference in the character and position of women, as set forth in the Iliad and Odyssey, and as we see them in the pages of the tragedians and comedians of the so-called classical period. No one can deny that the *status* of the higher class of women in the great Epics is a very distinguished and honourable one. We need only consider the examples of Andromache and Hekabe in the Iliad, of Helen in both the poems, and of Arētē and Nausicaa in the Odyssey. We see that marriage was regarded as a highly honourable estate, as an enduring and sacred bond. Where is the relation between man and wife more exquisitely represented than in the last sad meeting of Hector and Andromache on the walls of Troy? What woman has ever surpassed Penelope in long-enduring constancy in the midst of the greatest temptations and the most harrowing trials of her faith? What woman was ever more highly honoured by her husband and her people than Arētē, the wife of King Alcinoos? Who ever chanted a more eloquent eulogy of the bliss of pure and faithful wedlock than Odysseus in his prayer to the lovely princess Nausicaa?

In the culminating period of Greek culture and

Position of Women in the Classical Period

civilisation, in the most brilliant age of the "violet-crowned"[1] Athens, "the eye of Hellas," all this is changed. The men have ascended to intellectual heights never attained before or since; the great mass of the women have become mere household drudges, without part or lot in the great affairs of life, disregarded and despised as necessary evils. The change which took place between the age of Homer and that of Pericles is immense, and extremely difficult to account for. Even in Hesiod we find a change, very much for the worse, in the condition of women. The position of women in Greek tragedy and comedy, which only falls incidentally within our scope, and can only be treated briefly and superficially here, is fully and ably discussed by Mr. Benecke in his "Antimachus of Colophon: a Fragment for the use of Scholars." See also Professor Mahaffy's interesting chapters (second and third) of his work on "Social Life in Ancient Greece."

Of love, in our sense of the word, the crown and glory of the woman, there is hardly a trace in the Attic drama. Æschylus never brings a couple in love upon the stage, and prides himself upon the fact. "I never wrote of the adulteries of Phædra or Sthenoboia, nor do I know that I ever made a woman in love."[2] Sophocles employs the passion of love to enhance the tragic interest of his plots, as in the "Antigone," where Hæmon,

[1] Pindar, Fr. 46: Λιπαραὶ καὶ ἀοίδιμοι Ἑλλάδος ἔρεισμα κλεινοὶ Ἀθᾶνοι. *Cf.* Aristoph. Ach. 637.
[2] Aristoph. Ranæ. 1012:
    'Ἀλλ' οἱ μὰ Δί' ου Φαίδρας ἐποίουν πόρνας οὐδὲ Σθενεβοίας,
    οὐδ' οἶδ' οὐδεὶς ἥντιν' ἐρῶσαν πώποτ' ἐποίησα γυναῖκα,

The Women of Homer

her lover, commits suicide from despair at losing her. But he never makes love—the love of the sexes—the main feature of his drama, and his Antigone sacrifices herself, not for her lover, who plays a very subordinate part, but for her brother. *We* wander through a three-volume novel, or sit out a five-act play, to watch with breathless interest how the author will bring a young man and a young woman into the safe haven and heaven of matrimony. This would have seemed ludicrous to a Greek tragedian of the palmy days of Athens. Sophocles and Euripides, like Æschylus, are inclined to regard the passion of love as a νόσος—a fell disease sent by the gods in anger. Thus Helen excuses her escapade with Paris: "Punish," she says to Menelaos, "not me, but the goddess, and show yourself superior to Zeus, who rules over all the other deities, but is a slave to Aphrodite."[1]

What can be more alien to our view of love and marriage than the speech of Sophocles' noblest creation, Antigone, in which she shows her preference for a brother to parents, husband, or children?—or more shocking than the reasons she gives for it? "Never," she says, "had I been the mother of children, or if my husband had been mouldering in death, would I have taken this task upon me, in the city's despite. What law, ye ask, is my warrant for that word? The husband lost, another might have been found, and a child from another man to replace the first-born. But father and mother hidden in Hades, no brother's life could bloom for me again."[2]

---

[1] Euripides, Troades, v. 941 : τὴν θεὸν κόλαζε, καὶ Διὸς κρείσσον γενοῦ.
[2] Soph. Antigone, 905.

Controversy on Antigone's Strange Speech

A very lively controversy has arisen concerning the authenticity of this passage; and many commentators, and among them Professor Jebb,[1] maintain that it is an interpolation, taken from Herodotus. "The wife of Intaphernes, who, with all his kindred, had been convicted of treason against Darius, came and stood before the king, weeping and wailing." And Darius was touched with pity for her, and sent a messenger to her to say: "Lady, King Darius gives thee as a boon the life of one of thy kinsmen; choose which thou wilt of the prisoners."[2] Then she pondered awhile before she answered: "If the king grants me the life of one alone, I make choice of my brother." Darius, when he heard the reply, was astonished, and sent again, saying, "The king bids thee tell him why it is that thou passest by thy husband and thy children, and preferrest thy brother. He is not so near to thee as thy children, nor so dear as thy husband." She answered, "O king, if the gods will, I may have another husband, and other children, when these are gone; but as my father and my mother are no more, I cannot have another brother." *Darius was so pleased with her "wise answer"* that he gave her the life of her eldest son also; but he slew all the rest.

Besides the sentimental grounds which he thinks are sufficient to prove that the passage in the "Antigone" is an interpolation from Herodotus, Professor Jebb thinks that the composition of vv. 909–912 are unworthy of Sophocles. In a very interesting note

---

[1] See his edition of the "Antigone" (Cambridge, 1888), and the Appendix to v. 905 *et seq.*   [2] See Appendix XX.

The Women of Homer

on the passage he gives many weighty reasons for his opinion. Goethe, as a poet, was naturally "horrified" at the slur on the character of his favourite heroine, and fervently hopes that the scholars would unanimously reject the offensive lines. His wish has not been fulfilled. Authorities of equal weight take different sides in the controversy. Bellermann, Böckh, Moritz, Seyffert, and others either justify or excuse the passage. Hermann, who characterises it as sophistical, adds significantly, "Sed placebant talia scilicet Atheniensibus," but gives no decided opinion.

If it is an interpolation it is a very ancient one, for the whole passage was included in the text which Aristotle[1] had before him not later than 338 B.C. Those who reject it suppose that it was inserted very soon after the poet's death by his son Iophon, or by some actor of the play.

The argument against the authenticity of the passage is weakened, I think, by the fact that it does not stand alone in its strange and distasteful logic. In the "Eumenides" of Æschylus,[2] Apollo defends Orestes on the plea that a mother is not really a parent, but only a nurse; and Athene too votes for him, because she herself had no mother!

> "For as no mother gave me birth,
> My grace in all things, save the nuptial rites,
> Attends the male, as from my sire I drew
> The vigour of my soul."

---

[1] Rhet. iii. 16, sec. 9, where he quotes vv. 911, 912.
[2] 648 and 726.

Similar Passages in the 'Eumenides'

The reasoning of Antigone is hardly more surprising, more unromantic, we might almost say more absurd, than that of Apollo and Athene.

We find it difficult to enter into modes of thought so alien to our own, but, to be quite fair in our judgment in this controversy, it is necessary to do so as far as possible. We see that Herodotus relates the story of Intaphernes' wife, without expressing any disapproval; and Darius, we are told, was "highly pleased with her," and thought that "she had answered well." Herodotus must have been of the same opinion. The passages quoted above from the "Eumenides" have not been called in question, though they are equally repugnant to our taste. Why, then, should that which seemed reasonable and praiseworthy to Herodotus, Darius, and Æschylus, be thought so unworthy of Sophocles? It is, indeed, hard to have the fair image of the noble self-sacrificing maiden in any degree defaced; but, on the other hand, it is dangerous, in criticising ancient authors, to allow too much weight to æsthetic considerations. Even Shakespeare's maidens betray feelings and make use of language which we should gladly brand as spurious. And, after all, is the disputed passage so very inconsistent with the uncompromising sternness of Antigone's character, as shown in her treatment of her sister, the gentle Ismene, when she hesitates to defy the laws of the city? "I will not urge thee; no, nor yet if thou shouldst have the mind, wouldst thou be welcome as a worker with me." "Go and denounce me! Thou wilt be far more hateful for thy silence, if thou proclaim not these things to all."

The Women of Homer

We must also take into account the very low views of love and marriage which were prevalent in the age of Sophocles, and remember how weak was the tie of marriage compared with that of kindred blood. How little is Antigone concerned about her lover Hæmon! When she is being led away to death, she bewails, indeed, that "no bridal bed, no bridal song, no joy of marriage, no portion in the nurture of children" have been hers, but there is no mention of her particular lover. And how strange is the attitude of Hæmon himself when he hears that his mistress is condemned "to go living to the vaults of death." "Father," he says, "I am thine, and thou in thy wisdom tracest for me rules which I shall follow. No marriage shall be deemed by me a greater gain than thy good guidance." He then enters into a long academic argument with Creon, and gradually works himself up to the madness of suicide, but his whole bearing leaves us utterly cold.

It is generally supposed that Euripides has incorporated more of the element of love in his dramas than his two great predecessors. But even in his works the men take very little interest in the women. He too, like Æschylus and Sophocles, thinks of love as a furious disease. This is very clearly shown in his Medea,[1] when Jason, who owes everything to her, coolly tells her that he owes her no gratitude, as she was driven by the fury of her love to save him. The difference between what we mean by love and what Euripides meant by it, and the essentially sensual and selfish nature of love in his view of it, is clearly shown by the fact that, in the case

[1] v. 526. *Cf.* Eurip. Hippol. 477, 730, 764.

Euripides' Opinion of Women

of Medea, Phædra, and others, directly it is thwarted in its passionate desire, it turns to the most deadly hatred.

At the same time we must allow that Euripides did something to raise the estimate of women. He was certainly a misogynist, and speaks very bitterly of women, but he had a high idea of their intelligence and power. As wives he maintains that they ought to be in entire subjection to their husbands, never to leave the house or to see visitors at home. "No wise man," he says, "will give a woman her head; if he does he will probably get murdered."[1]

This absolute subjection of the wife to her husband—not because she loves him, but because he is her lord and master—is fully shown in the "Alcestis." She does not seem to care much for Admetus, and he thinks it quite natural that she should be ready to die for him, and makes very little objection to her doing so.

But subordinate and unromantic as the love represented in the noblest works of Æschylus, Sophocles, and Euripides, it is still further debased in the older and middle Attic comedy, and especially in the latter. It was, no doubt, the Ionian Greeks who first put women in the background, following Oriental example, and their influence soon made itself felt in Athens.

The early Attic comedy was almost exclusively political, and women are almost ignored, except Aspasia and other eminent *hetairai*, who, unable to bear the drudgery and monotony of the virtuous matron's life, preferred to gain their freedom even at the cost of their reputation.

---

[1] Fr. 463 (Cressæ), Fr. 464.

The Women of Homer

Cratinus, the first distinguished dramatist of the Old Comedy, was a bitter opponent of Pericles, on whom he lavishes the most pungent personal abuse. Crates, one of the principal actors of Cratinus' plays, also wrote comedies, the women of which belonged to the *hetairai*; and three of his plays are called after the notorious women of this class, Corianno, Thalatta, and Petale.

The earlier plays of Aristophanes, too, are also mainly political, and his keen satire is employed with terrible effect against Socrates and Cleon. In these there are but few allusions to women, and where they are brought upon the stage they are shown up in a revolting fashion, as incontinent and drunken.[1]

Yet some ancient critics maintain that in his "Cocalus," one of the very last of his dramas, is to be found the forerunner of the new romantic comedy of Antimachus, Menander, and Philemon.[2] How improbable, not to say impossible, this is, is clearly proved by Benecke.[3]

But it is in the Middle Comedy that women, love, and marriage are the most degraded and despised. Of love, as distinguished from brute passion, there is hardly a trace. The *hetairai* are in full possession of the field, and marriage is held up to contempt and ridicule. Athenæus[4] gives a passage from the "Athamas" of Amphis, in which the superiority of the *hetaira* over the wife are gravely set forth. The advantages of commerce with the *hetairai* over that of an intrigue with the wives of others

---

[1] Eccles. 877; Thesmoph. 383; the Lemniæ.
[2] Vita Aristoph. p. xxxviii.
[3] Antimachus of Colophon, p. 135 *et seq.*
[4] xiii. 559 A. See Appendix XXI. *Cf.* Athenæus, xiii. 562 C. We see a reflection of this style in the Truculentus, Mercator, Mostellaria, &c., of Plautus.

Love and Marriage in the "Middle Comedy"

are also dwelt upon with great force. "A girl that one is going to marry," says one of these poets, "has all the disadvantages of a wife but for one thing. While the wife *in esse* is, as a later writer expresses it, 'an immortal necessary evil,' and therefore cannot be altogether escaped from, there is no need to meet troubles halfway by drawing attention to the wife *in posse*. 'Let us eat and drink, for to-morrow we marry;' and while we do so, let us have no Alexandrian skeleton at the feast to remind us of the fatal hour."[1]

The contempt, we may say the hatred, for pure love in marriage appears throughout the Middle Comedy; and it was chiefly on account of their advocacy of a purer love that Plato and the much-maligned Sappho are held up to scorn and ridicule.

Benecke[2] gives amusing instances of this feeling from an unnamed poet,[3] who declares that marriage is worse than disfranchisement, and gives the reasons why: "When one is disfranchised, the law does not allow us to rule others; but when one is married, one is not even master of one's self."[4]

Still better is the passage in the "Philopator" of Aristophanes, where a man asks another about a common friend, and learns that he is married. "*What* do you say—married? *really* married! he whom I lately left alive and walking about!"

In Greek comedy, as we have seen, we find the women in the lowest state of degradation, and, morally speaking, in utter ruin. The "Ranæ" and the "Equites"

---
[1] Taken from "Antimachus of Colophon" by E. F. M. Benecke, p. 159.
[2] l.c. p. 162.   [3] Incert. 34.   [4] See Appendix XXII.

The Women of Homer

of Aristophanes present to us a picture of social decadence for which we can only find a parallel in the first French Revolution. We find there not only criminal excess of every kind, but even shameless cowardice, and deliberate treachery and meanness.

The Middle Comedy "goes one worse,"[1] and as no lower depth could be reached, we are hardly surprised to see in the New Comedy a powerful and wholesome reaction in the direction of decency and virtue.

It is difficult to draw a hard and fast line between the three comedies, Early, Middle, and New, because while in the one preceding there are sometimes indications of a coming change, so in the succeeding there is often a recurrence to the former evil tone. We may, however, fix the date of the improvement with Benecke at the years 315–310 B.C., somewhat later than that generally adopted, because many of the earlier comedies of Menander breathe something of the evil spirit of the Middle Comedy.[2] To whom this most salutary change is to be attributed is a matter of doubt and dispute, but the honours are divided between Antimachus of Colophon, Menander, and Philemon. Antimachus is mentioned in connection with Lysander and Plato. A story relates that he read his "Thebais" before a large audience, who, being wearied with it, gradually went away, till no one but Plato was left. But Antimachus consoled himself, saying that Plato outweighed a thousand others.

Antimachus is mentioned in terms of high praise by ancient authors, though Catullus calls him "*tumidus*"[3];

---

[1] For Xenophon's (Œcon. 7. 5) opinion of the young woman of his day see Appendix XXIII.   [2] Benecke, l.c. p. 194.   [3] Carmen, 95.

Antimachus, Menander, and Philemon

but as there are only a few fragments of his works left to us, we cannot form a judgment respecting his merits. His chief work, the "Thebais," was celebrated and read for centuries after his death. His elegy "Lyde,"[1] addressed to his wife after her death, was considered as a model of the virtuous love poem, and is referred to by Ovid in his "Tristia."[2]

It seems more than probable that the works of Antimachus influenced the great coryphæi of the New Comedy, Menander and Philemon, and first inspired them with a reverence for enduring affection, as distinguished from the momentary frenzy of passion, which is the only recognised form of love in the Middle Comedy. What could possibly seem more ludicrous to the writers of the latter than that marriage should be held up as the supremely happy state, the great object of the lover's hopes and wishes?

Respect for the sanctity of marriage was considered one of the chief features and the greatest merit of the works of Menander;[3] and Plutarch recommends them as especially suitable for the study of married men.[4] Among the chief followers of Antimachus, Philetas and Callimachus are especially mentioned and commended.

Whoever may have originated the romantic drama, it is quite certain that it differs *toto cælo* in respect to love and marriage from the Middle Comedy, and in

---

[1] See Appendix XXIV.
[2] i. 6. 1:—
"Nec tantum Clario Lyde dilecta poetæ,
Nec tantum Coo Battis amata suo est,
Pectoribus quantum tu nostris, uxor inhæres."
Cf. Asclepiades in Anthol. Pal. ix. 63.
[3] Epigram. C. i. G. 6083.   [4] Sympos. vii. 712 C.

The Women of Homer

fact from the works of the great tragedians. In the Middle Comedy love is purely sensual, and the *hetaira* is preferred to the wife.

To recapitulate. In the New Comedy, which was the forerunner of Alexandrian comedy and romance, we find woman restored to her natural place as the object of pure and even Platonic love, and marriage held up as the highest object of a lover's aspiration.[1] In the "Stichus" of Menander, two women remain faithful to their absent husbands for three whole years!

---

[1] *Cf.* the "Heauton-Timoroumenos" of Terence (ii. 51): "... Istæ formæ ut mores consimiles forent."

APPENDICES

APPENDIX I

(Page 3.)

Ὁποίας Ὅμηρον ἀναγραψώμεθα πάτρης
Κεῖνον ἐφ' ᾧ πᾶσαι χεῖρ' ὀρέγουσι πόλεις
Ητὸ μὲν ἐστιν ἄγνωστον ὁδ' ἀθανατοῖς ἴσος ἥρως
Ταῖς Μούσαις ἔλιπεν πατρίδα καὶ γενέην.
—Anthol. Pal. ii. 715.

Ὅμηρος μὲν οὖν τίνων γονέων ἢ ποιᾶς ἐγένετο πατρίδος οὐ ῥᾴδιον ἀποφήνασθαι, οὔτε γὰρ αὐτός λελάληκεν.
—Proclus, Life of Homer.

Οὐ γὰρ ἔφυ χθονὸς ἔργον, ἀπ' αἰθέρος ἀλλὰ ἑ Μοῦσαι,
Πέμψαν ἵν' ἡμερίοις δῶρα ποθητὰ φέροι.
—Anthol. Pal. ii. 715.

APPENDIX II

(Page 5.)

Wolf's Preface to the Iliad, p. xxii. :—" Quoties penitus immergor in illum veluti prono et liquido alveo decurrentem tenorem actionum et narrationum; quoties animadverto ac reputo mecum quam in universum æstimanti unus his carminibus insit color . . . vix mihi quisquam irasci et succensere gravius poterit, quam ipse facio mihi."

Appendices

APPENDIX III

(Page 8.)

" Nec sic incipies, ut scriptor cyclicus olim
Fortunam Priami, cantabo et nobile bellum,
Quid dignum tanto feret hic promissor hiatu?
Parturiunt montes, nascetur ridiculus mus."
—Horat. Ars Poet. 136.

APPENDIX IV

(Page 11.)

"Adparet Divóm numen, sedesque quietæ
Quas neque concutiunt venti, nec nubila nimbis
Adspergunt; neque nix, acri concreta pruina,
Cana cadens violat, semper sine nubibus æther
Inter et large diffuso lumine ridet."
—Lucret. iii. 18.

APPENDIX V

(Page 21.)

"Ομηρος πρῶτος καὶ μέσος καὶ ὕστατος
Παντὶ παιδὶ καὶ ανδρὶ καὶ γέροντι.

(Page 21.)

'Ηρωῶν κάρυκ' ἀρετᾶς μακάρων δὲ προφήτων
'Ελλάνων Βιοτῇ δευτερον ἀέλιον
Μουσῶν φέγγος "Ομηρος.
—Antipat. Sidon. Anth. Pal. vii. 6.

Appendices

(Page 21.)

The *Apotheosis of Homer*, by Archelaus, son of Apollonios of Priene, was found at Bovillæ, and is now in the British Museum. It is supposed that this relief formed one of a series made in the reign of Tiberius for the use of schools. It is arranged in four parallel stripes, of which only the lowest is represented here.

The first figures on the left, as we learn from the inscriptions under them, are Οἰκουμένη (the inhabited world), with a modius on her head (as a Chthonic deity?), and Χρόνος (time), standing side by side behind the throne of the deified poet. Oikoumenos, as representative of the human race, is in the act of crowning him, while Chronos, with his long, swift wings, is bearing the poet's works in his hand down the stream of ages. Before them is the immortal bard himself, enthroned, with a sceptre in his left hand, and a branch (or roll of paper?) in his right. He is no longer "the blind old man of Scio's rocky isle," as he is represented in busts, but appears in all the pride of renewed and immortal youth. On each side of him crouch two small figures, representing the Iliad, with a sword in his hand, and the Odyssey, with an aplustre (stern of a ship). On his footstool are a frog and a mouse, as reminiscences of the Batryomachia (the battle of the frogs and mice). Immediately in front of Homer, and turning towards him, is Mythos (fable), whose boyish form indicates the childlike character of Fable. He is bearing the oinochoe (ewer) and wine-cup, in the capacity of Hierodule (sacrificial attendant). To the right, again, is the flaming altar, behind which stands the victim, a Carian ox, with the hump peculiar to that breed. Next to the altar, on the right, stands History, of which Homer was the source, casting incense into the fire. Then follow Epic Poetry, holding a torch in each upraised hand; then Tragedy and Comedy, the germs of which lie in the works of Homer. The former of these is distinguished by superior height and more dignified carriage and dress, and especially by the lofty ὄγκος (the bushy top-knot of hair), intended to give greater height to the brow.

Appendices

This first and chief group of adorers is separated from the succeeding one by a small figure, apparently female, representing Φύσις (the native genius of the poet). The four figures crowded together on the extreme right, to balance the close arrangement on the extreme left, are Ἀρετή (manliness, virtue), with upraised face and hand, in ecstatic adoration; Μνήμη (memory), with her hand to her mouth; Πίστις (faith), the tall figure behind Arētē; and Σοφία (wisdom), meditating, with her hand under her chin.

The figures of this lower stripe are closed in by a curtain, as background to the scene.

APPENDIX VI

(Page 22.)

Μόνον Σοφοκλέα τυγχάνειν Ομήρου μαθητην . . . μόνος δὲ Σοφοκλῆς ἀφ' ἑκάστου τὸ λαμπρὸν ἀπανθίζει καθ' ὃ Μέλιττα ἐλέγετο. —Vita Sophocl. i. 131.

APPENDIX VII

(Page 23.)

See *infra*.

(Page 23.)

Ἀπώλετο πράν τοι Ὅμηρος,
Τῆνο τὸ Καλλιόπας γλυκερόν ὁτόμα καὶ σε λέγοντι
Μύρεσθαι. —Mosch. Idyll. iii. 71.

τίς δὲ κὲν ἄλλου ἀκούσαι;
ἅλις πάντεσσιν Ὅμηρος. —Theocr. Idyll. xvi. 20.

Appendices

(Page 23.)

'Αλλ' Όμηρός τοι τετίμακεν δι' ἀνθρώπων, ὃς αὐτόν
Πᾶσαν ὀρθώσαις ἀρετὰν κατὰ ῥάβδον ἔφρασεν
Θεσπεσίων ἐπέων λοιποῖς ἀθύρειν
Τοῦτο γὰρ ἀθάνατον φωγᾶεν ἔρπει
Ἔ, τις εὖ εἴπῃ τι. —Isthm. iii. 55.

APPENDIX VIII

(Page 23.)

"Traditum est etiam Homerum cæcum fuisse. At ejus picturam, non poesin videmus. Quæ regio, quæ ora, qui locus Greciæ, quæ species formaque pugnæ, quod remigium, qui motus hominum qui ferarum, non ita expictus est, ut quæ ipse non viderit, nos ut viderimus effecerit."—Cic. Tusc. Disput. v. 39.

APPENDIX IX

(Page 30.)

The Alexandrians in Schol. Alcibiad. I. cap. i. ed. Tur. p. 916, B. 33.

Ὁμήρῳ, ᾧ καὶ τόξον Ἀπολλων αὐτὸς ἔδωκεν.

APPENDIX X

(Page 32.)

Ὣς ἔφατ' οὐδ' ἀπίθησε διάκτορος Ἀργειφόντης
Αὐτίκ' ἔπειθ' ὑπὸ ποσσὶν ἐδήσατο καλὰ πέδιλα
Ἀμβροσια χρύσεια τὰ μὲν φέρον ἠμὲν ἐφ' ὑγρήν
Ἠδ' ἐπ' ἀπείρονα γαῖαν ἅμα πνοιῆς ἀνέμοιο.
  —Od. v. 43.

Appendices

APPENDIX XI

(Page 54.)

Ἄνδρας ὄντας καὶ δικαίους καλοῦστε κἀγαθούς
Καὶ τραφέντας ἐν παλαίστροις καὶ χοροῖς καὶ μουσικῇ.
—Aristoph. Ranæ, 745.

No mention of arithmetic (γράμματα), which seems to have been rather despised. Aristophanes says—

οὐ δὲ μουσικῇ ἐπίσταμαι
Πλὴν γραμμάτων καὶ ταῦτα μέντοι κακὰ κακῶς.

APPENDIX XII

(Page 72.)

ἐν τῇ ῥα μὲν γάμοι τ' ἔσαν ἐιλαπίναιτε,
Νύμφας δ' ἐκ θαλάμων δαΐδων ὕπο λαμπομενάων
Ἠγίνεον ἀνὰ ἄστυ πολὺς δ' ὑμέναιος ὀρώρει.
Κοῦροι δ' ὀρχηστῆρες ἐδίνεον, ἐν δ' ἄρα τοῖσιν
Αὐλοὶ φόρμιγγές τε βοὴν ἔχον ἁὶ δε γυναῖκες
Ἱστάμεναι θαυμαζον ἐπὶ προθύροισιν ἑκάστη.
—Il. xviii. 491.

APPENDIX XIII

(Pages 82 and 83.)

Isthmion and Hormos.

The Hormos fell from the nape of the neck over the bosom (Hymn. in Apoll. i. 103; Hymn. in Vener. iv. 88, vi. 11):—

δειρῇ δ' ἀμφ' ἁπαλῇ καὶ στηθέσσιν ἀργυρέοισιν
Ὅρμοισι χρυσέοισιν ἐκόσμεον οἷσι περ αὐταὶ
Ὧραι κοσμείσθην χρυσάμπυκες.

Appendices

These ornaments are found on clay figures of Astarte at Amalphus in Cyprus (see Cesnola-Stern, i. 50, 3.) Found also on old Greek and Etruscan figures (see Perrot et Chipicz, iii. p. 257), and on Tanagra figures in Necropolis of Kameira, and on Francois vase (see Helbig, Epos, 270).

(Page 82.)

The Isthmion was the ancestor of the classical necklace (Schol. to Od. xviii. 300):—

Ἴσθμιον ἰσθμὸς ὁ τράχηλος.

Such necklaces are found in bronze in the Apennine peninsula, in the Necropolis of Villanova. (See Helbig, Epos, 271; and Friederich's "Kleinere Kunst," pp. 124 and 527.)

APPENDIX XIV

(Page 89.)

"L'Art Mycen.," par M. W. Helbig, *Mémoires de l'Institut Nation. de France*, tome xxxv. p. 291:—"J'y ai supposé que les Phéniciens eurent une large part dans le développement de la civilisation que nous connaissons surtout par les monuments de Mycènes, et qui a prit, pour cette raison, le nom de Mycénienne . . . Les malheureux Phéniciens sont dévenus l'objet de la profonde antipathie de plusieurs savants. . . . On a voulu contester aux Phéniciens l'honneur d'avoir été les maîtres des Grecs primitifs."—P. 347.

(Page 92.)

"Les poètes épiques quand'ils parlent d'objets d'art, expriment la plus grande admiration pour les produits de l'industrie phénicienne. Nous sommes donc logiquement forcés d'attribuer à cette industrie les chefs-d'œuvre qui se trouvent en Grèce, parmi les restes 'mycéniens' et de remplacer le x par 'l'art phéniciens.'"

Appendices

APPENDIX XV

(Page 121.)

Κύπρι φιλομειδής, θαλαμηπόλε τίς σε μελιχρὴν
Δαίμονα τôις πολέμων ἐστεφάνωσεν ὅπλοις;
(Aphrod.) Εἰ γυμνὴ νικῶ, πῶς ὅταν ὅπλα λάβω;

APPENDIX XVI

(Page 175.)

Ότι ἐκ τούτου τοῦ ἴστου ἔλαβε τὸ πλείον τῆς Ιστοριάς τοῦ Τρωικοῦ Πολέμου ὁ θεῖος Ὅμηρος. —Aristarchus ad I. G. 125.

APPENDIX XVII

(Page 175.)

Οὐ γὰρ ἔβας ἐν νηυσὶν ἐυσέλμοις οὐδ ἵκεο Πέργαμα Τροιάς.
And the same idea is expressed by Euripides in the "Electra," v. 1278:—

Οὐδ' ἦλθεν Φρύγας
Ζεὺς δ' ὡς ἔρις γένοιτο καὶ φόνος βροτῶν
Εἴδωλον Ἑλένης ἐξέπεμψ' εἰς Ἴλιον.
—*Cf.* Eurip. Helena, v. 590.

APPENDIX XVIII

(Page 214.)

Athenæus (i. p. 20, E) says that Sophocles was a famous ball-player, and when he drilled his troop for his "Nausicaa" he represented her in the act of playing a game of ball:—

Μαλίστα δὲ φασι ἐπεμελήθησαν σφαιριστικῆς πόλεων μὲν κοινῇ

Appendices

These ornaments are found on clay figures of Astarte at Amalphus in Cyprus (see Cesnola-Stern, i. 50, 3.) Found also on old Greek and Etruscan figures (see Perrot et Chipicz, iii. p. 257), and on Tanagra figures in Necropolis of Kameira, and on Francois vase (see Helbig, Epos, 270).

(Page 82.)

The Isthmion was the ancestor of the classical necklace (Schol. to Od. xviii. 300):—

Ἴσθμιον ἰσθμὸς ὁ τράχηλος.

Such necklaces are found in bronze in the Apennine peninsula, in the Necropolis of Villanova. (See Helbig, Epos, 271; and Friederich's "Kleinere Kunst," pp. 124 and 527.)

APPENDIX XIV

(Page 89.)

"L'Art Mycen.," par M. W. Helbig, *Mémoires de l'Institut Nation. de France*, tome xxxv. p. 291 :—" J'y ai supposé que les Phéniciens eurent une large part dans le développement de la civilisation que nous connaissons surtout par les monuments de Mycènes, et qui a prit, pour cette raison, le nom de Mycénienne . . . Les malheureux Phéniciens sont dévenus l'objet de la profonde antipathie de plusieurs savants. . . . On a voulu contester aux Phéniciens l'honneur d'avoir été les maîtres des Grecs primitifs."—P. 347.

(Page 92.)

"Les poètes épiques quand'ils parlent d'objets d'art, expriment la plus grande admiration pour les produits de l'industrie phénicienne. Nous sommes donc logiquement forcés d'attribuer à cette industrie les chefs-d'œuvre qui se trouvent en Grèce, parmi les restes 'mycéniens' et de remplacer le x par 'l'art phéniciens.'"

Appendices

APPENDIX XV

(Page 121.)

Κύπρι φιλομειδής, θαλαμηπόλε τίς σε μελιχρὴν
Δαίμονα τοις πολέμων ἐστεφάνωσεν ὅπλοις;
(Aphrod.) Εἰ γυμνὴ νικῶ, πῶς ὅταν ὅπλα λάβω;

APPENDIX XVI

(Page 175.)

Ὅτι ἐκ τούτου τοῦ ἴστου ἔλαβε τὸ πλείον τῆς Ἱστοριάς τοῦ Τρωικοῦ Πολέμου ὁ θεῖος Ὅμηρος.   —Aristarchus ad I. G. 125.

APPENDIX XVII

(Page 175.)

Οὐ γὰρ ἔβας ἐν νηυσὶν ἐυσέλμοις οὐδ ἵκεο Πέργαμα Τροιάς.

And the same idea is expressed by Euripides in the "Electra," v. 1278:—

Οὐδ' ἦλθεν Φρύγας
Ζεὺς δ' ὡς ἔρις γένοιτο καὶ φόνος βροτῶν
Εἴδωλον Ἑλένης ἐξέπεμψ' εἰς Ἴλιον.
—*Cf.* Eurip. Helena, v. 590.

APPENDIX XVIII

(Page 214.)

Athenæus (i. p. 20, E) says that Sophocles was a famous ball-player, and when he drilled his troop for his "Nausicaa" he represented her in the act of playing a game of ball:—

Μαλίστα δὲ φασι ἐπεμελήθησαν σφαιριστικῆς πόλεων μὲν κοινῇ

Appendices

Λακεδαιμόνιοι, βασιλέων δὲ ὁ μέγας Ἀλέξανδρος, ἰδιωτῶν δὲ Σοφοκλῆς ὁ τραγικός, ὅς καὶ ὅτε φασί τὰς Πλυντρίας ἐδιδάσκε τὸ τῆς Ναυσικάας πρόσωπον σφαίρα παιζούσης ὑποκρινόμενος ἰσχυρῶς.

APPENDIX XIX

(Page 223.)

Ὦ γύναι βασιλεύς τοι Δαρεῖος διδοῖ ἕνα τῶν δεδεμένων οἰκητῶν ῥύσασθαι τὸν βούλεαι ἐκ πάντων. Ἡ δὲ βουλευσαμένη ὑπεκρίνατο τάδε εἰ μὲν δή μοι διδοῖ βασιλεὺς ἑνὸς τὴν ψυχὴν αἱρέομαι τὸν ἀδελφεόν. κ.τ.λ. —Herod. iii. 119.

APPENDIX XX

(Page 228.)

Εἶτ' οὐ γυναικός ἐστιν εὐνοϊκώτερον γαμετῆς ἑταίρα; πολύ γε καὶ μάλ' εἰκότως. ἡ μὲν νόμῳ γὰρ καταφρονοῦσ' ἔνδον μένει, ἡ δ' οἶδεν ὅτι ἢ τοῖς τρόποις ὠνητέος ἄνθρωπός ἐστιν ἢ πρὸς ἄλλον ἀπιτέον.

APPENDIX XXI

(Page 229.)

Τοὺς μὲν γοῦν ἀτίμους οὐκ ἐᾷ,
Ἀρχὴν λαχόντας ὁ νόμος ἄρχειν τῶν πέλας.
Ἐπὰν δὲ γήμῃς οὐδὲ σαυτοῦ κύριον
Ἔξεστιν εἶναι.

Τι συλέγεις; ἀληθινῶς
γεγάμηκεν, ὃν ἐγὼ ζῶντα περιπατοῦντα τε
κατέλιπον;

Appendices

APPENDIX XXII

(Page 230.)

Xenophon (Œconom. vii. 5) thus describes the young woman of his day, the latter half of the fifth century B.C. :—

Καὶ τί ἂν ἐπισταμένην αὐτὴν παρέλαβον ἣ ἔτη μὲν οὔπω πεντεκαίδεκα γεγονυῖα ἦλθε πρὸς ἐμέ τὸν δ' ἔμπροσθεν χρόνον ἔζη ὑπὸ ἐπιμελείας ὅπως ἐλάχιστα μὲν ὕψοιτο ἐλάχιστα δὲ ἀκούοιτο, ἐλάχιστα δὲ ἔροιτο.

And again (v. 13)—

Ἔγημας δὲ αὐτὴν παῖδα νέαν μάλιστα καὶ ὡς ἠδύνατο ἐλάχιστα ἑωρακυῖαν καὶ ἀκηκουῖαν.

Παῖς νέα means a fool in the Tragedians.—Æsch. Agam. 284; Eurip. Hipp. 429.

APPENDIX XXIII

(Page 231.)

The "Lyde" of Antimachus.

Λύδη καὶ γένος εἰμὶ καὶ οὔνομα τῶν ἀπὸ Κόδρου,
Σεμνοτέρη πασῶν εἰμὶ δι' Ἀντίμαχον.
Τίς γὰρ ἔμ' οὐκ ἤεισε; τις οὐκ ἀνελέξατο Λύδην
Τὸ ξυνὸν Μουσῶν γράμμα καὶ Ἀντιμάχου.
—Anthol. Pal. ix. 63.

CPSIA information can be obtained
at www.ICGtesting.com
Printed in the USA
LVHW050150130722
723331LV00006B/257